Guilt, Grace & Gratitude

Volume I

GUILT, GRACE & GRATITUDE

LECTURES ON THE HEIDELBERG CATECHISM

George W. Bethune

VOLUME I

THE BANNER OF TRUTH TRUST

THE BANNER OF TRUTH TRUST
3 Murrayfield Road, Edinburgh EH12 6EL, U K
P O Box 621, Carlisle, PA 17013, U S A

*

First published by Sheldon & Company, New York, 1864
First Banner of Truth Edition 2001

ISBN 0 85151 802 8 (2-volume set)

*

Printed in Great Britain by
The Bath Press

CONTENTS OF VOLUME I

PUBLISHER'S INTRODUCTION

G EORGE WASHINGTON BETHUNE, the author of these lectures on
the *Heidelberg Catechism*, 'stood in the front rank of ministers of the gospel'.[1] He was born in New York City in 1805,
studied at Princeton Theological Seminary, and chose to exercise
his ministry in the Reformed Church in America, previously
known, because of its origins, as the Reformed Dutch Church.
He served congregations in Rhinebeck, Utica, Philadelphia,
Brooklyn Heights and 21st Street, New York. Towards the end of
his life he also served the American Chapel in Rome (1859–60).
He died at Florence, Italy, on 28 April 1862.

A biographical account published by the Reformed Church in
America describes him in this way:

'Originally endowed with a fine mind, and furnished with
every possible facility for cultivating and furnishing it, he
achieved a very high degree of success in the pulpit and elsewhere.
A thorough master of English, of finished taste, fertile in
thought, rich in illustration, skilled in dialectics, familiar with the
stores of the past, yet with a quick eye to the present, a proficient
in *belles-lettres*, he had almost every literary requisite for the

---

[1] *A Manual of the Reformed Church in America, 1628–1902*, New York:
Board of Publication of the Reformed Church in America, 1902, p. 318.

composition of sermons. When to this it is added that he was sound in the faith and had his heart in the work, that he had a most musical voice, of rare compass and modulation, it is not wonderful that his reputation stood so high. He was a close and diligent student and never was ashamed to confess it. His platform efforts were always impromptu, but for the pulpit he felt conscientiously bound to make careful and thorough preparation . . . He was a man of very genial nature, sympathetic and companionable, destitute of formality and reserve, with a rich fund of anecdote and a sparkling wit, which gave a pungent zest to his conversation. He was the life of the social circle. Nor was this mere good-fellowship, for he had real kindness of heart, which was manifest in various ways to all who were near him.

The pulpit was the place where he loved to labour, and where he especially excelled and wielded his greatest power. His fame in his beloved work of preaching Christ is almost world-wide. For oratory he had a natural adaptation, which was very early shown. But he also studied the best authorities, and by wise culture and careful direction properly developed those qualities which God had given him, and the result was a natural, individual manner peculiarly his own . . . He realized very deeply that his pulpit was a consecrated place, and that his work there, whether as the mouth of God to the people or as the mouth of the people to God, was of the most responsible character. Hence it was with him a matter of special concern that the highest possible interest should be given to every part of the service. The selection of his hymns or psalms was very carefully made, and these were read in a manner to give them the fullest effect on the hearer; and no man understood better than he how to accomplish this.

His devotional exercises were what they claimed to be – the outpouring of a full heart at the mercy seat, tenderly alive to all the interests with which he was charged, and especially making himself one with his people, whom he loved most tenderly. All was solemn, humble, simple, earnest, with no rambling into the field of fancy, no proclamation of his views on the conflicting theories of theology, no attempt to show how much he knew and how well he could exhibit it, but all was truly devotional. One felt, as he joined with him in prayer, that he was really holding converse with an infinitely holy Being, and occupied a place very near the throne, and was bowed down by its overpowering holiness . . .

His preaching was eminently evangelical and biblical, and no hearer could avoid the impression that the treasures of the gospel were inexhaustible.

Christ and him crucified was the theme in which he delighted and on which he expended all his strength. And learned as he was, having great literary treasures at command, yet his sermons were marked with the utmost simplicity. He was also courageous and faithful as a preacher. The fear of men did not influence him. Hence he was ever ready to proclaim the most humbling and unpalatable doctrines of the Word of Life, as circumstances required. He did not hesitate to assume whatever responsibility fairly belonged to a servant of the living God. His theology was that of the Reformation. Yet he was no stranger to the metaphysics or the philosophy of modern theologians and those of the German schools.

In his pulpit exercises a special importance was given to Scripture reading. He felt bound to honour, on all occasions, the Bible, and his care was so to read that men should feel that it was God's Word they heard, and so to hear as to understand. His selections were most judiciously made with reference to the subject of his discourse, as was the case with the hymns chosen for praise, so that a perfect harmony reigned in the services of the sanctuary. Nothing was carelessly done or allowed to pass off in a slovenly manner.'[2]

Dr Bethune published a large number of sermons and addresses on various subjects, but his most substantial work seems to have been his *Expository Lectures on the Heidelberg Catechism*, first published, after his death. The title of the present reprint is taken from the threefold division of the subject-matter of the *Catechism*: 'First, the greatness of my sin and wretchedness. Second, how I am freed from all my sins and their wretched consequences. Third, what gratitude I owe to God for such redemption' (*Answer to Question 2*). The author was removed by death before he could complete the exposition of the *Catechism*,

[2] *Ibid.*, pp. 318–20.

but he evidently enjoyed, at death as well as in life, the comfort spoken of in its first answer: 'That I belong – body and soul, in life and in death – to my faithful Saviour, Jesus Christ', since he penned, on the day before his death, the following poem:

When time seems short, and death is near,
And I am pressed by doubt and fear,
And sins, an overflowing tide,
Assail my peace on every side,
This thought my refuge still shall be,
I know my Saviour died for me.

His name is Jesus, and he died
For guilty sinners crucified;
Content to die that he might win
Their ransom from the death of sin.
No sinner worse than I can be,
Therefore I know he died for me.

If grace were bought, I could not buy;
If grace were coined, no wealth have I;
By grace alone I draw my breath,
Held up from everlasting death.
Yet since I know his grace is free,
I know the Saviour died for me.

I read God's holy word and find
Great truths which far transcend my mind;
And little do I know beside,
Of thought so high and deep and wide.
This is my best theology,
I know the Saviour died for me.

My faith is weak, but 'tis thy gift;
Thou canst my helpless soul uplift,
And say, 'Thy bonds of death are riven,
Thy sins by me are all forgiven,
And thou shalt live, from guilt set free;
For I, thy Saviour, died for thee.'

Dr Bethune's widow placed the following Dedication in the original edition of the *Lectures*, published in New York in 1864:

'Dedicated to the Reformed Dutch Church of America, the Church of the author's adoption and love, to which the thirty-six years of his ministry were devoted, in the lengthening of its cords and the strengthening of its stakes. In this Church, may his words still win souls to Christ, is the prayer of his sorrowing widow.'

THE PUBLISHERS
March 2001

PREFACE

IN THIS WORK the public are presented with the best literary monument of its illustrious author. The subjects are the highest within the range of theological science; and Dr Bethune brought to their discussion the ripeness of his intellectual powers, a classic beauty of style, and the riches of a library well stored in this particular department.

In view of this exposition, he had collected the principal commentators on the *Heidelberg Catechism*. As the lectures were prepared for popular audiences, they are free from the stiffness of theological formulas, and will prove interesting to all classes of readers.

While this Catechism has been so widely received, and has become the standard of faith in two large churches of our country, while it has engaged the attention of so many commentators in Europe, it seems singular that this should be the first American attempt at a popular exposition designed for the press.

It is a misfortune to the church that the work remains incomplete. It has been carried forward with careful regard to the catechetical text to the Thirty-fifth Lord's Day, where the exposition ends with an introduction to the Second Commandment. Sermons on the Third and Fourth Commandments have been added because they are some of the finest productions of the author's pen, and because, while not textual, yet they may be considered a fair commentary on the Thirty-sixth and Thirty-eighth Lord's Days.

ABRAHAM R. VAN NEST, JR.
NEW YORK, 1864

EXPOSITORY LECTURES

ON

THE HEIDELBERG CATECHISM.

——◆——

LECTURE I.

THE ONLY COMFORT OF BELIEVERS.

INTRODUCTORY REMARKS.

IT is a peculiarity of our Church, that she not only directs her children to be taught by a Catechism the Christian doctrine, as every Church of the Reformation has done, but also orders her ministers to explain the Catechism which she has adopted, systematically and regularly before her congregations on the Sabbath day; thus securing the intelligent acquaintance of her people with the articles of our holy faith, and the fidelity of her preachers as expounders of all evangelical truth. Originally it was made the pastor's duty to go through the exposition once a year, each of the fifty-two Sabbaths having its assigned part; but the Church in this country, that the minister might have a more free choice of topics, sometime since, modified the rule, by extending the time over four years; and one lecture or more in each month will meet the requirement of that authority to which we happily owe submission. I undertake the difficult work the more cheerfully, because many of my hearers have but recently associated themselves with our denomination; because the method and the language of the Catechism is well chosen for such as desire the knowledge of the truth, that they may live by it; because many hurtful errors are lamentably prevalent; and because Christ's true disciples will always gratefully listen to plain, scriptural statements of sanctifying truth. At the same time, we protest against being thought " to hold the Catechism in equal estimation with the Word of God " (*Marck*); or " that orthodoxy should be decided by any other standard than the combined writings of the divinely inspired Prophets and Apostles, — the only rule of faith and practice " (*Zeigland, L'Enfant*); — but we do hold it as the symbol of our belief, and the test of adherence to our Reformed Church, into which no one has a right of entrance who does not acknowledge its published confessions. " If," as Van der Kemp says, " we believe the doctrines of the Catechism, it is not on account of the Catechism, but of God's own Word, out of which and according to which the Catechism was composed. If we prize this little book, we love the Word of God more. We commend it, because it recommends and explains clearly the Word of God to us."

Before, however, we begin its exposition, it may not be out of place to give a very brief sketch of its origin and history. It received its name from the city of Heidelberg, on the left bank of the Neckar, now in the Grand Duchy of Baden, but formerly of the Lower Palatinate, or Palatinate of the Rhine; the fertile territory of which is now divided into Prussia, Bavaria, Baden, Hesse Darmstadt, and other German States. Heidelberg became famous by the establishment of a University there, in 1386 (the oldest of the German seats of learning after those of Prague and Vienna), which contributed greatly to the enlightening of the Palatinate and the circumjacent countries. Early in the fifteenth century, Jerome of Prague came to Heidelberg, advocating the new opinions; and the University took an active part among the controversialists of that eventful time. In April, 1518, under the reign of the Elector Ludwig, Luther came from Wittenberg to his brethren, the Augustines, at Heidelberg, and set up public disputations in their monastery, gaining applause and followers among the members of the University and the nobility of the Palatinate. These eminent men, but especially Œcolampadius, Martin Tucco, and Brentz, pushed the cause of the Reformation with such vigor as to alarm the champions of Rome, who prohibited the disputations of Luther and his friends, citing Brentz and his associate, Theobald Bilikan, before the Chancellor of the Electorate (Von Banningen), to answer the charge of heresy, and for a time prevented their preaching; but Frederic II., who succeeded his brother, the Elector Philip, being well versed in the disputes, and zealously devoted to the new opinions, began at once the Reformation of the Church; and was accomplishing much good, when the disastrous battle of Mühlberg (24th of April, 1547, in which the Elector of Saxony, the leader of the Reformation, and the Landgrave of Hesse were made prisoners) gave the Emperor Charles V. the power to dictate the so-called Interim, by which the main tenets of Popery were enforced. The Emperor's triumph over the steadfast friends of truth did not last long, however; and by the memorable treaty of Passau, Aug. 2, 1552, the Germans obtained full religious freedom. The Elector, Otto Heinrich, following the example of Frederic II., whom he succeeded, 1556, abolished the mass, with other idolatries of Rome, ordered all images to be removed from the churches, and commissioned Heinrich Stolo, Michael Diller, and Dr. Marbach, from Strasburgh, to make a new Church order, or ritual, which he caused to be published and adopted by all the churches of the Palatinate. He also established at Heidelberg an " Ecclesiastical Council," the first members of which were Diller, the court chaplain, the electoral Chancellors Ehren and Eraft, and afterwards, on the recommendation of Melancthon, Tielman Hesshus. Already, however, the opinions of Zuinglius, who held the true doctrine, contrary to the consubstantiation of Luther, had many adherents at Heidelberg ; and disputes ran high between the two schools. The pious Frederic III., succeeding Otto Heinrich, 1559, at once declared himself on the side of the Zuinglians. He took and pursued his measures with great prudence, but no less zeal ; and, after a sharp controversy, he remodelled the churches of the Palatinate after the form of the Zuinglian-Helvetic pattern. He converted a college, which Frederic the Second had established at Heidelberg, into a theological seminary, and gave it professors of the Reformed (not Lutheran) opinions. After accomplishing this, he turned all his attention to the preparing of a catechism for the churches and schools of the Palatinate. There were already several catechisms, besides that of Brenhius and that of Luther, used among the Palatinate churches, causing many disputes from their discrepancies ; and they needed a symbolical book of their own, clearly setting forth the true Christian doctrine. The Elector himself says, in the Preface which he wrote to the first edition of the Heidelberg Catechism, 1563, that it was written in order to remove all error, false doctrine, and differences of opinion from the Church, and establish the Reformation firmly. The Elector proposed the composition of the Catechism, in

1562, to Zachary Ursinus, a learned professor at Heidelberg, and Casparus Olevianus, the court preacher, a favorite of Frederic. Each took part in the composition of the book. Olevianus arranged his as a simple illustration of the covenant of grace; Ursinus prepared two forms of a catechism, — one for children in the schools, another suited to the more advanced. From the labors of both, the Heidelberg Catechism was produced, — the system of which must be attributed to Ursinus. It is, however, certain that Frederic himself took part in the work, especially in the answer to the Seventy-eighth Question, which the Elector says he altered from the words of Theodoret, for reasons assigned.

The Catechism having been completed in the same year that it was begun, Frederic assembled in a synod at Heidelberg all the superintendents and preachers of the Palatinate, whom he expected to examine the book carefully, and see that it was every way according to the Word of God. Part of the church in which the synod met is still standing. They zealously performed the part assigned them, and, expressing their wonder at the learning and the precision shown in it, heartily approved it, particularly and as a whole, recommending its adoption and publication. It was immediately translated into Latin by two learned professors, Lago and Pithozao, and published in both languages at Heidelberg, 1563, by John Mayer, under the title of " Catechism, or Christian Instruction, according to the usages of the Palatinate Churches and Schools."

Though the Latin version was published at the same time with the German, the German, or original, is the authentic copy; " in which," says Alting, " everything is not only more elegantly, but also more impressively set forth."

The first edition is now extremely rare. It differs not a little from our present copies in form, words, and style, some things being wanting which were afterwards added, and some things supplied which were afterwards left out. It is not divided into the sections for the successive Lord's days. The paragraphs are not distinctly separated, questions and answers being thrown together. The scriptural proofs are few, and not always well chosen. The Eightieth Question, for some unknown reason, is wholly omitted.

The first edition was followed in the same year by another, having the same title and editor, so that it could not be recognized as distinct but for the insertion of the Eightieth Question, and a note at the end, stating that it was added upon the order of the Elector. The language of the Eightieth Question is not, however, the same with that which we now have, (probably from some desire not unnecessarily to offend the Papists,) but is in these words: "And is not the mass, in truth, nothing else but an idolatrous denial of the sole accepted sacrifice, the sufferings of Christ?" There was, probably, yet a third edition in 1563; as a copy, in other respects like the second, gives the conclusion of the Eightieth Question somewhat differently; possibly, however, a new page was substituted in later impressions of the second. The inconvenience of the early arrangement was so much felt, that the fourth edition (with same title) was issued by Mayer, 1573 (duodecimo), in which the questions and answers are divided and numbered, and marked for the fifty-two Lord's days.

The most valuable edition of these times is yet pub-

lished at Neustadt on the Hardt, 1595 (octavo), with
the title: " Catechism, or Brief System of Christian Doctrine ; together with the Church Ritual, Prayers, and
appropriate Proofs from Holy Writ. Also, the Defence
of the Heidelberg Theologians against the unfounded
charges and attacks with which this Catechism and its
excellent Proofs out of Scripture have been unfairly
pursued. Also, the Opinion of Martin Luther on the
Bread-breaking in the Holy Supper. Also, Answers
and Counter-questions on the Six Questions on the
Holy Supper, and in which particulars the Evangelical Churches agree or differ respecting the Holy Supper; arranged by Zacharias Ursinus." The Defence
given in this previous edition is masterly.

The division of the Catechism into its three principal
parts, as set forth in the Second Question and Answer,
was imitated from the order of Scripture in the Old and
New Testament, as we learn from the Prolegomena,
(preface) of Ursinus himself. It is also stated by several learned divines (Theo. Marck in his Catechetical
Defence, Dontrein in his Golden Treasure, and Von
Alpen in his Prolegomena), that the arrangement followed is that of the Epistle to the Romans.

The Catechism was the object of many and long-
continued attacks from various quarters, but was man-
fully and successfully defended until it gained the confidence and praise of all the Reformed Churches; editions
of both the German and Latin versions were numerous,
and many commentaries and expositions by way of sermons were written upon it, — the best of which is that
of Ursinus himself, published from notes taken from his
lectures on the work at Heidelberg, 1569–77, corrected
and edited by David Pareus, 1591–98.

The Catechism has been translated into nearly all the civilized languages. A Greek translation, intended for the churches of that name, was made by Frederic Sylburg, and sent at the expense of the States-General to the Patriarch of Constantinople. The Belgian government had it translated into Spanish, that it might be used in the West Indies. The Swiss churches reconstructed the Catechism of Zurich after its clearer expositions. The Reformed churches of Hungary ordered it to be taught and explained in their churches, schools, and universities. It received high commendations from the pious and learned in England; while almost universally on the continent it was acknowledged as a symbolical book of the Reformed churches. It was rendered into Hebrew, Greek, Dutch, Spanish, French, English, Italian, Bohemian, Polish, Hungarian, Arabic, and Malay, as well as in German and Latin. It has passed through not less than five hundred thousand editions, through the press of Germany alone.

But in no country was it more highly honored than in Holland. It was early made the symbolical book of the Dutch Church, ordered to be taught in their schools and universities, and expounded regularly from their pulpits. All their preachers, and teachers, and professors were sworn to hold and promulgate its doctrines ; nor was any one admitted to church-membership who did not profess its faith. In the most mournful times of persecution, Peter Gabriel encouraged the constancy of his suffering brethren by preaching from it at Amsterdam. It was first approved by the Dutch divines who were exiles for their creed, in an assembly at Wessel, 1568; the lesser national synod of Dordrecht, 1574, required that all their teachers of religion should sign the Catechism àt the same time with their Confession of Faith; and the great synod of Dordrecht directed their formularies to be prepared, — the first to be signed by professors of theology, the second by preachers, and the third by school-masters, — declaring and promising the strictest adherence to the Heidelberg Catechism. The first and second formularies are preserved in use among our churches here to this day. Many most learned theologians from all parts of Europe being present, by invitation, at that synod, united with their Dutch brethren in thoroughly examining it, and gave it the most unreserved and highest commendation. From the mother churches of Germany and Holland, it was brought by their children to this country, and is now the symbolical book of the Reformed German and Dutch churches of North America; where may God long maintain its holy teachings.

Thus you may see, dear fellow-Christians, through what care and unanimous devotion of pious, learned men the Lord of the Church has prepared and preserved this admirable compend of his pure truth for us. The little book which your children study, has stood the shock of Popery and heresy through bloody centuries, — strengthening the weak, and making heroic the strong. Well may we study, with devout and thankful hearts, a manual so sacred in its doctrines and associations.

You will remark, however, that, unlike most books of the kind, our Catechism takes the order of Christian experience; was prepared for those professing to be Christians, and should be expounded accordingly. May God aid me in the exposition, and bless you in the hearing, for the honor of his holy name. Amen.

FIRST LORD'S DAY.

THE ONLY COMFORT OF BELIEVERS.

QUEST. I. *What is thine only comfort in life and death?*

ANS. That I, with body and soul, both in life and death, am not my own, but belong unto my faithful Saviour, Jesus Christ, who, with his precious blood, hath fully satisfied for all my sins, and delivered me from all power of the devil; and so preserves me, that without the will of my heavenly Father, not a hair can fall from my head; yea, that all things must be subservient to my salvation; and, therefore, by his Holy Spirit he also assures me of eternal life, and makes me sincerely willing and ready henceforth to live unto him.

QUEST. II. *How many things are necessary for thee to know, that thou, enjoying this comfort, mayest live and die happily?*

ANS. Three: the first, how great my sins and miseries are; the second, how I may be delivered from all my sins and miseries; the third, how I shall express my gratitude to God for such deliverance.

THE answer to the First Question tells us in a few words, what those great doctrines of the Scriptures are, from which the Christian derives his sure and only comfort.

The answer to the Second Question states the order which will be followed throughout the Catechism, by a division of all Christian knowledge necessary for our salvation into three parts.

The several truths contained in both these answers will be discussed at length as we proceed, step by step, with our study of the book. At present, therefore, we shall only ask you to mark —

FIRST: *The comfort which a Christian has in his religious belief.*

SECONDLY: *The method by which he attains a knowledge of this comfort.*

FIRST: *The comfort which a Christian has in his religious belief.*

My beloved friends, — the Catechism does not err, but follows the high, infallible, binding example of the Holy Ghost throughout the Scriptures. When the evangelical prophet, moved by divine influence, proclaimed, as the voice of God, the blessings of Christ's approaching kingdom, he commanded the messengers of grace, saying: " Comfort ye, comfort ye my people, saith your God. Speak ye comfortably to Jerusalem, and cry unto her that her warfare is accomplished, that her iniquity is pardoned ; for she hath received of the Lord's hand double for all her sins." When the angel came to the shepherds with the annunciation of Christ's advent, what were his words? " Fear not ; for behold, I bring you glad tidings of great joy which shall be to all people." When Jesus himself preached, what was his argument to gain the ears of the people? " If any man thirst, let him come unto me and drink." " Come unto me all ye that labor and are heavy laden, and I will give you rest." What is the name given by the blessed Master to his truth but the *Gospel,* or good news, which he has ordained shall be preached to every creature ? Nay, does not the term salvation imply that there is a danger of misery from which we are to be rescued, and is not the hope of safety a comfort ? The Catechism is right in bringing religion to us under the name of comfort ; nor is the promise of comfort discordant with the inculcation of duty, as the subsequent teachings of the book will show.

The chief end of man, in his salvation, as in his creation, is the glory of God ; but the glory of our divine Maker and Redeemer is closely connected with the happiness of all who faithfully obey him. It was that he might have the satisfaction of seeing a family of creatures reflecting in their happiness his own blessedness, that he made our race; it is that he may behold a family of penitent sinners happy again and forever, that he has established the plan of redemption. The holy angels, who advance by their glad service the glory of their Lord, are happy in their ministry; and man, while he continued sinless, was happy in his heavenly Father's approbation. The relation of the creature to the Creator makes it necessary that the happiness and obedience of the subject should be inseparable, and also — his disobedience and misery. It is only when his intelligent creatures break the righteous laws which God has given for their guidance, and thus dash themselves against the immutable principles of his government, that, to manifest the glory of his justice, he makes them miserable in their sins, as the fallen angels are, and as fallen men are, except they be saved through faith in Christ and repentance toward God. The process of the Gospel is the conversion of the sinner from sin to holiness; that through holiness he may be restored to happiness. It is our duty to be happy, because happiness lies in contentment with all the divine will concerning us. Therefore, the Christian is not selfish or blameworthy in seeking his own happiness from that religion, by the avowal and practice of which he endeavors to glorify God on earth and prepare for glorifying him more perfectly beyond the grave. Indeed, it is our enjoyment of the Christian religion, which proves our sincerity, for when we truly love God we must find his service a great delight. Jesus, our divine Master and holy example, served God

for the " joy that was set before him," counting it his
meat and his drink to do the will of his heavenly Father, and we follow in his steps when we fight the
Christian fight, run the Christian race, and keep the
Christian faith, cheered by the hope of winning through
grace the crown of life, which God for Christ's sake
has prepared for all who love him.   It is because God
would animate our zeal by such motives that he has
given us so many exceeding great and precious promises, causing the holy Scriptures to be " written for our
learning, that we through faith and comfort in the
Scriptures might have hope."

There is much meaning in the use of the word comfort, to express the Christian's enjoyment of religion, as
it supposes that the person who is comforted would
otherwise be oppressed by trouble.   The angels are
happy in heaven, but they need no comfort, for they
have no sorrow.   Our first parents needed no comfort
until sin brought trouble upon them ; but Lamech
called the name of his son *Noah* (or *Rest*), because,
said he : " This same shall comfort us concerning our
work and toil of our hands, because of the ground
which the Lord hath cursed."   Religion does not at
once deliver us out of trouble ; on the contrary, " it
is good for us to be afflicted ; " but it comforts us in
tribulations, through which we enter the kingdom of
God, enabling us to bear with patience our many sorrows, and to resist with courage our many temptations,
by the assurance that God loves us now, and has provided for us an eternal rest hereafter.   When we reach
heaven we shall need no comfort, because our troubles
will be over forever.

Hence the Catechism speaks of our " comfort in life

and death." While life lasts our troubles will last, and death is a fearful trial to the stoutest heart; but when we have passed through and survived that final agony, our joy will be perfect and secure. Until then we have great need of comfort, and find it in our Christian religion, which, though it does not make our present life perfectly happy (for this is not our rest), is rich in comfort to all that believe. Hence the Holy Ghost, through whose gracious influences we receive the truths of the Gospel, is called the Comforter, and those who enjoy his grace are said to " walk in the comfort of the Holy Ghost." Of this the Apostle Paul, our best example of a Christian, and of a Christian preacher after Christ, had sweet experience, as we know from many texts in his writings, but especially from the preface of his Second Epistle to the Corinthians : " Blessed be God, even the Father of our Lord Jesus Christ, the Father of mercies, and the God of all comfort, who comforteth us in all our tribulation, that we may be able to comfort them which are in any trouble, by the comfort wherewith we ourselves are comforted of God."

This is the believer's " *only* comfort." They, who have never acquainted themselves with the God of salvation, may find some passing comfort in things of the present world, but at the end will reap shame and eternal disappointment, since things gross and perishable can never satisfy the spiritual and immortal soul; but the Christian looks up to God, saying : " Whom have I in heaven but thee? and there is none upon earth that I desire besides thee. My flesh and my heart faileth; but God is the strength of my heart, and my portion forever." He is conscious of his spiritual immortality, and knows that God alone can fill his immortality with blessedness. He draws many comforts through the creatures of God, but only through them as the channels in which they flow down to him from God, the overflowing Fountain. Without God, he has nothing; with God, he has all things. It is the truths of religion which assure him of the Divine favor to his soul; and, therefore, in religion he finds his only comfort. The Catechism is right in its first question, for it puts our religion to the closest proof, when it demands: " What is our only comfort in life and in death ? "

The believer's answer to this question, states, *first,* a main fact; *then,* the particulars contained in the fact.

I. A main fact.

" That I with my body and soul, both in life and death, am not my own, but belong unto my faithful Saviour, Jesus Christ."

The natural pride of man's heart resists the thought of subjection to God, and of dependence upon him. This was the essence of man's first sin, when, tempted by the devil, he sought to be a god unto himself. So, every man, unconverted from the iniquity of the fall, loves not to retain the thought of God, but walks after the choice of his own heart. He would, perhaps, shrink from denying the existence or sovereign providence of God; but, practically, every man who does not live in the fear of God, depending gratefully upon divine care and conscious of his responsibility to the Great Judge, is an atheist at heart. The Christian has been changed from this proud temper by faith in the Gospel; and he considers it his happiness that he is not his own but belongs to God in Christ; that he is the Lord's, not only by creation, for surely what is made out of nothing belongs to the Maker, but also by redemption, because having been rescued from eternal ruin, he is the rightful property of his Saviour; that his body is the Lord's, from whom its life with all its faculties is derived, and by whom, when death returns it to the dust, it will be kept for a glorious immortality; that his soul is the Lord's, with all its capacities and affections, to be taught, ruled, sanctified, and employed by him for his glory; that his life is the Lord's, to be spent in his holy, pleasant service; and that his death is the Lord's, because his closing triumph here, and his eternal being after, will praise the mercy of his Redeemer, through whose gracious power he is raised from the depths of sin to the heights of heaven.

He belongs to Christ by a threefold obligation. Christ has *bought* him. His life and happiness were forfeit to divine justice; but Christ has redeemed him from eternal death by the substitution of himself to bear the wrath of God, and so Christ has acquired a full right over him, as the purchase of his atonement. First, he belonged to God his Creator, then he was in the righteous hands of God his Judge, but now he belongs to God the Saviour. " Thine they were," said the blessed Mediator, speaking of his disciples to the Father, " and thou gavest them me." The Father, as the representative of the Godhead against whom they had sinned, gives them to the incarnate Son as the representative of both the Godhead and the Church in the plan of salvation; but gives them not without a price. They are delivered, transferred, set over to the Saviour by virtue of the eternal covenant. Christ has fulfilled his part in satisfying the honor of the divine law which they had broken, and now the Father fulfils his part in giving them to Christ as his own peculiar property. Wherefore the apostle says : " Ye are not your own, for ye are bought with a price : therefore, glorify God in your body and in your spirit, which are God's."

Again, we are exhorted to look for the " appearing of the great God and our Saviour Jesus Christ, who gave himself for us, that he might redeem us from all iniquity, and purify unto himself a peculiar people (or a people of his own) zealous of good works." Yet again : " Forasmuch as ye know that ye were not redeemed with corruptible things, as silver and gold . . . . but with the precious blood of Christ, as of a lamb (a lamb sacrificed for sin) without blemish and without spot." All the property which God, as Creator and Judge, had in the believer is now trans- ferred to God the Saviour.

This the believer acknowledges when he accepts the atoning work of Christ. He is, therefore, Christ's by *his own vow.* He gives, surrenders himself to Christ, making a covenant with him, promising on his part to serve the Saviour by divine help all the days of his life, and Christ on his part engaging to save him until the uttermost.

Then, as a gracious consequence, the believer belongs to Christ because he is *a member of that spiritual body,* *whose Head is Christ.* There is much meant by the mystery of the believer's union with the body of Christ, which he cannot at present understand ; but this we do know, that through faith he lives, because Christ's life is in him, that he is corporated with Christ in the en- joyment of all those blessings which the righteousness of Christ has obtained from the Father ; and that he is

one with Christ in all the future glory of his Head.
It is thus a *vital* union ; the believer is a member of
Christ's " body, of his flesh, and of his bones ; " it is
a *fruitful* union, Christ animating him to all good
works ; for, by another figure, he is said to be grafted
in Christ as a branch in a vine, which bears fruit from
the energy diffused through it by the vigorous stem ;
it is an *indissoluble* union, for the body cannot be separated from its immortal Head ; " because I live," says
the Saviour, " ye shall live also."

Therefore does the Christian rejoice that he is " not
his own, but belongs unto his faithful Saviour Jesus
Christ." Were he his own, he would be left to the
care of himself ; but now because he is Christ's, Christ
will take care of him as his own, as the purchase of his
blood, as a member of his body, as the instrument of
his glory, and as a trophy of his triumphant grace.
This leads us to consider —

II. The particulars included by the main fact.

1. *Pardon.* — Christ " hath fully satisfied by his own
blood for all his sins." Did he belong to himself, he
would be obliged to meet in his own person all the
guilty consequences of his many offences against God,
and be unavoidably overwhelmed by eternal wrath ;
but now Christ claims him at the hands of divine justice as his ; interposing his atonement between the vengeance of God and his ransomed one, covering the
unworthy with his merits, representing the penitent in
his ever-prevalent prayers, claiming for him acceptance
with himself, in whom the Father is well pleased. Oh,
how precious, in this light, is the fact that we belong
not to ourselves, but to our faithful Saviour Jesus
Christ !

2. *Deliverance from danger.* — " And hath delivered
me from all power of the devil." This deliverance is
twofold. The devil, full of malice against men, is
employed by God as an executioner of divine vengeance ; and in this permitted capacity he claims the
impenitent for his victims ; but our faithful Saviour,
stronger than our arch-enemy, and in his right as the
Redeemer, rescues the captive out of his cruel hands.
So far as sin had given Satan a right over the body
and soul of the sinner that calls to Christ for help, he
destroys death and him that has the power of death ;
placing the penitent, now his own, eternally beyond
his baffled rage. This deliverance, however, is a part
of pardon, which we have already treated of.

But sinners are said by the Scripture to put themselves wilfully under the control of the devil, when
they comply with his temptations. They admit his
sophisms, by which he leads the godless astray, into
their minds, and so their conscience is deadened or
perverted ; their crimes against God, often repeated,
acquire the fettering force of habit ; nay, they get a
fearful proclivity to evil, accelerating in impulse as
they go downward, until, if divine grace do not arrest
them, they plunge from the wickedness of this world
to the yet more awful wickedness of hell. Hence
they are said to be " sold (like slaves) under sin ; " to
be " led captive of the devil ; " to be " in bondage to
Satan." Oh, how shall the sinner, if left to himself,
break these more than iron chains ? How shall he deliver himself from this fatal bondage ? How shall he
escape from his cunning, cruel master ? " Blessed be
God ! " exclaims the penitent believer, " I belong to
my faithful Saviour Jesus Christ ; he is my master

now; he has bought me for his own with his most precious blood; he will not leave me in my helplessness; by his Holy Spirit he will break the fetters from my soul; he will give me liberty; his love will be a refuge where my old master cannot reach me. Stronger is he that is for me, than all that be against me." The deliverance may not be complete at once, for sanctification, in the wise process of grace, is a gradual work; the devil yields not his possession of our hearts easily, and the conflict there of sin with godliness may be sharp; but the deliverance is begun in regeneration; it is carried on by an Almighty Power; its certainty is assured by divine promise. The charm of Satan over the believer is met by a master charm in the name of Jesus, "for he shall save his people from their sins." The Seed of the woman has so bruised the old serpent's head, that the weakest saint shall break him down under foot, and trample over him into life, freedom, and joy eternal. Oh, thanks again to God, that Christ owns us, and we are not our own!

3. *Preservation.* — " And so preserves me, that without the will of my heavenly Father, not a hair can fall from my head; yea, that all things shall be subservient to my salvation." If, instead of belonging to his Saviour, the Christian owned himself, his condition were most miserable, for he would own nothing but himself, while all around him — all that is necessary to his happiness, all present and future events affecting his welfare, are the Lord's, and ordered by the Lord, on whose goodness he has no claim; he would be alone, helpless, utterly destitute and needy. Now, Christ owns him; and as a faithful master cares for his own servant, whom he has bought so dearly; and all things are

Christ's, and he turns all things for the good of his own. The God of salvation is the God of adoption. The believer is united to the only-begotten Son of God incarnate, therefore God adopts him as his child; and the heavenly Father will never suffer any real evil to come upon his regenerate children. When the Father gave to Christ the sinners whom he redeems, he gave all things into Christ's hands, that he might be Head over all things to his Church. All power is given unto Christ, and all his sovereign prerogative he employs for the benefit of his own peculiar people. He has made their eternal salvation his glory, and none can pluck those whom he preserves out of his affectionate embrace. Life is the time of the Christian's preparation for eternity; every thing that concerns him here has a bearing upon his state hereafter, therefore does his faithful Saviour take the tenderest care of him now and until he is brought home. He is " kept by the power of God through faith unto salvation ready to be revealed in the last time." So nice and intense is this care that the very hairs of his head are numbered. Not one of them falls to the ground without his Father's will. Nay, all things work together for his good. The process is begun, is now carried on, and will be steadily furthered until the design is consummated in the believer's full redemption. Cheerfully, then, does the believer commit his all to Him to whom he has committed himself; his time, to him who takes charge of his eternity, the regulation of his circumstances on earth, to him who has prepared for him a blissful heaven. If he had the care of himself, he might well despair; but now that Christ has the care of him, he knows he is safe, — his body safe, his soul safe, safe in life, safe in

death, safe forever. His griefs may be many, his
temptations strong, his infirmity extreme, and therefore
he cannot help being troubled; but he has comfort
amidst all, because he belongs to his faithful Saviour
Jesus Christ, whose grace is sufficient for him.

4. *Assurance.* — " By his Holy Spirit he also assures
me of eternal life, and makes me sincerely willing and
ready henceforth to live unto him." Man, left to his
own unassisted reason, could never have ascertained
the character or will of God, much less discovered the
plan of salvation through Jesus Christ; but the faithful Saviour having undertaken to rescue his own from
all the consequences of their sins, makes their instruction sure by the grace of his Holy Spirit. Holy men
of old were moved by the Holy Spirit to write the
books of the Old and New Testaments, which together
constitute the Word of God, our only rule of faith and
practice; and therefore all we know of religion we
have been taught by the Holy Spirit. The Scriptures
are, however, by themselves addressed to men or Christians (as the case may be) generally; and experience,
nay, the Word itself, shows that no man applies the
testimony of the revelation to his own case, until the
same divine Agent who inspired the testimony moves
the sinner's heart to perceive himself addressed by it;
but then discovering his guilt and danger, he also sees
the sufficiency of atonement offered on his behalf, and
trusts in Christ as his Saviour. Such personal faith —
the appropriating of the Gospel to our own souls — is
the effect of the Spirit's testimony in our hearts corresponding to his testimony in the Scriptures, and constitutes our assurance of salvation, — by which salvation
we mean, according to Scripture, the full accomplish-

ment of the Saviour's purpose of eternal love toward
the sinner that believes on his name.   Thus we read:
" No man can say that Jesus is the Lord but by the
Holy Ghost ; " and again : " He that believeth on the
Son of God hath the witness in himself; " and yet
again : "As many as are led by the Spirit of God,
they are the sons of God.   For ye have not received
the spirit of bondage again to fear ; but ye have received the spirit of adoption whereby ye cry, Abba,
Father.   The Spirit also beareth witness with our
spirit that we are the children of God ; and if children,
then heirs ; heirs of God and joint-heirs with Christ."
The promise assures complete salvation to all who believe ; when, therefore, we believe, God by his own
testimony assures complete salvation unto us.

But it will be asked, May not a sinner deceive himself in thinking that he believes when he does not ?
Is there not a counterfeit of true faith ? and if so, how
may we attain the assurance of our salvation ?   The
Catechism meets the inquiry.   There is indeed a counterfeit faith, but it may be detected by its fruitlessness,
while on the other hand a true faith shows itself in its
sanctifying effect on the life and character.   The purpose of the Saviour is to save his people from their
sins ; perfect salvation, which is perfect holiness, is
achieved only in heaven, but it is begun on earth.
Repentance is the beginning of salvation, the pulsa-
tions of a new life which is eternal.   The believer is
conscious of this great change.   He is yet a sinner, he
sees his sinfulness more plainly than ever, he feels his
weakness and utter inability to contend with the temptations that beset him ; but he no longer delights in
sin ; his desire is to do the will of God, and, by divine

help, to resist all evil. Amidst all his failures and imperfections he discovers a new principle at work in his soul which can have been engendered there only by divine power. This is the testimony of the Spirit. The same Holy One who testifies in the Scriptures and in the hearts of sinners, testifies in the believer's life, making him who was once a rebel now "sincerely willing and ready henceforth to live unto Christ." Oh what a happiness, what a comfort it is, that we belong unto Christ, who not only has died for us, but by his Spirit lives in us, working through us his holy purpose! When we can claim this comfort, "Christ is formed in us the hope of glory."

SECONDLY: *The method by which the Christian attains a knowledge of this comfort.*

This is not the time to dwell upon the answer to the Second Question, as it only sets forth in brief what will be shown more fully hereafter. The order given is, however, most natural, and according to the doctrine of the Scriptures.

I. He must know how great his sins and miseries are. Unless he knows himself to be a sinner, he will not feel his need of pardon; unless he sees his miseries, he will not see his need of a Saviour; unless he feels that his sins and miseries are great, he will not be zealous in escaping from them to the great salvation provided for him. None but those who are conscious of being lost can discover that Jesus is the Saviour they need. This is set forth in the second, third, and fourth Lord's days.

II. He must know how he may be delivered from all his sins and miseries. This includes a knowledge of the whole Gospel, — the purpose of God, the mediation of Christ, and the grace of the Holy Ghost, which is taught from the fifth to the thirty-second Lord's days.

III. He must know how to express his gratitude for such deliverance to God his Saviour. This includes all his duty, to which the Catechism gives the yet higher name of gratitude; the true Christian being moved to render it with a cheerful zeal, not only because God has a right in him, but also because he delights in recognizing and meeting the claims of a Benefactor so gracious, upon all his heart and mind and life. This is treated of from the thirty-second to the last Lord's day.

May God assist our farther studies by his Holy Spirit, that we, being convinced of sin and made to know the preciousness of Christ, may find our only comfort in his choice of us, and our choice of him as our Saviour, Master, and eternal Friend. Amen.

LECTURE II.

THE KNOWLEDGE OF OUR MISERY.

SECOND LORD'S DAY.

THE KNOWLEDGE OF OUR MISERY.

QUEST. III. *Whence knowest thou thy misery?*
ANS. Out of the law of God.
QUEST. IV. *What doth the law of God require of us?*
ANS. Christ teaches us that briefly, Matt. xxii. 37–40: "Thou shalt love
the Lord thy God with all thy heart, and with all thy soul, and with
all thy mind," and with all thy strength. "This is the first and great
commandment; and the second is like unto it: Thou shalt love thy
neighbor as thyself. On these two commandments hang all the law
and the prophets."
QUEST. V. *Canst thou keep all these things perfectly?*
ANS. In no wise; for I am prone by nature to hate God and my neighbor.

THE blessed Master himself declares the reason and
purpose of his mediatorial work, when he says:
" The Son of Man is come to seek and to save that which
was lost." Had not God been angry with us we should
not have been miserable; had we not sinned against
God, he would not have been angry with us; had we
the power of reconciling ourselves to God, we should
not have needed a Saviour; had not our condemnation
been very great, we should not have needed so great a
Saviour; and had not God, our righteous Judge, been
infinitely merciful, he would not have "sent his Only
Begotten Son, that whoso believeth in him might not
perish but have everlasting life." It was our ruin that
moved the pity of God, our helplessness that brought
his Son to be our Saviour, our guiltiness that made the
Saviour a sinless sufferer in our nature, obedient until
death on our behalf. To understand and appreciate
the salvation by Christ, it is necessary that we should
know our misery, its source, its extent, and our utter

dependence upon divine grace through Christ for pardon, favor, a new life, and immortal happiness. To teach us this is the design of the Church, as opened in the section of her Catechism for the second Lord's day ; from which we learn,

FIRST : *The Test of our condition :*
The Law of God.

SECONDLY : *The Requirements of the Law :*
Supreme love to God our Lord, and love to our neighbor as ourselves.

THIRDLY : *Our Inability to fulfil those Requirements :*
Being prone " by nature to hate God and my neighbor."

FIRST : *The Law of God is the test of our condition :*
According to the Second Question and Answer, the first branch of Christian inquiry is : " How great our *sins* and *miseries* are." The Third Question is : " Whence knowest thou thy *misery ?* " the term *sin* not being repeated ; yet the answer is : " Out of the *Law* of God ; " which is an implied assertion that our misery is penal or the effect of sin, being our punishment as sinners, and, therefore, in proportion to our sins. The word and character of God allow of no other conclusion, since we cannot believe that he who delights in goodness and mercy would willingly, or without reason, afflict his creatures. Our misery can come only from his anger, and he is angry only with the wicked. His favor, which includes all blessings, is promised to the obedient ; his curse, which includes all miseries, is threatened against the disobedient. The degree of our sin is, therefore, the measure of our misery, and that we may ascertain this we must look into the Law of God ; for if we have not kept its precepts, the pen-

alties annexed show the guilt, or obnoxiousness, liability to punishment, which we have brought upon ourselves. Hence the Law of God is the only true test of our condition.   This is the argument in brief, which we may, not without profit, examine more particularly.

1st.   God is Sovereign ; by which we understand, that he has the right to rule, that he has the power to rule, and that he does rule over all.   To deny this were atheism ; for the fundamental idea of God is : The First Cause of all things.   The First Cause must be self-existent and independent of all.   The same will which alone could create, alone can preserve ; and, therefore, God must rule over all.   The creation includes moral beings, or beings who have a sense of right and wrong, with powers to act accordingly ; therefore, the administration of the Supreme Will must be a moral government.   Thus the fact of our existence proves that we belong to God ; the fact of our preservation, that we are under the control of God ; and the fact of our moral consciousness, that we are subject to the moral government of God.   If our lives be in harmony with the principles of the divine government, no evil can reach us, because our Preserver is Sovereign over all ; but if we are at variance with his will, no good can reach us for the same reason.

But how may we obtain a knowledge of the divine will which should be the rule of our lives, and in our conformity or opposition to which we are to find happiness or misery ?   The Catechism answers : " Out of the Law of God ; " that is, out of the Law which God has revealed in the Holy Scriptures.   For it is clear that none but God, whose infinite wisdom arranged and ordained the principles on which he administers his will, can discover what those principles are. These may be dimly perceived in the processes of Providence around us, or what is sometimes called the fitness of things; but not sufficiently, for besides that we cannot, from the weakness of our reason, accurately trace the visible effects back to their unseen causes, the development of those effects is as yet very partial. If we were left to learn the will of God concerning our duty from the manifestations of his providence, we should have to wait until eternity before we could begin our obedience, for only in eternity those manifestations are complete. There are a thousand seeming discrepancies in the providential administration of human affairs, which God will not vindicate until he consummates his mighty scheme at the catastrophe of the Judgment. So oppressively embarrassing are these difficulties, that the very advocates of Natural Religion, who bid us learn the character of God and our duty from the fitness of things, make them their strongest, but far from satisfactory, argument for a future state of reward and punishment.

Neither can conscience be a trustworthy oracle. For conscience does not itself determine right or wrong, but is only our faculty of recognizing the distinction between the right and the wrong, when they are presented to us. Recognition is very different from discovery. It is one thing to perceive a path when it is marked out for us, and another to find out a path for ourselves; so it is one thing to see the right when God makes it known, and another to decide upon what is right without his aid. This last is utterly beyond the prerogative or the power of conscience. Indeed, conscience needs education like any other human faculty, and education supposes some fixed fundamental rules to which it must be conformed. No faithful parent leaves his child to learn morals from its conscience, but presses rules of right upon its conscience. The variety of moral opinions among men is so great, that were it possible to hold an œcumenical council of consciences, there is scarcely a point of morals on which their decree would be unanimous. Nay, the revolutions of moral sentiment in the same man at different stages of his experience and knowledge, show how uncertain and even capricious the judgments of conscience are when left to itself.

Besides, obedience to the dictates of conscience, without a distinct reference to the will of God, is not right, since that were making conscience and not God our Judge and Lord. For a man to think that he can do no wrong while he follows his conscience, unless his conscience be regulated by the will of God, is a self-idolatry and an atheistical pride. A human government does not try its subjects by their consciences, but by its own laws; and excuses a violation of its laws only in those who are not capable of perceiving what those laws require. So will God try us by the laws of his kingdom, not by our own imaginations.

The judgments of individuals being so imperfect, the general opinions of mankind must be also unworthy of confidence. A long and traditional experience of the good or ill effects consequent upon certain courses of action, may have led the world to agree respecting some matters immediately affecting our interests; but history proves the failure of all attempts to frame a system of morals without wisdom from above. The best and wisest of the classical philosophers differed widely among themselves as to the very definition of virtue;

while some, especially Socrates, the most exalted of them all, humbly confessed that the line dividing right from wrong could be drawn only by the finger of him who presides over the universe.

God has himself excluded all question on the subject, by giving, in his own revealed word, the law to which he commands our conformity on pain of his curse.

The Christian, therefore, goes directly to God for instruction, trusting neither to the discoveries of his reason, the dictates of his conscience, the opinions of men, nor the practices of the world. God has the sole right to his service, and he asks from God only how that service should be rendered. Thus he makes the law of God the sole test of his condition, sees his crimes in his transgressions of it, and his misery in the punishment which it threatens. Until he looks at himself in that mirror of infallible truth, he can never judge of his moral character; until he gets a response from that unerring oracle, he can never know what awaits him at the hands of his God. He learns his " misery out of the law of God."

SECONDLY : *The requirements of that law.*

These the Catechism shows by citing the words of our blessed Lord, Matt. xxii. 37–40 ; though it must be noted that, in giving the first great commandment, the last clause, " and with all thy strength," is added from the parallel passage, Luke x. 27 ; and that our translator of the Catechism, by carelessly neglecting to copy the Scripture immediately out of his Bible, has allowed a slight but displeasing variation from the English text, which difference we shall correct.

" Thou shalt love the Lord thy God with all thy heart, and with all thy soul, and with all thy mind ; "

and, from Luke, " with all thy strength." " This is
the first and great commandment. And the second is
like unto it : Thou shalt love thy neighbor as thyself.
On these two commandments hang all the law and the
prophets."

Our divine Saviour did not give these comprehensive
precepts as of himself, but brought them together from
separate parts of the Pentateuch ; the first from Deut.
vi. 5 : " Thou shalt love the Lord thy God with all
thine heart, and with all thy soul, and with all thy
might ;" the second from Lev. xix. 18 : " Thou shalt
love thy neighbor as thyself." All that the older scriptures contain of divine morals, of our duty to God and
our service to man for God's sake, are summed up in
these two commandments. As the Apostle Paul says,
Rom. xiii. 10 : " Love is the fulfilling of the law ;"
and again, 1 Tim. i. 5 : " Now the end of the commandment is charity (*love*), out of a pure heart, and
of a good conscience, and of faith unfeigned ; " and
the Apostle John in his first epistle, iv. 16 : " He that
dwelleth in love, dwelleth in God, and God in him ; "
iv. 21 : " This commandment have we from him : That
he who loveth God, love his brother also."

Here is the legislation infinitely perfect. The statutes of human governments fill many volumes, and are
then proverbially indefinite, while every attempt to con-
dense them has only made the uncertainty worse ; but
the whole law of God is written in two sentences, the
whole duty of man in one word : Love. This clear, con-
cise rule covers all the specifications of service which
God requires of us in all the various circumstances in
which we can possibly be placed. Love is the bond of
perfectness, the golden chain, which, depending from the

throne of our Father God, and returning to it again, is cast around the brotherhood of his human children, binding us in sweet harmony with him and with each other.

LOVE has never been accurately defined, nor can it be ; but we know its meaning from our consciousness and from its effects. We love that being whose character we approve, of whom we delight to think, whose excellences we endeavor to imitate, whose wishes we desire to fulfil and in whose favor we find happiness. Such affection we may, without inconsistency, have at the same time towards several, even many of our humankind, according as they have, through Providence, claims upon us ; but our supreme love, comprehending all exercises of love towards his creatures, is demanded by God for himself alone : " Thou shalt love the Lord thy God with all thy heart, and with all thy soul, and with all thy mind, and with all thy strength."

These several terms : " heart," " soul," " mind," " strength," do not, it should be stated, convey to us the precise meaning of the Greek or Hebrew originals which they translate, but collectively in the entire verse they give the full meaning of the Scripture. To define each of them particularly would not be easy, and, if practicable, would require a nice criticism too prolix for the aim of our present discourse. Let us, therefore, devoutly consider the scope of this first and great commandment, which is, that *We must render the Lord our God a supreme, intelligent, zealous love, freely consecrating all our faculties to his praise, and all our energies to his service.*

We are to love God *supremely.* " Thou shalt love the Lord thy God with all thy heart." Every motive which prompts love, should urge us to love God above all. If intellectual excellence attracts our admiring regard, God is omniscient, the author of all light, the source of all truth ; if moral beauty wins our affectionate esteem, his holiness, justice, goodness, and mercy are infinite ; if favors received and favors expected, claim our gratitude, from him alone is our being, with all its capacities of enjoyment, and all we do or can enjoy ; if rightful authority, administered in faithfulness and considerate kindness, be entitled to a prompt, unswerving, devoted loyalty, he is our Owner because our Creator, our Ruler because our Preserver, our Lawgiver because Supreme Lord of the universe, whose precepts are our sure only guides to happiness, because obedience is accordance with his will; and his chosen glory, the design of his government, is the best good of his intelligent subjects, comprehending all, yet overlooking none. No creature, therefore, should be allowed to rival him in our affections ; he must have all our hearts, and none be admitted there except in harmony with our highest reverence, esteem, and love for him who is the Lord our God.

We are to love God *intelligently*. " Thou shalt love the Lord thy God with all thy mind." God has endowed us with understanding and reason, that we may know him and perceive the arguments which he addresses through our minds to our affections. The faculty of will or choice which he grants us, cannot be exercised rightly unless intelligently. We are not to love even the Lord our God without motive, or an appreciation of his claims upon our love. We are, therefore, to employ our minds, above all else, in the study and contemplation of those claims that we may by the very force of logic, cheerfully, yet, as it were, of a moral necessity, fix our hearts supremely upon him to whom of right they belong. We must diligently read his Word, in which he reveals himself for our learning; we must observe his works, in which he demonstrates himself to our senses; we must investigate his doctrines, meditate on his attributes, apply his laws to our consciences, trust in his promises, set his threatenings between us and what he has forbidden, while we practice his commands, that through experience we may be continually acquiring greater proof of their wise goodness; and especially must we seek by earnest, humble prayer the sanctifying grace of his illuminating Spirit, that in close, personal, habitual communion with God, we may grow more like him as we know more of him. Thus consecrating all our faculties to his praise, we shall love the Lord our God with all our hearts and with all our minds.

We are to love God *zealously.*

"Thou shalt love the Lord thy God with all thy soul, and with all thy strength."

Soul, here, according to both the originals, signifies the will, or rather the determined purpose of a man; and *strength,* his powers of external action. The two, therefore, may be expressed by *zeal,* which, as we ordinarily understand it, is ardor of pursuit, or earnest purpose carried out in correspondent action. A supreme, intelligent love for God our Creator, Sovereign, and Judge, cannot be inoperative. The reasons for which we love God, his authority and character, show how our love is to be proved. If we love him as our Creator, all our faculties should be consecrated to his glory; if we love him as our Ruler, we should delight to obey

all his commandments; if we love him as our Benefactor, gratitude should make us continually intent upon
rendering him returns for his kindness. Thus we truly
love him with all our hearts and with all our minds,
only when we endeavor to serve him with all our powers in their utmost energy. Hence, love comprehends
our fidelity to God as his subjects, and our dutifulness
as his children. If we love him with all our hearts,
and know what he requires of us, the entire conformity
of our lives to his will is certainly secured.

This is the only service which God can accept or a
rational creature render. The laws of man refer only
to the external conduct, because the human eye can
look no further; yet is an unwilling obedience admitted
to have no merit, and we always consider the good or
evil of an act to lie in the motive. But God looks in
upon the heart, and according as he sees that love to
him is or is not the ruling principle of our actions, will
he accept or disown us, whatever our overt acts may
be. He, who refuses his love to God, the perfection
of moral beauty and the centre of all obligation, does
not love goodness or justice or holiness, evinces a spirit
at war with the welfare of the universe, and is justly
punished for so monstrous a depravity. On the other
hand, he who renders such love to God is justly rewarded for an obedience which on every opportunity
will be overtly shown.

Such service is necessary to the happiness of the
creature. Our happiness can come only from God who
has so fenced us in by his laws, that our welfare depends on our conformity to them; but to obey one
whom we do not love, is to do what we hate, thus turning our seeming compliance with right into a source of

misery. The highest reward of obedience is love, and love alone can earn it. Love is the strong charm by which God prompts the discharge of every duty springing from the relations of life, — as the duty of the husband, the wife, the parent, the child, the friend, or the patriot. How much more is love necessary for our duties to God! If we love him, we can never do enough for him, all our inclinations will be absorbed by a desire to please him, and his honor will engross all our energies.

The Second Commandment is like to the first; like in authority, because emanating from the same divine source; and like in the character of the duty which it enjoins, Love. " Thou shalt love thy neighbor as thyself." It is included in the first, because he, who has a right to all our heart and all our service, has the right of commanding our love and service for those whom he commends to our regard.

Our blessed Master, in his parable of The Good Samaritan, has clearly defined " our neighbor " to be every human being brought by the providence of God within the reach of our kindness. The duty is to God the Father of all men, and required for our fellow-man as his child. Selfishness may restrict itself within narrow boundaries, but a soul elevated to the love of God looks over all such littlenesses and comprehends the whole brotherhood of mankind.

The degree of loving service which we are to render our neighbor is to regard his welfare as we do our own. The precept clearly allows a certain degree of self-love, and insists upon no fanciful, impracticable disinterestedness. I am to love my neighbor, because God is his Father; but for the same reason I am to love myself, since he is my Father also, and he has in a

peculiar degree committed my happiness to my own
keeping. Our love for ourselves is taken for granted,
being the standard by which our love for our neighbor
must be adjusted, and therefore, not inconsistent with
it; so that we should err if we regarded another's welfare to the neglect of our own. Nor can we love all
men alike, since we are commanded by Scripture and
Providence to love some especially, as those of our own
household and those of the household of faith. We
are to love ourselves consistently with the law of God,
and according to its directions; so we are to love our
neighbor, rendering them all that affectionate service
which God enjoins with the same readiness that we
would benefit ourselves.

The Master himself has given us the best commentary on the law of love to our neighbor, in Matthew
vii. 12, where he says: " All things whatsoever ye
would that men should do to you, do ye even so to
them." That is, Whatever we could properly, according to the law of God, expect from others in certain
circumstances, we are in similar circumstances to do
readily for them, though they be never so unworthy
of such kindness, since it is a duty which we owe not
to them personally, but to God, and to them for his
sake. At the same time, the promise is distinctly con-
veyed that such service of our neighbor has sure tendency to advance our own welfare.

How clear is this rule, and how universally applicable, when we carry the measure due to others within
our own bosoms! How happy would the world be, if
all men acted towards each other on this principle!
But how vain must be all attempts to secure the common welfare of the race, upon any system of ethics

short of that which first lifts man out of all sinful selfishness to the love of God, and then enables him from
that generous fountain to mingle his love with the love
of the universal Father as it descends in blessing upon
all his children !

Farther discussion of these two commandments is
reserved for the time when we must consider the precepts of the Two Tables, given on Mount Sinai.

THIRDLY : *Our inability to fulfil these requirements.*

" Canst thou keep all these things perfectly ? "

" In no wise ; for I am prone by nature to hate God
and my neighbor." This melancholy truth the Christian
learns from the Word of God and from experience.

1. The terms, ability, power, and the like, originally
referring to physical matters, become very vague when
applied to our moral being, the exercise of our will,
judgment, and affections ; nor, though some have in-
geniously but unsatisfactorily dogmatized on the question, could we readily show where man's moral impotence lies, except we be content with acknowledging,
what is the fact, that it is a disorganizing corruption of
the entire soul. But, putting such lame metaphysics
aside, and going to the unerring Word, we find there un-
equivocally stated the fact of our own utter insufficiency
to keep the law of God. The testimonies to it pervade
the whole Scripture, and the Divine Spirit labors to
express, in our imperfect language and by such figures
as we can understand, our complete ruin as moral creatures. It is declared that " there is none that doeth
good, no, not one ; " that " the heart of man is evil, and
only evil, and that continually ; " that " all are concluded
under sin," conceived in sin, and brought forth in iniquity ; that we are not only weak, but, so far as godly

virtue is concerned, without any strength, nay, " *dead* in trespasses and sins." The plan of salvation proceeds on this fact. When we were impotent, " without strength, Christ died for the ungodly." " If righteousness " could have " come by the law (*i. e.* through our keeping of the law), then is Christ dead in vain." That this is true only of some is disproved by the offer of the Gospel to all men: " God so loved the *world*, that he gave his only-begotten Son, that whosoever believeth in him should not perish, but have everlasting life. For God sent not his Son into the world to condemn the world, but that the world through him might be saved. . . . He that believeth on the Son hath everlasting life ; but he that believeth not the Son shall not see life ; but the wrath of God abideth on him."

So the sanctifying or illuminating and strengthening grace of the Holy Ghost, is radical in every one that is saved. He renews us by a fresh begetting, a re-creation, a resurrection from the dead ; and no man, " except he be born again " " of the Spirit," " can enter the kingdom of God." So we see that " there is no difference, for all have sinned and come short of the glory of God." " The carnal mind (*i. e.* the mind of man in his natural state) is enmity against God ; " and since, as we have seen, love to our neighbor proceeds from our love to God, man is by nature at enmity with his neighbor.

This enmity against God and our neighbor may not at once be utter and extreme, for living, as we do, under a remedial system, the restraining grace of God is round even the unregenerate ; but we are prone to it, and were the grace of God entirely taken from us, as it will be from the lost in hell, there is no depth of depravity to which we should not sink. Our enmity against God may not appear against his goodness, or his mercy, or his love; but it is naturally strong against what is equally his character — his holiness and justice; for whenever his law or his providence clashes with our inclination, it is rampant, bitter, and obstinate. So are we enemies of our neighbor, when he crosses our supposed interest. Whence also could come such malicious crimes, such bloody wars, such envious calumnies, as those which fill the earth with clamor and rapine and cruelty! Thus, the Apostle describes the heathen who had departed from God as filled with evil, stained by the most hideous pollutions, " covenant-breakers, without natural affection, implacable, unmerciful." It is the proneness, not of the individual, here and there, but of human nature, of the race; for everywhere we see symptoms of this depravity; everywhere men make laws to guard against it; every penal statute, every gibbet, every prison, every lock on our doors, testify to man's belief that his fellow-man is prone to hate God and his neighbor. Christianity, or other restraining influences of God's government, may modify, and to some extent hold back the tendency, but in what man has been and what man now is, when grace is not exercising some control, we see what he would be were he left alone.

The Christian's experience confirms the divine declaration. Who that looks upon these two precepts of God's law can say he has kept them, or that he could keep them perfectly? Who of us can love God, with all his heart, and his neighbor as himself? The believer knows he cannot; he knows that there is within him a tendency downward, which none but God can change; that there is a lack in him, call it what you will, and place it where you will, which nothing but God's grace can supply, but without which he is lost, — powerless to do good, and prone to all evil. It is this that he expects through Christ; this he asks of God by the Holy Spirit; this he relies upon alone for eternal life.

O blessed Gospel, that thus meets us in our last extremity, turning our despair into joy! O blessed Law of God, whose very terrors drive us to welcome Christ! O blessed Bible, which thunders on the one page from Sinai the curse of eternal death, and on the next shows us Christ on the cross dying in our stead; then beyond it, Christ on his throne beckoning the penitent to eternal life! Glory to God the Lawgiver! Glory to God the Redeemer! Glory to God the Sanctifier! Glory to God, Father, Son, and Holy Ghost, our Covenant God, throughout all ages! Amen.

LECTURE III.

THE FALL OF MAN.

THIRD LORD'S DAY.

THE FALL OF MAN.

QUEST. VI. *Did God, then, create man so wicked and perverse?*

ANS. By no means; but God created man good, and after his own image, in righteousness and true holiness, that he might rightly know God his Creator, heartily love him, and live with him in eternal happiness to glorify and praise him.

QUEST. VII. *Whence, then, proceeds this depravity of human nature?*

ANS. From the fall and disobedience of our first parents, Adam and Eve, in Paradise; hence our nature is become so corrupt that we are all conceived and born in sin.

QUEST. VIII. *Are we, then, so corrupt that we are wholly incapable of doing any good, and inclining to all evil?*

ANS. Indeed we are; except we are regenerated by the Spirit of God.

THE lesson of to-day sets forth a doctrine of Christianity at which, more than any other, infidels and heretics have aimed their assaults; and no wonder, since, if it be not true, our whole creed is without consistency and must fall to the ground; but the purpose of this discourse is not to establish or defend it by any argument of our own. The Catechism undertakes no more than to teach, systematically and very briefly, what doctrines God himself has declared throughout the Holy Scriptures; and the Church, when commanding her ministers to preach upon the Catechism, intends no more than that they should teach only what the Catechism teaches, assisting her people to understand it by farther explanations conformable with the Scriptures and the other articles of evangelical faith. Our duty, therefore, is to bring before you what God asserts to be true; if after that there be any questioning as to how these things can be, the dispute is not with us but God, and we leave the objector in his hands who needs no help from our logic.

You will also remember that on the point before us, has turned a long, extensive controversy, filling many volumes by the most acute pens ; and that it is not possible in a single hour even to touch many things, which the most candid hearer might wish made clear.

The section for the Second Lord's Day having taught, that we are " prone by nature to hate God and our neighbor," inquiry is supposed to arise respecting the origin of such an evil tendency :

6th. " *Did God create man so wicked and perverse ?* " which being denied, and contrary facts stated, it is asked :

7th. " *Whence, then, proceeds this depravity of human nature ?* "

And the answer gives the true history of our most mournful ruin ; whereupon another question is put as to the degree of our moral decay :

8th. " *Are we, then, so corrupt that we are wholly incapable of doing any good, and inclined to all wickedness ?* "

The reply confirms the doctrine already asserted, pronouncing our condition, if left to ourselves, utterly desperate ; but, at the same time, points out a sure way of escape through the gracious power of the Holy Ghost, the Spirit of Christ, and the Author of all life.

Thus we have our subject and the order of handling it :
The subject :
The origin of human depravity.
The order :
FIRST : *It is not from our Creator.*

SECONDLY : *It is from the sin of our first parents.*

We need not treat of the answer to the last question separately, as the first part is properly included by our second head, and the latter will be fully discussed under a subsequent division of the Catechism.

Before, however, we enter upon the explanation supplied us by our Church, it should be remarked, that the origin of evil is a difficulty not peculiar to the Christian creed.   The actual existence of evil, physical and moral, is a fact not to be denied.   Death, with all its painful precedents, is upon all men.   Crime or wrong-doing, by which we mean violation of laws regulating our own and the common happiness, is seen everywhere, among all nations, in all circumstances.   There are degrees of wrong-doing, and there may be exceptions as to particular kinds of wrong-doing, still a tendency to do wrong is as much, or as really, a characteristic of human nature as liability to death.   Every civilized community, and, though less formally, savage tribe ordain statutes for the punishment of murder, theft, adultery, not because this or the other individual is particularly suspected of a purpose to commit any of those crimes (which, at the moment, may or may not be the case), but because the nature common to all men makes the commission of such grievous wrong so probable that severe restrictions, with penalties, are necessary to prevent what all agree would be evil ; nor are any of us affronted at being put under a government of the kind.   Nay, from our own consciousness of human weakness, we consent to laws for the control of all.   Thus, those who reject the Bible are as much bound as we are to account for this fact of human corruption, which, because it is universal, cannot have been fortuitous, but must come from a source involving all men. Philosophers of all ages, people, and sects, have sorely felt this difficulty at the very outset of their ethical observations ; and a Christian does not create, but obeys the necessity, when he seeks in the Word of God for an answer to the sad question, — whence originated the depraved tendency of our world-wide race ? Our present duty, therefore, is to consider that answer as it is brought before us by the Catechism.

FIRST : *Human depravity is not from God.*

As the depravity is in human nature, and human nature sprang from the creating will of God, our first thought is : Can it be that man came into being with such an evil disposition ? or, as the Catechism has it :

"*Did God, then, create man, so wicked and perverse ?* "

But at once we shrink from such an impious suggestion with horror, which revulsion is strengthened by the scriptural account :

" By no means ; but God created man good and after his own image in righteousness and true holiness, that he might rightly know God his Creator, heartily love him, and live with him in eternal happiness to glorify and praise him."

1. A positive denial : " *By no means.*"

There can be no thought so shocking as that God is in any way the author of evil, which he would be if he had created man wicked and perverse ; since, then, the inference would be irresistible that the will of God is evil, and the sovereign rule of the universe held by the hands of ONE who can be neither wise, nor just, nor good. Where, then, could his moral creatures look for a standard of right, for the reward of virtue or the punishment of vice? Better the blankest atheism than such a belief, — better the wildest chance than such a government, — by whose capricious cruelty all the elements of happiness and misery are thrown into dark, waning, destructive confusion. No! It cannot be! "By no means" can it be! Let man's wickedness and consequent misery come whence they may, they cannot have come from the creating will of God. "Yea, let God be true, and every man a liar." Some may ask here, if it be not asserted in Scripture that God made men wicked, where the Wisdom says (Prov. xvi. 4), "The Lord hath made all things for himself; yea, even the wicked for the day of evil." But that text bears no such interpretation. God, who made all things for himself, certainly made wicked men, yet that is very different from making men wicked. He made them, and they became wicked; and what the Wisdom means, is that the wickedness of men does not put them beyond the control of God, neither will it defraud him of his glory; for they are still his creatures, therefore in his power; and on the great day of retribution (a most evil day to them), he will abundantly display the glory of his justice by their signal punishment. So says the Psalmist (lxxvi. 10), "Surely the wrath of man shall praise thee; the remainder of wrath shalt thou restrain;" *i. e.* God in the wisdom of his providence will overrule the malignant passions of men to the praise of his government, and suffer them to go no farther. The same principle is woven through our whole subject.

II. The contrary account in Scripture.

(1) "God created man good; (2) and after his own image in righteousness and true holiness; (3) that he might rightly know God his Creator, heartily love

him, and live with him in eternal happiness, to glorify
and praise him."

Here we have 1. The creation of man good. 2. The
form of his goodness; after the image of God in righteousness and true holiness. 3. The design of his creation after the divine image; that he might be capable
of glorifying God by an eternal, spiritual, and happy
obedience.

The logical order of the thoughts is the reverse of
the words.

1. The design of God in creating man was, that he
might be capable of glorifying his Creator by an eternal, spiritual, and happy obedience.

The English translation of our Catechism is not well
done, and there is an obscurity in the last phrase of the
answer now before us, which is made worse by defec-
tive punctuation. As it now reads, it would seem that
the words, " to glorify and praise him," had reference
only to man's " living with God in eternal happiness,"
while, really, they relate to all that has gone before.
A comma put after happiness, will greatly help to clear
the sense; but there should have been inserted some
such phrase as,— "And this as the method" " to glorify
and praise," or "for the purpose of glorifying and prais-
ing him."

By the *glory* of God is to be understood the manifestation of his infinite attributes; and he is glorified
by his works, when they show proofs of his attributes
exerted upon them. The radiant sun, the fruitful
earth, the cunning anatomy of plants and animals, all
that is discoverable in unconscious nature, glorify God.

Yet it is necessary to such glorification of God that
there should be creatures capable of perceiving and

recognizing the glory so manifested. Being created with these spiritual faculties, they exhibit in their own nature proofs of the divine glory as much more wonderful than those of unconscious nature, as conscious spirit is more wonderful than mere matter. But they render a higher tribute of glorification, when they give their adoring praise before kindred intelligences to the Author of all. The glory of God in the revelation of truth to his creatures, whom he has gifted with capacity to receive, is unspeakably more noble than his glory in his works ; and those creatures return him a correspondent glory when they acknowledge his truth with homage for his divine wisdom ; but the highest degree of glorification which intelligent creatures can yield, or God can receive, is their perfect happiness derived from conformity to his will, for then are the power, wisdom, goodness, and holiness of God most fully manifested.

It was to give man a fitness for thus glorifying his Creator that God made him, as Scripture everywhere testifies. God had already, according to many scriptural intimations, created various orders of intelligences ; but, so far as we know, they are all pure spirits, living, acting, serving, and adoring, only in spheres of thought. Man alone was a union of the material and spiritual. Man alone was intrusted with lordship over material things, was capable of deriving happiness from God in a legitimate use of them, and charged with the office of glorifying God by such a happy obedience, on a theatre where mind and matter are united and coöperative. In him the things of heaven and earth are brought together. In him, as the connecting link, the two grand divisions of the Almighty's works are met. It is true that this is seen very dimly in the first Adam ;

yet when we know of the woman conceiving from the
Holy Ghost the Second Adam, and see Jesus, our
Brother, at the right hand of God, the demonstration
is complete.

The design of God was to give man a *fitness* for thus
glorifying him; but the divine purpose was not absolute that man should so glorify him, as the immediate
sequel shows, though the ultimate issues of redemption
will triumph gloriously over the ruins of the fall. The
design was carried out. Man did receive from his
Creator entire fitness to glorify and enjoy him; though,
as we shall see, there was necessarily in that very fitness
an element which made his defection possible. " God
made man upright; but they have sought out many
inventions."

2. The form of man's moral creation was "after the
image of God in righteousness and true holiness."
"And God said, Let us make man in our image, after our
likeness. . . . So God created man in his own image;
in the image of God created he him; male and female
created he them." What is meant by the image of
God in which man was created? The parallel and
nearly synonymous term "likeness," used by God himself, gives us the key to the explanation.

Man being designed to reflect, spiritually, the spiritual glory of God, by his enjoyment of God through an
intelligent conformity to the divine will, it was necessary that he should have a correspondent capacity, and
be, so far as a finite creature may, a counterpart of his
infinite Creator. This could not be properly true of
his body, for organized matter cannot resemble the
spiritual ONE, " whom no one hath seen or can see; "
and the language of the text cited guards us against

such a mistake : " In the image of God created he him," *i. e.* man irrespective of bodily distinctions, as " in Christ there is neither male nor female ; " but when those corporeal differences are spoken of, it is simply said, " Male and female created he them ; " no mention being made of the divine image. It must, therefore, relate to the soul, and in fact proves that man has, besides his body, a spirit, because he is like God who is a spirit, and he " must worship " the spiritual God " in spirit and in truth."

Man is a creature : therefore, all that he is, and has, must be derived, and, for the same reason, finite ; God, the origin and source of all, must, on the other hand, be infinite. Still there will be a correspondence between the finite receiver and the infinite imparter. The happiness of the spiritual creature must come from the same causes as the spiritual creature ; and hence there must be a spiritual resemblance.

Thus this image, likeness, or counterpart of God in man may be seen threefold.

1. In understanding : all knowledge is original with God, but he imparts truth to man, and man must have understanding as the capacity to receive it. Hence the Catechism gives as one reason why man was made in the image of God, — " that he might rightly know God his Creator."

2. In affection : by which we mean what is among us commonly understood by heart ; that is, a capacity of being so affected by the character and disposition of those to whom we have relations that we return them love, or the reverse. But God manifests his love towards us, and requires our love in return. Hence, man must have affections correspondent to the relations

which he has with God, and in the economy of God
with his fellow-creatures. So the Catechism gives as
another reason why man was made in the image of
God, " that he might . . . love his Creator ; " and the
Apostle John: " He that dwelleth in love, dwelleth in
God, and God in him."

3. In will: by which we mean a power of choice, or
of determining our actions, within our sphere. The
will of God is supreme over all things, for it is the only
source whence they exist. He rules over unintelligent
things by mere force, and they, being unconscious,
cannot resist or obey. But, having given man understanding and affections, he presented to his understanding, — and through his understanding to his affections,
— arguments or motives for the determination of his
choice, that man might act freely according to his own
will ; and an intelligent, hearty choice of that which
God approves is the service which the Creator required
at man's hands. Here, then, you see the triple likeness of the creature, man, to the Creator, God. God
understands, man understands ; God loves, man loves ;
God chooses, man chooses.

But there must have been something more to complete the correspondence of the creature to his Creator ;
and what this was we learn from the description which
the Apostle gives of regenerated man, or sinful man in
whom the original likeness is reimplanted by the Holy
Ghost. We find it in two nearly parallel texts : one,
Ephes. iv. 23, 24 : " And be renewed in the spirit of
your mind ; and that ye put on the new man, which
after God is created in righteousness and true holiness ; " the other in Coloss. iii. 9, 10 : " Ye have put
off the old man with his deeds ; and have put on the

new man, which is renewed in knowledge after the image of him that created him." Here we see that the image of God consists in knowledge, righteousness, and true holiness. In knowledge, that is, a right use of the understanding; in righteousness, that is, a proper discharge of relative duties, to which love, as the two great commandments teach, is necessary, for " love is the fulfilling of the law"; and holiness, which is conformity of will to the will of God, or choosing as God chooses. God, being unchangeably, because essentially, perfect, never makes an error in understanding; never fails in righteousnesss toward his creatures; never is inconsistent with himself, which is his holiness. Man, therefore, when he had the divine image, was sound in understanding, disposed to a loving discharge of all his relative duties, and conformed willingly to the will of God. But, being a creature, he was unlike God, neither infallible nor unchangeable; and, having the power of choice, he might choose evil or good. This was necessary to his original constitution as a moral creature; for else his conduct, however in accordance with the divine rule, would not have been the result of his knowledge, his love, or his will. You could not predicate of him either right or wrong any more than you could of a brute, a plant, or a stone. Still, though he had this faculty of choice, he was under no bias to wrong, but, on the contrary, received from his Creator with his being a disposition to do well. Hence, the Catechism gives a third reason why man was made in the image of God, " that he might live with God in eternal happiness," which he could not do unless he chose as God chooses, partaking of the divine blessedness as he agreed with the divine character, which is the reason of the divine blessedness. The blessedness so acquired would have been for ever, because death came in only as "the wages of sin;" and the soul of man being immortal would have lived perpetually with God. Nay, his body also would have been incorruptible, and the whole man happy through conformity to the divine will. But of this we need not now speak further, as it will come under consideration in another place.

Thus, God created man good, with no evil in him, or disorder tending to evil, but fitted for the duties and circumstances which should be assigned him; so that in no sense has the evil, moral and physical, which subsequently came upon man and is now upon all his descendants, been the fault of his Creator.

SECONDLY: *Human depravity is from man himself.*

The 7th Question asks: "*Whence, then, proceeds this depravity of human nature?*" If man was not created wicked and perverse, how became he so?

The Catechism answers:

" From the fall and disobedience of our first parents, Adam and Eve, in Paradise; hence our nature is become so corrupt that we are conceived and born in sin."

This asserts: the cause of the corruption to be the sin of our first parents; and: the manner of its transmission to be our conception and birth in sin; which together give us the doctrine held by the Reformed Churches, according to the Word of God, that all men are involved in the fatal consequences of Adam's sin.

Or, as the clear language of the Westminster divines expresses it: " They sinned with him and fell with him in his first transgression."

The word *fall*, though nowhere it has such reference in Scripture, is commonly used by believers of Christian doctrine to signify man's loss of the high place which he had when originally created. This was brought about by the disobedience of our first parents, Adam and Eve, in Paradise. The particular act of disobedience on which such fatal consequences ensued, must, therefore, have been the first of which man was guilty, because before that he was blameless, and immediately after it, he was cast out of Paradise. It is, then, for us to inquire how our race were so deplorably concerned in that one sin of our first parents? This we may learn from a collation of Scripture: Gen. ii. 15: "And the LORD God took the man, and put him into the garden of Eden to dress it and to keep it. And the LORD God commanded the man, saying: Of every tree of the garden thou mayest freely eat;" (mark, the tree of life was among those not forbidden to him;) "but of the tree of knowledge of good and evil, thou shalt not eat of it; for in the day thou eatest thereof thou shalt surely die." Mark here, that from the nature of this command with the threatening, there is implied a covenant by which God promises life on condition of his obedience, since death could come only through his disobedience. Chap. iii. 1 . . . " Now the serpent was more subtile than any beast of the field which the Lord God had made." (Other Scriptures warrant us in believing that the devil was here under the form of the subtle reptile: " That old serpent called the devil," Rev. xii. 9.) " And he said unto the woman: Yea, hath God said, Ye shall not eat of every tree of the garden? And the woman said unto the serpent: We may eat of the fruit of the trees of the garden; but of the tree which is in the midst of the garden, God hath said, Ye shall not eat of it, neither shall ye touch it, lest ye

die." (The covenant had been made with the man
before the woman was formed; but she rightly judged
herself involved by it, as making with man the human
nature.) " And the serpent said unto the woman, Ye
shall not surely die; for God doth know that in the
day ye eat thereof, then your eyes shall be opened,
and ye shall be as gods, knowing good and evil. And
when the woman saw that the tree was good for food,
and that it was pleasant to the eyes, and a tree to be
desired to make one wise, she took of the fruit thereof,
and did eat, and gave also unto her husband, and he
did eat. And the eyes of them both were opened,
and they knew that they were naked; and they sewed
fig-leaves together and made themselves aprons. And
they heard the voice of the LORD God walking in the
garden in the cool of the day; and Adam and his wife
hid themselves from the presence of the LORD God
amongst the trees of the garden. And the LORD God
called unto Adam, and said unto him, Adam, Where
art thou? And he said, I heard thy voice in the garden, and I was afraid because I was naked, and I hid
myself. And He said, Who told thee that thou wast
naked? Hast thou eaten of the tree, whereof I commanded thee that thou shouldest not eat? And the
man said: The woman whom thou gavest to be with
me, she gave me of the tree, and I did eat. And the
LORD God said unto the woman, What is this that
thou hast done? And the woman said, The serpent
beguiled me and I did eat. And the LORD God said
unto the serpent, Because thou hast done this, thou art
cursed above all cattle, and above every beast of the
field; upon thy belly shalt thou go, and dust shalt thou
eat all the days of thy life: and I will put enmity

between thee and the woman, and between thy seed and her seed; it shall bruise thy head, and thou shalt bruise his heel. Unto the woman he said, I will greatly multiply thy sorrow and thy conception; in sorrow thou shalt bring forth children; and thy desire shall be to thy husband, and he shall rule over thee. And unto Adam he said, Because thou hast hearkened unto the voice of thy wife, and hast eaten of the tree, of which I commanded thee, saying, Thou shalt not eat of it, Cursed is the ground for thy sake; in sorrow shalt thou eat of it all the days of thy life; thorns and thistles shall it bring forth to thee, and thou shalt eat the herb of the field; in the sweat of thy face shalt thou eat bread, till thou return unto the ground; for out of it wast thou taken; for dust thou art, and unto dust shalt thou return. . . . . . And the Lord God said, Behold, the man is become as one of us to know good and evil; and now lest he put forth his hand, and take also of the tree of life, and eat and live for ever; therefore the LORD God sent him forth from the garden of Eden, to till the ground from whence he was taken. So he drove out the man. And he placed at the east of the garden of Eden cherubims and a flaming sword, which turned every way, to keep the way of the tree of life." Gen. v. 3. "And Adam . . . . begat a son in his own likeness, after his image."

Now compare with this the doctrine of the Apostle, when opening the way of redemption by Jesus Christ; Rom. v. 12: "Wherefore as by one man sin entered into the world and death by sin; and so death passed upon all men, for that all have sinned. . v. 18. Therefore as by the offence of one judgment came upon all men to condemnation; even so by the righteousness of one, the free gift came upon all men unto justification of life." So, also, 1 Cor. xv. 21. . . . " For since by man came death, by man came also the resurrection of the dead. For as in Adam all die, even so in Christ shall all be made alive." 45. " The first Adam was made a living soul; the last Adam was made a quickening spirit."

There are many things in the original story and the apostolical comments, upon which it might not be unprofitable to remark, if we had time; but since we have not, we shall be confined to the inferences immediately touching our subject. Let us, however, be on our guard against the sceptical notion that the Mosaic account is an allegory; for it is in no way so distinguished from what follows or from what goes before. If part be allegory, the whole is allegory; the account of creation is allegory, man is but an allegorical being, and all human beings, you and I and the rest of our race, are mere figments of a poetical description. The facts of the curse are present with us now, — the creeping serpent, the ungenerous earth with its thorns and thistles, the pains of childbirth, the necessity of toil, the death which returns us all to the dust. The whole reasoning of the apostles respecting the plan of redemption assumes the facts given by Moses to be actual and not figurative. Nay, if the first Adam fell not, there is no redemption by the second, Christ Jesus our Lord. The simple means by which the obedience of our first parents was tried, so far from being puerile, as some profanely think, were in perfect accordance with the general economy of God, and show more plainly than more complex or imposing arrangements could have done the importance of the principle that a holy safety lies in obedience to God. Innocent man was yet dependent on his Maker for daily food, and God put the test there that it might be most obvious.

From the whole, then, we learn, —

a. That Adam forfeited by sin the favor of God, lost the upright likeness, which he originally had, to his Creator, and came under condemnation to death, being driven out of the garden where God held communion with him, and shut out from all access to the tree of life, the fruit of which was the means of immortality. How a pure being could fall into sin, we have not philosophy enough to explain, nor has the Holy Ghost answered such curiosity. He had the faculty of choice, from the exercise of which God could not directly restrain him without destroying the essence of his moral being. But that he did sin, we know from the testimony of God; and that the punishment of sin came upon him, we know by experience.

b. When he fell, he fell not alone, but all his descendants fell with him, as the Apostle expressly asserts: " In Adam all died." " By one man sin entered into the world, and death by sin." When the covenant was made with Adam, it was made with human nature, for he was then the whole of human nature, and, by his progenitive character, the head and representative of all the human nature that should proceed from him. Had he remained sinless, no doubt his posterity would have been sinless; but he fell, and his posterity fell with him. Had he retained the holiness which constituted the image of God, he would have begotten his children in the image of God; but having lost that image, his children were begotten and conceived in his own image. The natural faculties of understanding, affection, and choice, his nature retained, but greatly shattered and under a fatal bias to sin; for, though one may be free to fall from a precipitous height, he is not free to regain his lost place. His moral likeness to God was gone from him and he could not give it to his offspring. Death moral, death natural, death as the result of sin, death as the punishment of sin, was upon him, upon his very nature; and, therefore, upon all who derived their nature from him. Death was distinctly threatened as the punishment which would follow Adam's breach of the covenant, and that death involved the moral being of his soul as well as the decay of his body. " The wages of sin is death;" and the consent of Evangelical Scripture declares that the death now visible is but the faint yet sure foreshadowing of death eternal, which, as the favor of God is life, must be the wrath of God on body and soul forever. Death is upon us all. We have the evidences of it in our frames. We are of a mortal race. Our forefathers are dead. We too must die, for we have derived death from them with our life. As we all die with Adam, we must all be condemned with him, and are corrupt with him. The evidences of our moral depravity are as plain as those of our bodily death; and so as we fell in Adam, are we depraved with him. " We are," says the Apostle, " by nature the children of wrath;" and again: " The Scripture hath concluded all under sin." God deliver us from the death eternal!

c. Our corruption is derived from Adam through our conception and birth: " Behold," says the Psalmist, when accounting for his foul transgressions, " I was shapen in iniquity, and in sin did my mother conceive me." In the same manner that we have our descent from Adam, we have our fallen evil nature. Whatever be the difficulties which lie about this fact, it is true. The parental relation of Adam to us involves us with him. Our whole nature, in some proper sense, is from him. Our sins are imitations of his; we commit wilfully personal sins, but behind all these there is sin in us and guilt upon us; we "are by nature the children of wrath," begotten in the likeness of man after he had lost the image of God. So certainly as we are his children, are we sinners prone to all evil, except we be regenerated by the Spirit of God.

Such, my dear hearers, is our sad state by nature. Our cavils cannot change the fact; but the grace of God can change our condition by changing our nature. Let us cease to challenge the justice of God in condemning us, and invoke his ever ready mercy to create in us clean hearts and renew right spirits within us.

Let us seek the same blessing for our fellow-sinners, our brothers in human fallen nature; and strive by all the means which the Gospel offers to bring them under the headship of Christ, the second Adam; that, as in the first they died, so in him they may all be made alive by his quickening Spirit unto eternal holiness.

Especially do you, who are parents, look upon those who are, through you, children of sin because your children; and leave no method untried that you may be, by divine help, their fathers and mothers in Christ, to whom with the Father and the Holy Ghost be Glory. Amen.

LECTURE IV.

PUNISHMENT OF SIN.

FOURTH LORD'S DAY.

PUNISHMENT OF SIN.

QUEST. IX. *Doth not God, then, do injustice to man by requiring from him in his law that which he cannot perform?*

ANS. Not at all; for God made man capable of performing it; but man, by the instigation of the devil and his own wilful disobedience, deprived himself and all his posterity of those divine gifts.

QUEST. X. *Will God suffer such disobedience and rebellion to go unpunished?*

ANS. By no means; but is terribly displeased with our original as well as actual sins; and will punish them in his just judgment, temporally and eternally, as he hath declared: "Cursed is every one that continueth not in all things which are written in the book of the law to do them."

QUEST. XI. *Is not God, then, also merciful?*

ANS. God is indeed merciful, but also just; therefore his justice requires that sin, which is committed against the most high majesty of God, be also punished with extreme, that is, everlasting punishment, both of body and soul.

THE section of the Catechism for the Second Lord's Day taught us the utter inability of man to keep the law of God; that for the Third, how our nature, which God created good, became so corrupt; and the lesson of to-day, declares the certain, most terrible punishment of sin by the wrath of God.

An inquiry is supposed, whether or not the obligation of man to obey the commands of God is removed by his inability:

9th. " *Doth not God, then, do injustice to man by requiring from him in his law that which he is unable to perform?* "

This being denied for reasons given, farther inquiry

is made respecting the consequences of man's wickedness :

10th. *"Will God suffer such disobedience and rebellion to go unpunished?"*

The answer to which is, that God has not only made known his holy anger with us because of our innate depravity and overt crimes, but has pronounced an awful curse upon every transgressor of his law. Nor will the compassion of God mitigate the severity of his vengeance, for the answer to question the

11th. *"Is not God, then, also merciful?"* reminds us that executive justice is essential to divine sovereignty, and that no one attribute of God can oppose another.

Thus we have our subject and its order : —

The subject :

The Punishment of Sin.

The order :

FIRST : *The accountability of fallen man.*

SECONDLY : *The sentence passed upon him.*

THIRDLY : *The certainty of its execution.*

FIRST : *The accountability of fallen man.*

The original obligation of man to obey God, with his consequent responsibility for his actions, was shown on the Second Lord's Day, and springs necessarily from the relation of the moral creature to his Creator. The difficulty before us is, how, since man has lost his ability to keep the law, he can be held liable to punishment for not keeping it ; and whether it is or is not charging God with injustice to assert that he so holds him. The Catechism answers :

" Not at all, for God made man capable of performing it ; but man, by the instigation of the devil, and his own wilful disobedience, deprived himself and his posterity of those divine gifts."

The truth of the principle that ability must precede obligation is admitted, but its applicableness to the case of fallen man is denied; and the argument takes the form of a syllogism, thus: God made man able to keep the law given him; But man by his own wilful act deprived himself and his race of that ability; Therefore, the law with its penalties is justly binding upon us. The first was shown in answer to the fifth question; the second in answer to the sixth; the third, though following irresistibly, we may briefly discuss.

The law with its penalties is justly binding upon us, notwithstanding our inability to perform its requisitions.

1. God has declared it to be so in both his word and providence. In his word, he makes the law the rule of our duty, as: in the promulgation of its two tables on Sinai, and the confirmation of it by our Lord in the two requirements of love to God and love to our neighbor; while he pronounces us utterly unable to keep it, and describes us as " without strength," " dead in trespasses and sins," needing a new life, a new nature, and the imputed righteousness of Christ before we can be saved, because " by the deeds of the law no flesh shall be justified;" at the same time forewarning us of the judgment when he will render unto every man according to his deeds, and denouncing the fearful curse, which is no less than the wrath of God forever, against "every one that continueth not in all things which are written in the book of the law to do them." If God condemns us for not keeping the law, which he himself says we are unable to keep, who will dare deny his justice?

Shall we set up our opinion against his, who, while he pronounces us guilty, " so loved the world that he gave his only begotten Son, that whosoever believeth in him should not perish, but have everlasting life ? "   Surely, one so merciful cannot be unjust.

His providence agrees with his word, for death is the penalty of the law, and " death hath passed upon all men," which is clear proof " that all have sinned." The full infliction of the penalty is reserved for the next world, yet here we see that mainly the happiness or unhappiness of men springs from their conformity to the law of God or their transgression of it ; so much so, that those governments which copy most nearly their laws from the divine, offer the best security for the common good ; and, that those nations which violate the rules of righteousness and purity divinely laid down are sure, if not at once, in succeeding generations to bring disaster and ruin on themselves ; showing, beyond a doubt, that the law with its penalties originally imposed on man is still the law of his nature under which his Creator holds him.   Nor, as has been intimated by these examples, are those penalties of sin always sent only upon the actual transgressor : posterity suffers from the crimes of their ancestors ; children through many generations, often until families become extinct, inherit disease and weaknesses of both mind and body through the vices of their forefathers ; while a very large majority of deaths, with the ordinary accompaniments of pain and distress, is of children too young to have contracted guilt by their own voluntary sin. How can we account for these facts (which no one can deny) otherwise than by the theory of the Scriptures, that the primeval law is still dominant over us ;

that the corruption of man is derived with his nature ; and that all his race, in consequence of Adam's sin, are held guilty (that is, obnoxious to the penalties of the divine law) before God.

2. The law under which man was created, with its penalties, is unchangeable. God adapted it to his nature and his nature to it. It is the result, as has before been said, of his relations, moral and physical, to his Creator, and to the system of things in which the Creator has placed him. Unless all the laws of this world, as created by God (which we must believe are in harmony with the laws of the universe, because the Legislator is one and the same), be changed, the particular law, under which man was at the first subject, must remain unaltered. We distinguish sometimes, for the sake of argument, between the natural and the penal consequences of sin ; between the mischief which sin brings about in the condition of the sinner, and the miseries which the wrath of God inflicts on him because he is a sinner ; but the distinction is nominal, and has no warrant from fact. The Creator is the Lawgiver, and he, who is both Creator and Lawgiver, is the only Judge. He would allow no hurt to reach the innocent, and has arranged all things for the happiness of the obedient ; consequently, whatever evil comes upon any moral creature must come from the wrath of God and is a punishment of guilt. The skeptic, making out of his own purblind fancy a law according to which he would fashion the righteousness of the infinite Creator, may presumptuously deny that our good God can be so severe as to send misery on the whole race of man through Adam ; but the denial is in the teeth of fact. Misery has come upon the

whole race; depravity, physical and moral, has been and is characteristic of every individual who has a human nature. Whence came that misery, if not from the Creator? and why from the Creator, if it be not the punishment of sin? If the fact of human misery were not obvious, we might tolerate for a moment the hypothesis of the objector; but, when we see and feel a fate so universal, we cannot doubt that it is from God, and when we know that it is from God, we cannot doubt that it is just.

Besides, when the law was ordered and given as both the rule of man's duty and the method of his happiness, he was able to keep it; since he has so lost his ability that (in the language of Scripture) he " cannot please God;" must then God lower the demands of his law and accommodate it to our fallen nature? No one can soberly contend for that. Should a law punishing murder restrain its operation against the wretch who has become so malignant and brutal that he cannot keep from shedding blood for revenge or rapine? Or should the poisonous effects of strong drink cease in the constitution of the drunkard, because he cannot resist the terrible thirst which he has wickedly acquired? Upon such a principle, the worse a man is, the less pure and exacting the law over him should be. It is not the fault of the law, but of the sinner, that he comes under its penalties, which are intended, not to make man miserable, but to deter him from sin, which will certainly make him miserable.

3. The inability of man to keep the law of God, which we derive through our descent from Adam, is not of such a nature as to free us from blameworthiness. There may have been, there probably has been,

all along with our reasoning, an objection in the minds of some, that the absence of power to obey renders obedience on our part impossible, which seems to go far towards relieving us from guilt. But let us consider more closely the nature of this inability, and where it lies. It is, doubtless, a moral inability, for it respects moral acts; and as morality (or right and wrong) belongs to the will, the inability must lie in the will. Mark, — in asserting that our inability is of the will, we are far from asserting, as some with more art than correctness have done, that we have a natural ability to keep the law of God. To speak of a natural ability to do a moral act, is a confusion of terms utterly unjustifiable, and can lead to no sound result. The exercise of what are termed our natural faculties, (not those of our bodies but of our souls,) such as the faculty of understanding or loving, have a moral character only, because of the exercise of the will through them. Morality is, we know, inseparable from the exercise of those, so called, natural faculties, because the exercise of them is always by the will; but, for the same reason, their moral character is derived from the will. To know God is our duty, yet could not be our duty if we were without the faculty of knowing; to love God is our duty, yet could not be if we had not the faculty of loving; but as both our understanding and our heart are exercised by our will, there can properly be no ability to do what is moral where the will is not concerned and engaged. To deny the moral ability to do right (by which is understood ability of will) is to deny all ability to do right. At the same time, it must be seen that there is a reflex action of the understanding and affections upon the will, biasing it,

and, where it is weak, controlling it, because the will
itself is determined (so far as we can discover the laws
of its mystery) by the motives presented to it.   This,
however, strengthens the objection to the claim of natural ability to serve God, because both Scripture and
experience teach us that the understanding is darkened
and weakened by sin, while our affections have from
the same fatal cause acquired a proneness to evil, thus
influencing the will to wrong as well as being directed
by it.   In fact, our whole spiritual being is disorganized
from its proper balance and adjustment, needing an entire renovation as a whole, and in each part.   So the
Apostle declares that God worketh in the believer "both
to will and to do of his good pleasure;" his understanding must be enlightened and his heart changed.
This corruption of his so-called natural powers does
not free the sinner from guilt, because he has himself
corrupted them wilfully.   Had God created man without eyes, he surely would not have required from him
an admiring study of visible creation; but if man,
after having received sight, had wilfully deprived himself of his eyes, he would not by so criminal an act
have escaped from his duty, because his acquired inability would have been a sin involving all the consequent omissions; just as human law holds a drunken
man responsible for all the wrong he does while in a
state of self-assumed craziness.   God gave man a sound
reason and unpolluted affections; but he depraved those
faculties wilfully, and is justly responsible for the consequences of that depravity.

It is clear, however, that much of the difficulty thrown
around this subject arises from the insufficiency of our
human language to state clearly what concerns spiritual

or moral things. Power, strength, ability, are terms
primarily expressive of physical faculty ; and cannot
apply with parallel force, or corresponding sense, to
the will of the spiritual soul. When the will is exercised, there is choice ; and when we say that man
cannot, before he is regenerate, choose the service of
God, we do not mean that he is compelled to evil
by a force without himself, as a stream runs downward or a flame points upward ; but that he is so
wicked by nature that his choice is inevitably fixed on
what is wrong. He cannot do right, because he is so
bent on doing wrong. Can any of us say that he is
forced to sin whether he will or not ? Can he say that
his bondage to sin does not include his will, or that,
when he sins, he is not a voluntary agent ? There is
no reasoning on this ; we know it, in the same way that
we know we exist, from our consciousness. If, then,
we sin of our own accord, can we be innocent ? Nay,
if we are without a disposition to obey God, there can
be no doubt of our guilt. It is the want of a heart to
serve him for which God condemns us. The inability
spoken of by the word of God and the Catechism, is
nothing else than that depravity of our nature through
sin by which our heart is alienated from God, our understanding blinded, and our very conscience perverted.
Therefore, (in the language of the Episcopal Church,)
" the condition of man after the fall, is such, that he
cannot turn and prepare himself, by his own natural
strength and good works, unto faith and calling of
God."

It may be objected that the Apostle speaks of " doing
the thing he would not," and our Church in the Communion service, of " sin remaining against our will in

us ; " but in those passages we must understand " would " and, " will " to mean the general purpose and desire of a believer, which is for the consecration of his whole being to God.

4. The method of God in salvation justifies his condemnation of us under Adam ; for Christ takes the place of a second Adam, and holds the same federal relation to the elect, whom he represents, as the first Adam did to his natural posterity. In him the believer is justified, as in the first man he was condemned ; by the righteousness and expiation of Christ in his stead, he is pardoned, accepted, and rewarded ; the blessing comes on Christ the Head first, then on every member of the Church which is his body ; and the strength enabling him to do right is not his own, but the grace of the Holy Ghost, the Spirit of Christ dwelling in him. It is only through such representation or suretyship of Christ that he can be saved from either the guilt or the power of sin, as the Apostle says : " For, if by one man's offence death reigned by one, much more they, which receive abundance of grace and of the gift of righteousness, shall reign in life by one, Jesus Christ."

To deny the justice of representation as a principle on which God may deal with us, is to take away all hope of our salvation. Indeed, when handling the subject of the fall, we should have constant reference to the condition of sinners under the Gospel, as a remedial system, for such is our condition ; and, therefore, every other method of considering it would be more curious than practical ; since God leaves us who hear the Gospel not irrecoverably lost through Adam, but with the gracious opportunity of restoration through Christ.

In conclusion, let every believer ask himself if he does not feel that of his own nature he is utterly unable to obey God, yet that he is guilty for not obeying him ; and, at the same time, that " it is God who worketh in him both to will and to do of his good pleasure ? " Such conviction of Christian experience is the doctrine of the Catechism.

Secondly : *The sentence passed upon fallen, sinful man.*

Our guilt, because of our sins, having been demonstrated, the question recurs : *Shall we be suffered to go unpunished by the good God, whom we have rebelled against ?* And the Catechism answers : " By no means ; but (he) is terribly displeased with our original as well as actual sins ; and will punish them in his just judgment, temporally and eternally, as he hath declared : ' Cursed is every one that continueth not in all things which are written in the book of the law to do them.' "

From the line of argument which we have chosen, much, which otherwise should come under this head, has been anticipated, yet several important things are yet to be noted : The *terms* of the condemnation ; the *reason* of it ; and its *extent*.

1. The terms of the condemnation : " Cursed is every one that continueth not in all things which are written in the book of the law to do them." This is the language of God himself as given by the Apostle Paul out of the older Scripture. Curse is the opposite of blessing ; both imply the action of God, for he alone can curse, and he alone can bless ; blessing is the happy consequence of his favor, cursing is the miserable consequence of his anger. Sometimes

these opposite terms are applied to unconscious objects, as : "a field which the Lord hath blessed, which for that reason is fruitful; or "cursed is the ground," which for that reason brought forth thorns and thistles ; yet such merely material things are not themselves properly objects of divine blessing or cursing, but only the means through which God blesses or curses man. Blessing or cursing are often restricted to particular concerns or parts of men's interests, but when used generally, or without specification, they comprehend the whole of man's being and experience ; and are then synonymous with life and death in their full sense, — for the favor of God is life, and the anger of God is death.   Thus Moses, having declared the law with its sanctions of reward and punishment, says : " I call heaven and earth to record this day against you, that I have set before you life and death, blessing and cursing ; therefore choose life, that both thou and thy seed may live."   So in the sentence before us, " Every one that continueth not in all things, which are written in the book of the law, to do them," is denounced as " cursed," that is, condemned to death, or to all the awful effects of divine wrath ; God not only withdrawing from him his favor, but also pursuing him with his vengeance.   How extreme must be the misery of one whose enemy is God omnipotent !

The sentence is passed : " Cursed *is* every one who continueth not in all things which are written in the book of the law to do them."   God has, it is true, " appointed a day in which he will judge the world," but his wrath does not linger until then ; for the day of judgment is rather the time of the public final award to the righteous of life eternal, and to the wicked of death eternal, at the close of the mediatorial scheme. Doubtless, there will then be a great increase of happiness on the one hand, and of misery on the other, because the sentence either way will be fully carried out, the intercession of Christ being ended ; but the sentence against the sinner is already passed, and partly put in force the moment he is a sinner ; nay, the only reason why it is not executed at once is the stay of divine vengeance to give opportunity of salvation through the Atoner. So the language is not " cursed will be " the sinner, but " cursed is he." " In the day thou eatest thereof thou shalt surely die," and in the day he ate he did die ; he lost the favor of God which is life, he came under the anger of God which is death ; death in his body which then began to die ; death in his soul which then became corrupt ; death in his entire humanity, because under condemnation ; death upon all the race which he represented : " By one man sin entered into the world, and death by sin, and so death passed upon all men for that all have sinned ; " and again : " By the offence of one, judgment came upon all men to condemnation." How dreadful is this thought ! We are already condemned ; and unless we have escaped to the shelter of Christ's mediation, the unspeakable weight of the curse of God may at any moment crush us into hell forever ; all the woes we suffer now, unless they have been changed to fatherly discipline by the adopting grace of God in Christ, are but faint presaging shadows of our eternal doom.

The sentence is passed upon *all* sinners : " Cursed is every one," &c. " The Scripture hath concluded all under sin," for " there is none that doeth good, no not one." " Death hath passed upon all men, for that all have sinned." In our mortality and moral corruption we have the proof of both our sin and our condemnation. We cannot escape on the plea that we have broken only one or a few of the divine precepts and kept the rest; even if this were possible, the sentence is against every one that continueth not *in all things* which are written in the book of the law to do them;" so that to escape the curse we must not only keep all the commandments, but keep them continually, without exception and without intermission. But it is not possible; "for," says the Apostle James, "whosoever shall keep the whole law, and yet offend in one point, he is guilty of all. For he that said do not commit adultery, said also, do not kill. Now if thou commit no adultery, yet if thou kill, thou art become a transgressor of the law." The sin lies not merely in a particular offence, or in the breach of one particular commandment; but in rebelling against the authority of him who ordained the whole law, showing plainly that the sinner is not restrained from breaking the rest by the reverence he has for God, but only through temperament, or absence of trial, or lack of opportunity. He, who would for sound religious reasons keep one precept, would from the same conscientious motive abstain from breaking all the rest. Therefore is the sinner condemned for having rebelled against the majesty of the Lawgiver. Who, then, my hearers, can stand? Who among us has always and at all times made the law of God, because it is God's law, the rule of his conduct? Who of us can abide the scrutiny, when God searches our inmost hearts?

2. The reason of the condemnation.

God is terribly displeased with our original as well as actual sins.

The word GOD is not only the distinguishing name of the infinite Being, but also a title of his supreme office. We cannot use it rightly without understanding by it the Moral Governor, as well as the Creator of the Universe. As belief in an all-wise First Cause throws chance entirely out of the physical system, bringing all things under law; so it is impossible that the Sovereign can be indifferent to the character and acts of his moral subjects. The freedom of their agency does not· put them beyond his authority, else they would become more than creatures and he less than supreme. They,. therefore, must be under law, and their happiness or misery be in proportion to their conformity or lack of conformity with the divine law; so that, giving to their freedom its widest definition, it can be nothing more than freedom to work out their happiness or misery under the law of the Creator. But the law, under which they act, must spring from the very nature of God, and, as he is essentially holy, whatever in the moral creature is contrary to the divine holiness, must bring upon him the hostility of the divine power.

Again: whatever definition may be given to right, the rule of right for the moral creature can be no other than the expressed will of his divine Lord; he has, as a subject, reason to look for such a declaration of the divine will respecting his acts, (since "sin is not imputed where there is no law,") and God has revealed that law clearly to us; a transgression of the revealed law is, therefore, a rebellion against our rightful Sovereign, and the transgressor must be dealt with as a

traitor. Yet again: no man is alone in the world, nor
do his actions affect only his own well being, but he
belongs to a vast community of human beings, moral
creatures like himself, so interlinked that their actions
necessarily bear upon each other and upon their posterity; God is the Governor and Defender of the whole
as he is of each, and therefore any breach of the law
given to conserve the happiness of all, must be regarded
by him as a grievous offence against him, because
against the peace of those under his care.

Once more: all his intelligent creatures have a
right to ask from God his estimate of right or wrong,
the degree in which the one is meritorious, the other
damnable; nor can they learn this except from the
reward he attaches to obedience and the penalties he
denounces against disobedience. Were he to overlook
his creatures' good or evil, were he to reward lightly or
punish lightly, even in a single case, the consistency of
his administration would be shaken, and doubt as to
the very principles of truth or happiness would darken
over the universe. The dreadfulness of the curse
against sin is the expression of the sense he has of its
enormity, and meant to deter his subjects from it; but
when any will, notwithstanding, transgress, the penalty
they defy must take its course. Thus we see that God
is terribly displeased with sin from the holiness of his
nature, from jealous vindication of his authority, from
his regard for the happiness of his subjects, and from
his design to teach his moral universe the only way of
life.

Sin, therefore, in any form that may be chargeable
on us, must excite his severe displeasure; our actual
sins not only, but, also, our sin in which we are born;

for, if the overt act be a trangression of his law, the
disposition or tendency to transgression which is in our
nature must be offensive to him as the root or fountain
of all sin.

As to our actual sins, the testimony of the word of
God is so clear, that none of them will escape his righteous anger, as to need nothing from us, especially after
our previous reasoning. But the Catechism, by our
innate or born sins, (" original " as the English translator has it,) evidently means not only our native corruption, but also the sin of our first parent in whom
we fell. This we shall now argue no farther than to
say, upon the testimony of afore-cited Scripture, and
upon the proof everywhere seen of the whole race
being as a race under the curse pronounced upon
Adam, that God holds us guilty because we are children of Adam, the progenitor of us all. How else, we
ask again, can we account for the suffering and mortality of babes before they are capable of actual sin?
Not that we can believe in the damnation of infants, as
has been falsely charged on those who hold our creed;
on the contrary, only we can consistently hold the doctrine of their salvation, because we believe that they
are saved through the merit of Him who has said:
" Of such is the kingdom of heaven." Are we asked:
What would have been their fate, if the redemption
had not been provided? We answer that of such
contingencies we have no knowledge, and, therefore,
no right or room for conjecture, except that in no circumstances God would do unjustly. Sufficient is it for
us to know that we are all condemned, all under the
curse, all born in sin ; and (thanks be unto God for his
unspeakable gift!) that there is full redemption through
Jesus Christ for all who believe on his name.

O my friends, how terrible must be the displeasure
of God, and how base that sin which clouds with
frowns against his creatures the face of him, whose
names are Life and Light and Love!

3. The extent of the condemnation.

God " will punish them (our sins) in his just judgment, temporally and eternally."

The penal consequences of sin, included by the curse
are temporal and eternal, on (as the answer to the
next question states) both body and soul."

Man, as God created him, consists of both body and
soul. His soul, having a life peculiar to itself, may
exist without his body, and will so exist from the time
of his so called death until the Last Day; but then
it is not the entire man; neither is it the design of God
that the soul should be disembodied, except for a passing purpose; nor can the soul have its full sensibility
or put forth its full energy when apart from the body.
God contrived the body with its faculties to be the
dwelling and instrument of the soul; he created and
fitted the soul (unlike angelic spirit) to live in the
body and act through it. The relations of body and
soul are, therefore, most intimate. As we see it in this
life, the sympathy of each with the other is close and
necessary. Through the bodily appetites, the soul
maintains or impairs its natural vigor; through the
bodily senses, it perceives and derives ideas from external things; through the bodily faculties, it acts out-
wardly its will; through the passions, which belong
both to it and the body in combination, it enjoys or
suffers. The soul, it is true, has faculties and affections
peculiar to itself, and alone has will, but it has not the
complete powers intended for its action without the

means and implements supplied by the body; for which reason a "spiritual body" (as the apostle characterizes it) as well as a sanctified soul is necessary to the entire felicity of man in heaven, not less than in paradise on earth; which makes the clear-sighted Paul, even while lamenting the impediments of a corrupt body, desire not to "be unclothed, but clothed upon, that mortality might be swallowed up of life." It follows, therefore, without dwelling now longer on this most interesting topic, that the punishment of sin, and the reward of righteousness as well, must be both on body and soul, or on the entire man. The body is the instrument of the soul's ungodly acts and unholy pleasures and contaminating influences, so through and in the body must the sinful soul suffer punishment; yet, as the soul has its peculiar properties which it prostitutes to sin, the punishment must also be heavy on the soul itself immediately.

This, we have seen, is the case temporally, because the curse has passed upon all men, and many specific punishments occur on every hand. Yet it should be remarked that these inflictions of divine wrath are for the most part warnings against the wrath to come, that men may repent; and that what remains of them on the believer have the curse so taken out of them as to make them parts of the divine discipline, educating his yet sinful though penitent child for the glory above.

The punishment will be eternal, upon the impenitent sinner, body and soul in this life, upon his soul after death until the Last Day, and ever after upon him body and soul, for his body will then be raised to the resurrection of damnation. The eternity or perpetuity of the sinner's punishment is plainly declared in the

word of God.   Let one text out of many suffice :
" These (the wicked) shall go away into everlasting
punishment."   This proof is, however, objected to by
some on the plea that the original word, rendered
" everlasting," seldom or never in Scripture means
everlasting, but only a long period.   Our answer is
easy and prompt, that the same word is applied in the
other part of the verse to the blessedness of the righteous, " into life eternal."   If the criticism were sound,
the happiness of the righteous as well as the misery of
the wicked will be for only a limited period.   But men
are immortal.   Where, then, will the wicked immortal
be after having passed through the age of hell ?   Where
the immortal righteous, after the age of heaven ?
Where the immortal soul, when heaven and hell are
both past ?   The objection is absurd.

Besides, if, as has been shown, the natural effects of
sin are misery, and the justice of God requires the
punishment of the sinner, those consequences, natural
and penal, must remain upon the sinner so long as he
continues to be a sinner, every moment of his sinfulness working out fresh misery and provoking anew the
wrath of the Judge.   But the Scriptures teach us that
there is no repentance after death, and that with death
all opportunities of God's converting grace are closed ;
wherefore it must be that the impenitent soul will grow
worse from the downward tendency of sin, and so his
misery increase constantly forever.   Let us, then, dear
friends, hasten while we may to flee from the wrath to
come, for there is no escape across the gulf which God
has fixed between hell and heaven !   " To-day, if
' we ' will hear his voice, let us not harden our hearts,"
lest he " swear " unto us in his " wrath : Ye shall not
see my rest."

THIRDLY : *The certainty that the sentence will be executed.*

After the previous reasoning, but one objection to the doctrine of the sinner's punishment remains for us to answer, which is, that God is merciful, and, therefore, will not be so severe against his human creatures, even though they have broken his law. The reply of the Catechism is ours : " God, is, indeed merciful, but also just: therefore his justice requires that sin, which is committed against the most high majesty of God, be also punished with extreme, that is, everlasting punishment both of body and soul."

That God is merciful, we rejoice in knowing from countless passages of Scripture, but those which assert his justice are scarcely less numerous. His justice demands that sin, every sin, against his law should be followed with appropriate punishment. His law has been proclaimed with its penalty of curse, and so the punishment is now demanded by the truth of God. Sin is an offence not only against God himself as our Creator and owner, but also against him as the most high Sovereign of the universe, whose office is to teach all his intelligent subjects what is the way of right and the consequences of keeping or departing from it ; but also to defend and vindicate them from the evil of sin by which the disobedient may assail the welfare of the faithful. It is clear, therefore, that his mercy, when exercised, must be consistent with his justice, and in no case can remit the punishment of sin. If by mercy is meant mere pity for the transgressor, which allows him to escape the righteous sentence against him, it would be a weakness utterly inconsistent with the perfection of God ; for where, then, would be the force of his law, where the consistency of his administration, where the knowledge of his wrath against sin? What should we think of a human sovereign, presiding over a considerable community, if he should cease to execute, or irregularly execute, the laws out of pity for the offenders? Should we not say that he was unfit to govern, that his miscalled mercy to the criminal was cruelty to the many, because encouraging crime by the prospect of impunity; and that if such a course were continued, it would end in anarchy and utter ruin? Would this be less true on the enlarged scale of the divine dominion? So long as we attribute to God the moral government of the universe, we must believe that so principal a part of executive sovereignty as the punishment of offences against organic law will be faithfully administered. If God punish not wrong, where shall we look for the vindication of right?

God is merciful, but his mercy cannot contradict his justice. There must, therefore, be a method by which the divine mercy is justified, and the divine justice administered through mercy. This is the purpose and end of the redemption through Christ, the delightful doctrines of which it will be our privilege to consider on the subsequent Lord's Days. There we may see that, though "all have sinned and come short of the glory of God," all who believe are "justified freely by his grace, through the redemption which is in Christ Jesus; whom God hath set forth to be a propitiation, through faith in his blood, to declare his righteousness for the remission of sins that are past, through the forbearance of God; to declare, I say, at this time his righteousness; that he might be just, and the justifier of him which believeth in Jesus." Yes, beloved breth-

ren, here is our hope: " Cursed," indeed, " is every one
that continueth not in all things which are written in
the book of the law to do them ; but Christ hath redeemed us from the curse of the law, being made a
curse for us." Death by Adam, life by Christ; lost
ourselves, redeemed by Jesus ; guilty through our own
sin, justified by the righteousness of Him in whom we
have believed. God grant us all this faith, that we
may not perish, but have everlasting life ! Amen.

LECTURE V.

NECESSITY OF A MEDIATOR.

7

FIFTH LORD'S DAY.

NECESSITY OF A MEDIATOR.

QUEST. XII. *Since, then, by the righteous judgment of God, we deserve temporal and eternal punishment, is there no way by which we may escape that punishment, and be again received into favor?*

ANS. God will have his justice satisfied; and, therefore, we must make this full satisfaction, either by ourselves, or by another.

QUEST. XIII. *Can we ourselves, then, make this satisfaction?*

ANS. By no means; but, on the contrary, we daily increase our debt.

QUEST. XIV. *Can there be found anywhere one who is a mere creature able to satisfy for us?*

ANS. None; for, first, God will not punish any other creature for the sin which man has committed; and, further, no mere creature can sustain the burden of God's eternal wrath against sin, so as to deliver others from it.

QUEST. XV. *What sort of a mediator and deliverer, then, must we seek for?*

ANS. For one who is very man and perfectly righteous; and yet more powerful than all creatures, that is, one who is also very God.

HITHERTO our meditations on the Catechism have been sad and bitter, though, I trust, not unprofitable or without glimpses of comfort. The shadows of the curse have been heavy, yet the morning light of the Sun of Righteousness has gilded the horizon. It is the method of Christ's Spirit thus to humble that he may exalt us, and, by convincing us of our guilt, to prepare us for hearing with great joy the glad tidings of salvation; nor could we understand how we may be saved through the representative righteousness of Christ, did we not first see our ruin through the fall of our first father. " The law " is " our schoolmaster to bring us unto Christ, that we " may " be justified by faith." Blessed be God, that when our sense of eternal danger

makes us cry out : What must we do to be saved ?
He has himself given us the answer by his only begotten Son, our Elder Brother ! Yea, blessed be his holy
name, that he honors sinful men with the happy office
of proclaiming the full and free salvation to their fellow-sinners ! O that his grace would strengthen me,
his most unworthy servant, this day and at all times of
my ministry, to make known the methods of his mercy
so clearly that all of you, my dear hearers, may by the
same Spirit be comforted and built up in the faith of
Jesus Christ, the only " name under heaven given
among men, whereby we must be saved ! "

Hereto assist us, the Almighty God and Father of
our Lord Jesus Christ.   Amen !

Having shown us our condemnation under the curse
denounced against sinners, the Catechism leads us to
ask if there be any way of deliverance from the irresistible wrath of God, and gives a gleam of hope in the
answer to Question the 12th.   " God will have his justice satisfied ; and, therefore, we must make this full
satisfaction, either by ourselves or by another."

If, then, we may escape through a full satisfaction,
for the dishonor we have done to the holy law of God,
can we ourselves make such a satisfaction ?   This is
declared to be impossible, in the answer to Question the
13th.   " By no means ; but, on the contrary, we daily
increase our debt."

But if we look for help to the creatures of God, is
there any one of them all who could make such satisfaction for us ?   The Catechism replies, in the answer
to Question the 14th, " None ; for, first : God will not
punish any other creature for the sin which man hath
committed ; and, further : no mere creature can sustain

the burden of God's eternal wrath, so as to deliver others from it."

Thus denied all hope from mere creatures, what kind of a surety must we look for ? Ans. 15th. " For one who is very man, and perfectly righteous ; and yet more powerful than all creatures, that is, one who is also very God."

This is our lesson proper for to-day ; but if you glance over that of the Sixth Lord's Day, you will see the doctrines of the 14th and 15th Questions and answers there more thoroughly opened, for which reason we shall now touch them but lightly, giving our attention chiefly to the 12th and 13th, comprising, however, the treatment of the whole doctrine in both Lord's Days under the following heads :

FIRST : *The impossibility of our salvation by our own works.*

SECONDLY : *The possibility of our salvation through the righteousness of a sufficient substitute.*

THIRDLY : *The qualities necessary to a sufficient substitute, or mediator, for us with God.*

FOURTHLY : *The provision of such a substitute, or mediator, in our Lord Jesus Christ,* as we learn from the Holy Scriptures of the Old and New Testaments.

FIRST : *The impossibility of our salvation by our own good works.*

This is taught us, according to Scripture, in the 12th and 13th Questions and answers : 1. " God will have his justice satisfied." 2. " We cannot," of ourselves, make such satisfaction, " but, on the contrary, we daily increase our debt."

1. " God will have his justice satisfied." This, you will remember, we argued at length in our lecture on

the Fourth Lord's Day, when treating of the 10th and 11th Questions and answers ; but we may, not unprofitably, repeat the main points.

a. The *truth* of God demands it ; for he has expressly and repeatedly declared that " the soul which sinneth, it shall die ; " " Cursed is every one that continueth not in all things which are written in the book of the law to do them "; and that he " will by no means clear the guilty." It cannot, for a moment, be supposed that God will deny himself. What he has said, he will execute. Whatever sophisms the carnal heart may invent, " let God be true and every man a liar."

b. The *holiness* of God demands it ; for there is such a contrariety in sin to his own purity that he cannot look upon the sinner without abhorrence ; and, as his infinite blessedness results from his infinite holiness, it must be that the result of sin will be misery.

c. The *authority* of God demands it ; for if, as the Supreme Ruler, he has promulgated his law, and one of his subjects break that law, he is defied to his face, and, should he not execute the penalty incurred, the transgressor will seem to triumph, and the divine rule cease to be infallible, giving encouragement and immunity to sin.

d. The *care of God for the welfare of his subject-creatures* demands it ; since his law was given to guard the happiness of each from the injurious encroachment or remissness of any, and sin is a positive and wide-spreading injury, any tolerance of sin on his part would be to allow of wrong being done by the sinner against his fellow-subjects, who should have the divine protection.

e. The *moral instruction of God's rational subjects*

demands it ; for, only from his revelation of his will in his word and works can we know what he requires of us, the distinction in his sight between right and wrong, and the estimate he sets upon righteousness and upon wrong-doing. If, therefore, he allow sin to pass without punishing the sinner, how can we or any observer of his doings know the way of right and reward from the way of wrong and punishment ?

Thus we see that the escape of a single sinner from punishment, though he may have committed but a single sin, would cause a fatal doubt of the divine truth, of the divine holiness, of the divine authority, of the divine goodness, and of the divine will. Truly, therefore, asserts the Catechism : " God will have his justice satisfied," and until that satisfaction be rendered, we cannot escape punishment. As certainly as God is unchangeable, the unjustified sinner must die.

2. " We cannot, of ourselves, make satisfaction to the divine justice ; but, on the contrary, we daily increase our debt."

Debt, though now commonly used for pecuniary obligation, really signifies that which is due, whatever it be. Our debt to God is twofold : The penalty we have incurred, and the constant obedience required ; both the discharge of that penalty, and the rendering of that obedience, are necessary to the satisfaction of the law to which we are subject ; but in neither part can we render satisfaction to divine justice.

a. Not by discharging the penalty. For, as has been shown, the guilt of man, that is, his desert of punishment, God considers so great that no suffering of man can ever expiate it, and hence his punishment will be so long as any guilt of his remains ; which, consequently, if man be left to himself, will be perpetual or eternal. We should be continually enduring punishment, but never finishing the payment of the penalty; and our expiation, being ever imperfect, would be prolonged forever.

But some may ask: Will not God allow us to atone for our past offences by future obedience, or, in other words, make up for past transgressions by our repentance and faithful service after this? The answer must be in the negative. When a penalty has been deserved it must be suffered. No remorse can destroy the sinful act done or its consequences. The law has been broken, the authority of God has been insulted, the evil against our fellow-creatures has been wrought, the sentence has been pronounced; no regrets can annihilate the past. Is it not so under human law? Is remorse ever considered an expiation of crime, or accepted in lieu of the penalty? The thief goes to prison, the murderer to the gallows, though they weep never so bitterly or promise never so well. Sometimes, indeed, the penalty may be mitigated, but it would be only because the moral sensibility displayed by the culprit shows that his guilt was less, not that his tears had washed it away. Is it not so under God's natural laws? Can the remorse of the sensualist repair the peace he has destroyed? or the tears of the drunkard restore to him the health and vigor he has wasted? And shall a few pangs of the sinner's soul, caused rather by dread of suffering than honest sorrow for crime, suffice to hide from the holy God all trace of his offences against wise, good, and just law? Let it once be admitted as a principle, that sorrow for sin atones for it, and the value of law is at an end. Again: The

law of God is so broad that it requires all our service
at all times. Every thought, every word, every act,
every moment of our lives belong to God. All our
mind, all our heart, all our soul, all our might, belong
to God. We cannot, without sin, alienate our strength
for a single moment from the duty which belongs to
that moment. If, therefore, we have at any time failed
to render an entire obedience, we can never compensate
for it; because, even though we should afterward render an entire obedience, it is no more than what we
owe to God at the time, and there can be no excess or
surplus of service which may be put to the supply of
the former deficiency. This principle is acknowledged
in the administration of human laws; for they, requiring good conduct at all times, admit no previous or subsequent virtue as an expiation of crime. Though a
man be honest all the rest of his life, if he, in any one
moment, steal, he is punished as a thief; if he commit
but one murder, he is executed. The penalty may
sometimes, through a merciful policy, be mitigated, but
can never, in strict justice, be remitted.

b. Neither can we satisfy divine justice by a constant
obedience; which is the other part of the debt we owe
to God. Granting, for the sake of argument, that all the
penal consequences of our past sins were removed from
us, and we were allowed to begin anew our probation,
we could not, if left to ourselves and our present
nature, satisfy the requirements of the divine law, but,
" on the contrary," should " daily increase our debt;"
for, as has been shown in our previous lessons (particularly on the Second and Third Lord's Days), the
natural consequence of sin is the depravity of our
moral disposition and faculties, so that we are from

our very birth " wholly incapable of doing any good, and inclined to all wickedness," " except we be regenerated by the Spirit of God." Upon this depravity of our nature we have already argued so fully that no farther proof need be adduced. It is clearly a doctrine of all Scripture, especially that which declares, on the one hand, that by the deeds of the law no flesh can be justified, and, on the other, that sincere repentance and its fruits of a Christian life are wrought in the believer by the grace of the Holy Spirit, converting and sanctifying his soul. The Holy Spirit is the Spirit of Christ, and the grace of the Spirit is bestowed only upon those who by faith receive Christ as their Saviour because the Saviour of sinners. If reformation does occur, it is only through the operation of faith in the Gospel which reveals the atonement, and is, therefore, consequent on the atonement. Even then the reformation is never complete in this life, and the more a penitent receives of divine grace, the more is he convinced that " it is God who worketh in " him " both to will and to do of his good pleasure." Without the Spirit of Christ we are utterly unable to render any of that service which the law requires for our justification ; and if we be regenerated so that we lead good lives, the credit is due, not to us for our justification, but to him, whose is the only righteousness which God will accept as sufficient to honor the law under which we live and by which we shall be tried.

Thus we see that in no sense are we able to satisfy for ourselves the justice of God, but are daily increasing our debt, and heaping up for ourselves wrath against the day of wrath. Such would be our miserable condition in this world, and such our terrible fate in the

world to come, were there no method provided for our
salvation, other than that originally proposed to man:
our personal innocence and obedience. But, blessed
be God, we are not so cut off from hope; for we
learn:

SECONDLY: *The possibility of our salvation through
the righteousness of a sufficient substitute.*

" God will have his justice satisfied, and, therefore,
we must make this full satisfaction either by ourselves
or by another." (Ans. 12th.)

The necessity of satisfaction having been shown, and,
also that we cannot make it of ourselves, a new question arises: *Will God accept of satisfaction rendered
for us by another?*

The whole evangelical Scriptures, and our Church
in all her confessions according to Scripture, answer:
Yes. We freely admit that no such method of salvation could have been discovered by the reason of men;
but contend that, having been revealed to us by God
himself, the infinitely wise and holy Sovereign, it is
perfectly consonant with the highest reason.

1. God has declared that the righteousness of Christ,
when accepted by the faith of the sinner as offered on
his behalf, is accepted as a sufficient ground of his justification; as says the apostle: " All have sinned, and
come short of the glory of God; being justified freely
by his grace, through the redemption which is in Christ
Jesus; whom God hath set forth to be a propitiation
through faith in his blood, to declare his righteousness
for the remission of sins that are past through the forbearance of God; to declare, I say, his righteousness;
that he might be just and the justifier of him which
believeth in Jesus." This puts beyond doubt the fact,

that God does justify the believing sinner on the ground that a sufficient righteousness has been offered on his behalf by another. We may not, therefore, deny the propriety of such an arrangement without impeaching the justice of God. But,

2. It is also perfectly consonant with sound reason. The design of God in the denunciation of penalties on the breaking of his law, certainly was not the destruction of his subjects, but to maintain the divine authority of his law and to deter man from transgression. Now, if by the provision of a sufficient substitute for the sinner, three things can be secured, God is just in receiving the sinner again into favor. Those three things are: *a.* The honor of the divine law. *b.* The maintenance of the divine authority, so that no encouragement is given that sin will go unpunished. *c.* The reformation of the transgressor, so that he returns to obedience.

a. For the first: The honor of the divine law; it is necessary that God should show his infinite estimation of its excellence. This is done by the perfect submission and obedience to the law of the sufficient Surety, that in the greatness of his service, the dishonor which we have done the law may be covered by a transcendent glory. And what greater honor could God have given to his law than by sending forth his only begotten and coequal Son to become in our nature its faithful servant, and obey all its requisitions, actual and penal, on our behalf? Must not the spectacle of the divine Lawgiver himself condescending to fulfil all its demands as a voluntary servant, yield in the sight of all holy creatures a testimony to its excellence and invest it with a glory infinitely higher and more convincing than the obedience of our whole race, or of myriads of worlds like ours?

b. For the second: The maintenance of the divine authority; it is necessary that God sternly require the penalties which we have incurred to be fully endured by a sufficient Surety, in such a manner as will show beyond a doubt the displeasure of God against sin and his determination not to allow it to go unpunished. And how could God more plainly indicate his just will that no sin shall be tolerated with impunity, and display his deep abhorrence of transgression, than by requiring the penalties which we have incurred to the uttermost from his own beloved Son, when incarnate as our representative? Could the eternal suffering of all our race, of myriads of worlds like ours, exhibit the divine wrath against the sinner, in any degree approaching the terrible anguish of body and soul which the innocent holy Jesus endured under the displeasure of the Father?

c. For the third: The reformation of the sinner who is pardoned on account of the substituted righteousness, so that he returns to obedience; it is necessary that the same grace which pardons should inspire him with a new life, with desire, and strength to keep the law he before has broken; else the pardon would be to let loose a rebel unsubdued, and an evil-doer unreclaimed. And how wisely and certainly has God secured the repentance and sanctification of the ransomed transgressor, by making the same faith which admits him to a discharge from condemnation effectual, by the grace of the Holy Ghost, to purify his heart, to work in him love, and to strengthen him for overcoming the world. For Christ saves none from wrath whom he does not save from the power of sin ; none have the grace of faith without the grace of repentance ; none have a part in Christ who do not receive the Holy Ghost to dwell in their souls ; and none are admitted to heaven without being first made holy and pure. Where can be found such generous and persuasive arguments to cease from sinning and do the will of God, as are forced upon the soul by the mercy of God through the devoted love of Christ ? Who, that has a heart at all sensitive to grateful emotion, would wilfully insult his deliverer that died for him ? How are we encouraged, notwithstanding our weakness, and the pressure of temptation from within and without, to attempt the difficult path of duty, when we are assured that God, for Christ's sake, will work in us " both to will and to do of his good pleasure ; " that all power is in the hand of Christ to overrule all circumstances for the safety of his people ; and that heaven, with all its benedictions and felicities, is before us as an eternal recompense for our brief trials, an exceedingly glorious reward of our perseverance in the footsteps of Christ ?

While presenting to you this condensed argument for the vindication of divine justice in redeeming the penitent sinner, we should be far from the thought that we have all the divine reasons for such an arrangement. There are depths in the divine purposes which no created mind can fathom, as there is a range of the divine operations which no created mind can comprehend. Divine truth, so far as it is revealed to us here in our present state, must be communicated through the medium of human language, which has been framed (a very few words excepted) with reference only to things of this world, and all illustrations of the divine working must be taken from facts of which we are conversant. Thus, the Scriptures (and our Church according to the Scriptures) exemplify the juridical proceedings of our divine Sovereign by the methods of human jurisdiction ; borrowing from them its terms, as debt, penalty, guilt, pardon, justification, atonement, and the like ; or, at the farthest, we look for explanations to what we can discover of the divine administration in providence over this present economy. But what is the narrow sphere of this little world, so petty a province considered by itself, to the vast empire over which our God sways his sovereignty ? What is the brief time of the earth's few ages to' the eternity past and future, through which the omniscient purposes of God are carried on by the mighty working of his omnipresent will ? What is the aggregated fortune of all our race, if separated from the rest of the spiritual creation, to the moral well-being of the countless families, who depend on our God for all that constitutes the life of life? Of what we can discover respecting God's dealings here and among men, though we push our inquiries to the utmost limit, we must say with the adoring patriarch : " Lo ! these are parts of his ways ; but how small a portion is heard of him ? " The full doctrine, or, if the expression be allowed, the complete theory of the atonement ; the reasons for its methods ; the extent of its purposes ; the variety of its results ; the number and character and condition of the moral beings that are and are to be affected by its consequences, can be understood only by the Infinite Author of the scheme. There must, after all our study and reasoning out of the Scripture and the analogies of providence, remain mysteries in the plan of

salvation utterly above our reach; and our best illustrations fall infinitely short of the vast idea.

Suppose, for example, that the Allwise Father were
himself teaching his heavenly servants the doctrine of
the redemption provided for man, would he employ the
terms and the analogies with which the Holy Spirit in
the Scriptures condescends to teach us? Must we not
believe that he would uplift the attention of those apt,
long-disciplined intelligences to great principles of the
divine government, but partially revealed to us because
we are capable only of partially understanding them?

We cheerfully and with devout reverence admit,
nay, would earnestly contend, that the principles of the
divine government on which the atonement is based, as
it is revealed to us, must be the same throughout all its
extent — and, especially, that main principle of justification for the believing penitents of our human race
through the substituted obedience and suffering of the
Son of God in our nature as our representative; but
what we mean to assert is, that that very principle is
and can be only partially, very partially understood by
us even through the revelation God has given of it to
us, because from the condition we are in, the revelation
must be confined within comparatively narrow limits.
Thus the Apostle Paul speaks of "the unsearchable
riches of Christ," and of "the love of Christ which
passeth knowledge;" and again with the same reference
he exclaims: "O, the depth of the riches both of the
wisdom and knowledge of God! how unsearchable are
his judgments and his ways past finding out!"

This is certain, the testimony of Scripture being so
clear as to allow no doubt, that the influence of the
plan of redemption extends far beyond the Church

which it translates from the depth of condemnation to
the height of heavenly glory ; nay, we may believe that
the radiance of the Sun of Righteousness sheds fresh
magnificence over all the spiritual universe of God's
creation.   The Apostle Peter declares that " the angels
desire to look into the things of redemption ; " and Paul
that " principalities and powers in heavenly places "
will be taught and are now taught " by the church
(that is, by God's dealings with the church) the manifold wisdom of God "   Jesus is declared to be the
observed " (seen) of angels ; " and the Lamb that
was slain will be eternally in the midst of the throne ;
the eternal object of admiration, adoration, and praise
to all the angelic hosts, who will alternate their respon-
sive hallelujahs with glorified believers, and join with
them in the unanimous, unending choruses of acclaim-
ing homage before the throne of God and his Christ.
What the effects of the evangelical scheme on other
worlds may be, we know not and dare not conjecture ;
but this we are certain of, that it reveals to all his holy
creatures who contemplate the divine character, its
very highest glory, his most manifold wisdom and love
and power.   It is " to the praise of the glory of his
grace that he has made us accepted in the Beloved."

God has manifested the glory of his majestic attributes in many ways, some of which we know, but more
of which we cannot understand ; yet it may without
irreverence be asserted, that were it not for the shining
of his glory in the face of his Son Jesus Christ, the
full beauty and the most attractive charm of his
infinite love would not be known.   His holy servants
would forever have adored his several excellences, but
could not have perceived their admirable harmony as

now they behold his wisdom devising and his power
executing the wonderful plan of salvation for the sinner, in which justice and goodness combine to reveal
mercy.   The justice of God, had it taken its unquali-
fied course in punishing the sinner, — the goodness of
God, had its bounties been confined only to the deserving and guiltless, — would indeed, have received and
been worthy of all praise from all holy creatures.   Still
those most glorious attributes are naturally essential to
the divine Sovereign ; we could not imagine the Holy
Father of intelligent creatures otherwise than just and
good.   The exercise of those divine qualities is necessary to the idea of God ; but that they could meet in
blessing on the souls of guilty sinners, no created mind
could ever have conjectured or believed to be possible
had not God made it manifest.   His mercy surprises
and startles the moral universe with a mild and
exquisite glory, transcending all other emanations from
the light unapproachable in which the mystery of his
being dwells.   It is brighter than justice, softer than
goodness ; for it is justice and goodness blending their
beams in mercy, — his choice, his delight, the good
pleasure of his sovereign will.

Now, dear hearers, let us learn and carry away with
us the practical inferences, from the doctrine thus far
developed.

FIRST: Our utter helplessness under our deserved
condemnation.

God will have his justice satisfied.   Who of us can
escape from his hands, or bear the fiery vengeance of
his curse ?   O, vain and impious is the expectation of
the sinner from the goodness or pity of God, while his

justice with flaming sword stands between to execute the sentence of the law.

SECONDLY: Our certain salvation, if, with penitent hearts, we accept of the suretyship of Christ.

It is the method God has provided, because he delights to save. It is the method which magnifies his justice infinitely more than our eternal death. It is the method by which we may be transformed from deep corruption into holy servants of his will forever.

THIRDLY: Our gracious obligation to spread the knowledge of this mercy among our fellow-sinners, for their immortal good ; the joy of angels ; our own reward, and the glory of God our Saviour.

LECTURE VI.

QUALITIES OF THE MEDIATOR.

SIXTH LORD'S DAY.

QUALITIES OF THE MEDIATOR.

QUEST. XVI. *Why must he be very man, and yet perfectly righteous?*

ANS. Because the justice of God requires that the same nature which hath sinned, should likewise make satisfaction for sin; and one who is himself a sinner cannot satisfy for others.

QUEST. XVII. *Why must he in one person be also very God?*

ANS. That he might by the power of his Godhead, sustain in his human nature, the burden of God's wrath; and *might obtain for, and* restore to us righteousness and life.

QUEST. XVIII. *Who is, then, that Mediator, who is in one person both very God and real righteous man?*

ANS. Our Lord Jesus Christ; who of God is made unto us wisdom and righteousness, and sanctification and redemption.

QUEST. XIX. *Whence knowest thou this?*

ANS. From the holy Gospel which God himself revealed first in Paradise, and afterwards published by the patriarchs and prophets, and was pleased to represent it by the shadows of sacrifices and the other shadows of the law; and, lastly, has accomplished it by his only begotten Son.

THE lesson for the Fifth Lord's Day set forth in the 12th Question and answer: The necessity of a satisfaction being made for our sins in order to our salvation; in the 13th: Our utter inability to make such satisfaction for ourselves; and in the 14th: The insufficiency of any mere creature to make satisfaction for us; which led to the 15th Question: What sort of Mediator and Deliverer must we then seek for? The answer given to which, is: " For one who is very man, and perfectly righteous; and yet more powerful than all creatures, that is, one who is also very God."

But those who were attentive to our lecture on the Fifth Lord's Day will remember the statement, — that the doctrine of the Mediator between God and man, which is opened in the 14th and 15th questions and answers, is more thoroughly discussed throughout those for the Sixth Lord's Day ; and that, therefore, for greater convenience, it was proposed to consider the whole subject under four heads : —

First : *The impossibility of our salvation by our own works.*

Secondly : *The possibility of our salvation by or through the righteousness of a sufficient substitute.*

Thirdly : *The qualities necessary to a sufficient substitute or mediator for us with God.*

Fourthly : *The provision of such a substitute or mediator in our Lord Jesus Christ, as we learn from the Holy Scriptures of the Old and New Testaments.*

The first two of these heads were then discussed at considerable length, leaving the third and fourth for discussion to-day ; which, imploring divine help, we shall now pursue.

Thirdly : *The qualities necessary to a sufficient substitute or mediator for us with God.*

The answer to the 14th Question denies that he may be " a mere creature," because, " first : God will not punish any other creature for the sin which man has committed ; and, further, no mere creature can sustain the burden of God's eternal wrath against sin, so as to deliver others from it." The answer to the 15th Question asserts that " our Mediator and Deliverer" must be : " One who is very man, and yet perfectly righteous, and yet more powerful than all creatures, that is, one who is, also, very God."

He must be " very man, and yet perfectly righteous," says the answer to the 16th Question : " Because the justice of God requires, that the same nature which hath sinned should likewise (*i. e.* also) make satisfaction for sin ; and one who is himself a sinner cannot satisfy for others." He "must also in one person be very God," says the answer to the 17th Question : " That he might, by the power of his Godhead, sustain in his human nature the burden of God's wrath ; and might obtain for and restore to us righteousness and life."

This instruction of the Catechism is so full and clear as to render any prolonged commentary of ours needless ; yet some more specific explanations may not be without use ; and they will be given under two propositions : —

I. The Substitute and Mediator must be " very (or truly) man, and perfectly righteous."

II. He must " also be very God in one person " with his human nature.

I. He must be " very man, and perfectly righteous."

1. No other mere creature can be accepted as a substitute for man.

A. " God will not punish any other creature for the sin which man has committed."

a. God would not compel any other creature to suffer for man's sin. If that creature be himself a sinner, he must suffer the punishment of his own sin, which he can never sufficiently expiate ; and, therefore, no sufferings of his can be put to the credit of the sinner of another nature. There are various ranks of spiritual creatures, and we have reason to believe that among the angels who have fallen there are some of very high rank originally ; but according to their original height has been the depth of their fall ; according to the eminence of their duties has been the guilt of their rebellion. They suffer for themselves; they cannot be made to suffer more than they deserve; nor, if that were possible, would the infliction of any additional sufferings on them for man's sake be just to them, or give any honor to the law which man has broken. Neither, if the other creature be innocent, would it be just to impose upon him sufferings which he does not deserve, that man might be relieved from sufferings which he does deserve. The authority of God could never be vindicated by such treatment of a creature who is entitled to reward for his obedience.

b. Nor, again, may such a creature, however highly exalted, voluntarily assume the place of man, either to endure man's punishment for the sins he has committed, or to perform the duties which he has omitted, both being necessary to the satisfaction demanded. For every creature, from the fact of his creation, is a servant of God, bound to use all his faculties with the utmost energy of which he is capable in the sphere where God has placed him, and can never do more than his duty. To take man's place, therefore, he must desert his own; to endure man's punishment, to perform man's duties, he must use faculties and time which already belong to God. The just authority of God would be aggrieved, not honored, by the disobedience of an angel to the law under which he is placed, that he might obey the law under which man is placed. A creature of God cannot change his sphere of duty any more than he can change his nature, for they are by the divine appointment necessarily relative to each other, not matters of the creature's choice, but absolutely of the divine will.

B. " Further : no mere creature can sustain the burden of God's wrath against sin so as to deliver others from it."

Even if it were possible that another mere creature, however holy and exalted, could take our place, no amount of suffering on his part would be sufficient to make up for the sufferings we need to be released from.

a. The punishment appointed to the sinner is everlasting, because he can never, by any sufferings he is capable of, exhaust the penalty. Yet the distance in dignity between any other creature and man is, of necessity, limited ; how, then, can our punishment, which is unlimited, be substituted by any sufferings of his short of eternal ?   The substitution, if undertaken, can never be accomplished.

b. Besides : the sinners to be redeemed are a great multitude, whom no man can number, and the substitute would have to bear in his single person the aggregate responsibility of them all ; if, then, the punishment of one sinner be so heavy that he cannot exhaust it, but must suffer on forever, what mere creature could endure the imputed sufferings of the whole Church ? A proper idea of the atonement will not tolerate for an instant the substitution of a mere creature to satisfy the wrath of God which we deserve.

2. The character of our responsibility is such that it cannot be assumed except by one in human nature, yet himself guiltless.

A. " The justice of God requires that the same human nature which hath sinned, should likewise make satisfaction for sin." (16th Ans.)

Even were another creature found capable of enduring the weight of our punishment, the circumstances of our sin are such that he could not assume its guilt or render a satisfactory obedience on our behalf; for —

a. The law which has been outraged was given to man, was adapted to his nature, and ordered for his sphere of service. Righteousness, it is true, must be ever and everywhere the same in its essential qualities. The same great principles of right must rule over all the subjects of God ; yet, as the natures of those subjects are various, and different theatres of action are assigned to their different natures, it follows, that the manner in which the obedience is to be rendered must be peculiar to each class. The service demanded of a pure spirit, which has been created to live without a body, must be different from that demanded of a spirit created to live in a body ; for example, the service of angelic spirit from that of a human being. Take the ten precepts of the law given to man, and you see that there are human duties which a holy angel cannot perform, as there are offences which a wicked angel cannot commit. Even one class of angels or unembodied spirits may have duties assigned them for which they are fitted, differing from those for which other classes of angels are fitted, each class being under its peculiar law, within its peculiar sphere, beyond which it cannot go. How much less can an angel, or unembodied spirit, come under the peculiar obligations of man ? The law, given to man for his obedience on earth, can be obeyed or satisfied only by human nature on earth, or in man's proper sphere. That law, imposed by the Creator on human nature, to be obeyed in his body on earth, man has broken ; and the earth is full of his rebellion. Whatever laws, therefore, are obeyed, if the law given to man remain dishonored, the government of God is shaken. Whatever classes of his moral creatures are faithful, if man be a successful, unpunished sinner, the justice of God is uncertain. Whatever provinces of his empire are loyal and tributary, if in this world his authority be not vindicated, it ceases to be sovereign. Whatever, decrees of his will are fulfilled, if the sentence against sinful man be not executed, his truth has failed. The satisfaction necessary for our safety must, therefore, we repeat, be made to the law appointed for us, in our nature and upon our earth. So we read that: " God sent forth his Son, made of a woman, made under the law, to redeem them that were under the law."

b. The penalties denounced against sin are of such a nature that none but man can endure them so as to free us from guilt. The sentence pronounced on man is death, — death of body, and death of soul, — which we know includes all the sicknesses, pains, and corruption of the body, with all the sorrow, anguish, and degradation of spirit which is occasioned by the withdrawal of God's favor and the weight of his wrath. This death of our entire human nature, temporal and eternal, is the punishment we deserve and must suffer, except we be delivered from it by a sufficient satisfaction rendered for us. None but man can know and feel the sorrows and agony of man in body and soul; none but man can suffer the pains and distresses of our mortal life, or our eternal death, the death " passed upon all men because that all have sinned." So we read of our Redeemer: " Forasmuch, then, as the children are partakers of flesh and blood, he also himself took part of the same, that through death he might destroy him that had the power of death, that is, the devil; and deliver them, who through fear of death were all their lifetime subject to bondage. For, verily, he took not on him the nature of angels, but he took on him the seed of Abraham. Wherefore in all things it behooved him to be made like unto his brethren, that he might be a merciful and faithful high-priest in things pertaining to God, to make reconciliation for the sins of his people."

There are other and most important reasons why the Mediator should be very man, which we may not now enter upon, but hope to consider fully when they are brought before us by subsequent sections of the Catechism. Yet we may ask: How may sinful man dare approach unto God; how may he know that God will again dwell with men ; that his fallen nature may again enjoy the felicity of his presence and the light of his love, unless he saw one made in the likeness of his own sinful flesh holding intimate communion with God, glorious himself from communications of the divine glory, and standing before us as the medium through whom we may look upon God and not die, — unless God be again with man on earth, as he was once in Paradise, speaking to man as to his dear child?

B. The Mediator in our human nature must be " perfectly righteous," because " one who is himself a sinner cannot satisfy for others." This point is so clearly stated, that no argument of ours is needed to make it clearer ; but it is stated so distinctly to prepare us for faith in him who has been constituted by God as our Mediator and Substitute. The perfect righteousness of the man who is our surety must be twofold; innocence and active obedience.

a. *Innocence.* — He must be without sin. If he had committed sin, his own guilt would be upon him ; and he would be rejected by God in his own person, much more as a mediator for his fellow-sinners. So we read of our Lord and Saviour, that " he did no sin, neither was guile found in his mouth."

b. Active Obedience. — The satisfaction for us required by God, is not merely a sufficient suffering in room of that which we deserve on account of our transgression, but an honoring of the law by an active obedience sufficient to be substituted in room of that which we are bound to render, and which is necessary, according to the divine justice, for our re-admission within the divine favor, vouchsafed only to those who are righteous in his sight. Such positive, energetic righteousness, no sinner, whose faculties have been depraved by the corruption of human nature consequent upon the fall, can render. " He made him to be sin for us, who knew no sin, that we might be made the righteousness of God in him."

The inference from this is, that the mediator or substitute we need must be man, partaker of all other human characteristics, but not of sin ; and, therefore, as all our race are fallen in Adam, guilty of overt, personal sins, and utterly without moral strength to honor God by keeping his law, the mediator or substitute for us in human nature, must be man after some extraordinary method which excepts him from the otherwise universal entailment of guilt and corruption, while he inherits all our weaknesses which are not sinful. Our guilt and corruption are derived from Adam in the same manner that our being is derived from him ; " Adam begat his ' children ' in his own likeness ; " we are " conceived in sin and brought forth in iniquity ; " that cannot be human nature, which is not born of woman ;

that cannot be sinless human nature which is begotten by man ; hence, our surety in human nature must be conceived from some " extraordinary generation," conceived without sin, brought forth without iniquity, yet, because his flesh and blood are derived from woman, having the physical weaknesses of humanity, being subject to all those infirmities, but without sin. So we read of our Lord's miraculous conception, in the words of the angel to the Virgin Mary (Let "all generations call her blessed!") "The Holy Ghost shall come upon thee, and the power of the Highest shall overshadow thee ; therefore also that holy thing which shall be born of thee shall be called the Son of God." The germ of the body was in the woman, and in her womb it grew till its birth, and from her bosom was it nourished after its birth, but the impregnating power was of God, and, therefore, was the flesh and blood of the "child wonderful" holy ; of the seed of Adam, Abraham, Judah, and David, through his mother, but sanctified in the first beginning of his human nature by the energy of the Holy Ghost.

II. Our Mediator and Substitute " must also be very God in one person " with his human nature.

For this two reasons are given by the Catechism (17th Ans.)

" That he might by the power of his Godhead sustain in his human nature the burden of God's wrath ; " and

" Might obtain for and restore us to righteousness and life."

1. " That he might, by the power of his Godhead, sustain in his human nature the burden of God's wrath."

A. Because the burden of God's wrath is too great for human nature, unsupported, to endure.

It is the wrath of God against the sinner. The sentence denounced against the sinner is death, which we have seen to be the utter withdrawal of the divine favor and the actual infliction of his vengeance. The moment that this sentence comes upon the sinner in its full execution, he must be crushed — he must die. There can be in him no vital energy left, no recuperative force — the weight presses him down forever. The substitute must be man, because it is the penalty of the law given to man. But if he were mere man, though himself righteous, the weight of the imputed guilt of a single sinner would crush him in death forever. He could never react from under it ; his power would be lost ; he would be dead. Nor could the strength of any creature avail for his help in so extreme an emergency. How, then, shall the one mediator be enabled to sustain the otherwise intolerable burden? All the wit of men and angels could never resolve the difficulty ; we must go for our answer to the revelation of the Gospel. " God " is there " manifest in the flesh." Man still stands forth the substitute of man, to receive upon his head the terrible curse ; one person is still to meet it alone ; but that Person is not merely man ; by an ineffable mystery, the coequal Son of God assumes that humanity to himself, so that the Son of God and the son of the woman, very God and very man, their natures still distinct, yet in their distinctness united, constitute one Person, the Substitute of the sinner. The Son of God thus makes the human nature of the Son of man his own. The wrath divine comes not on the Son of God, for divinity can in no sense suf-

fer or be put to shame ; it falls on the human nature
alone, because the justice of God requires that the
nature, which has sinned, should bear the penalty of
the sin ; but the divinity in the person of the mediator
sustains by its almightiness the humanity in the person
of the mediator to bear up under the curse, and, while
fully satisfying the wrath of God, yet to retain a vital
energy sufficient for its recovery from the imputed
death.   The human nature alone endures, but endures
by the strength of the divine, to which it is personally
associated.   Thus, the apostle speaks of the " Church
of God which he hath redeemed by *his own blood ;* "
i. e. by the blood of the human nature which through
his incarnation he made " his own."   " God sent forth
his Son " (elsewhere called his only begotten Son,
therefore Divine, as the begotten is of the nature of
the begetter) — his Son must have existed before he
sent him forth — sent forth his preëxistent Son " made
of a woman," that is, united to the Son of man as the
Saviour of sinners.   So again, we read, that Christ
Jesus, " being in the form of God (*i. e. existing as
God*) thought it not robbery to be equal with God ; but
made himself of no reputation, and took upon him the
form of a servant and was made in the likeness of men ;
and, being found in fashion as a man, he humbled himself and became obedient to (until) death, even the
death of the cross." · Great as must have been the
wrath of God which came on the human nature of our
Substitute, the strength of God could enable that human nature to bear it.

B. Because the merit of no suffering endured by a
mere man would be sufficient for the redemption of the
Church, saved through the Mediator.

If the wrath of God against a single sinner be so intolerable, how could a single man, as their substitute, sustain the wrath due to such a multitude?

A ready answer is, that the divine strength of the Immanuel could uphold his human nature under any degree of penal suffering; but the reply goes not far enough, for it will be asked again, Upon what principle of justice can one man be accepted in the room of many? If he be a mere man, how can the divine law be magnified by his suffering, let him suffer never so much, so that many sinners may escape by his substitution? It is obvious that where one stands forth as a substitute for very many, he cannot be accepted unless he has in his single person a dignity, or worth, far excelling that of a private individual man, and commensurate to the vast representativeness which he would assume. It is true, that by one man, Adam, condemnation to death came on our whole race; but Adam acted not merely as a private individual; nor became he man by ordinary generation; he was created immediately by God, so that the sacred genealogist hesitates not to call him "the Son of God" ("Enos, which was the son of Seth, which was the son of Adam, which was the son of God," Luke iii. 38): and, deriving his nature in this extraordinary way, he was constituted in the dignity of head of his race. He could justly represent all human nature, because all human nature was in him. All his descendants fell with him; all are under the condemnation which he brought upon them: where, then, among those guilty descendants can one be found of competent worth to take the place of a second Adam, the headship of a new race, the Redeemer of sinful men who are represented by his sufferings expiatory of their offences? It is obvious, again, that the Second Adam, like the first, must be the Son of God, of sufficient dignity to be constituted, and actually constituted by God, Head or Representative of all who are to be redeemed through him. There must also be such a worth, or legal value, in his sufferings, as fully to vindicate the justice of God in accepting them on behalf of the sinners saved. But we have seen from our previous reasoning that no mere creature could be accepted to bear, or could bear, if accepted, the sufferings due to us. How, then, shall this difficulty in the way of a just mercy be met? (O the matchless wisdom of divine love!) The Only Begotten, eternal Son of God himself, becomes incarnate as our Elder Brother; he assumes to himself, out of a woman's flesh and blood, a perfect human nature, begotten by the Holy Ghost, and by thus uniting it with his own divinity in one person, not only sustains the humanity under all the suffering of imputed guilt, but presents a surety of infinitely sufficient worth to represent all the redeemed. Therefore, was "laid upon him the iniquity of us all;" therefore, did it please the Father to bruise him, and put him to grief; therefore, did he forever "put away sin by the one sacrifice of himself," and by that "one offering perfect forever them that are sanctified." Our sufferings on account of sin would have been everlasting, because no sufferings of ours could ever have satisfied the penalty due to the sinner; but such is the incalculable merit of our Surety's sufferings for us, that in a portion of three days, the law was fully vindicated, and the whole Church absolved. Adam was made in the likeness of God, so far as a creature could reflect the likeness of the Creator, yet was he sustained only by a creature's strength, and he fell; but in our Second Adam dwelt " the Lord from heaven," the Son of God himself; the first Adam was made " a living soul;" the Second Adam is a quickening Spirit, for in him is not only a life derived, but he is the Life-giver. Therefore did he, " through death, destroy him that hath the power of death," and become the Author of eternal salvation unto all them that obey him."

2. Our Mediator must also be " very God in one person with his human nature," that " he might obtain for and restore to us righteousness and life."

Here are two offices of the Mediator for which his Divinity is necessary : —

The obtaining for us righteousness and life; and the restoring of righteousness and life to us.

A. The obtaining for us righteousness and life.

It is the part of the Mediator to act for us with God, and, therefore, is it requisite not only that a sufficient satisfaction be made to the law under which we are condemned, but that such satisfaction be duly presented and pleaded before God; and our justification, with its consequence, our readmission to the divine favor, acknowledged and secured. This justification and divine favor are meant by the terms " righteousness and life," used by the Catechism; for, according to the method of grace, the sinner who believes is not personally, that is, through his own merit, righteous, but considered and treated as righteous or justified solely on account of the satisfaction rendered to the law for him by his substitute; and the favor of God, which is life, goes out to him again only through his substitute, with whom, as the atoning representative of the sinner, God is well pleased. Is it not, then, clear that only he, who could make the satisfaction, can plead its merit before God and claim its reward? Who less than divine can thus speak with God? Who less than divine can take into his grasp such great blessing as life for all the host of the redeemed? If nothing less than divine strength could sustain the humanity of our surety under the wrath due to his people, an equal capacity is needed to contain the immensity of favor vouchsafed by the love of the reconciled Father to all his ransomed family. So reasons the Apostle of our glorious Mediator: "For it pleased the Father that in him should all fulness dwell; and having made peace through the blood of his cross, by him to reconcile all things unto himself;" and again: "For in him dwelleth all the fulness of the Godhead bodily. And ye (all believers) are complete in him, which is the head of all principality and power." And in the same strain, John the Baptist testified of our Lord: "Of his fulness have all we received and grace for grace." All the grace we need we receive of Christ; therefore all fulness dwells in Christ, and that he might contain all this fulness, in him dwells the fulness of the Godhead. It was necessary that the divine nature should sustain the humanity of the substitute, in the work of atonement; so it is necessary that after the merit of the work is provided, the divine nature should qualify the Mediator to obtain and receive by his intercession eternal redemption for us.

B. The restoring of righteousness and life to us.

It is the part of the Mediator to act for God with us; therefore is it requisite that not only the justification of the sinner, and the consequent life be obtained for

us, but, also, that those benefits be actually conferred,
and we restored to the enjoyment of all we have lost
through sin.   Who less than God can accomplish this
in us?   Who can justify where God has condemned,
but God himself?   Who can give life back, but the
Lord of life?   Who less than God can visit the hearts
of all the Church, and by the Holy Spirit incline them
all to receive by faith the pardon God extends, and
strengthen them all for the new obedience which God
requires?   If our Mediator be not divine, how can he
be omnipresent to hear every prayer of each one of all
his people; omniscient, to know their every thought
and every need; omnipotent, to sustain them all against
every temptation, under every duty, amidst sorrows
innumerable, and throughout time to a glorious eternity?   God adopts the penitents, but it is Christ who
"gives power to as many as believe," to become the
sons of God;" God strengthens them with all might,
but it is through Christ strengthening him that the
believer can do all things; God assures comfort, but
the comfort reaches us only through him, who, having
been the man of sorrows, is now the Lord of joy; God
has prepared unspeakable glories for them that love
him, and they are kept by his power unto salvation;
but Christ who is the Author, is also the Finisher of
their faith, and when they enter the full blessedness of
heaven, it is into the joy of their Lord.   Christ is the
beginning, Christ the continuance, Christ the end;
Christ first, Christ always, Christ last, Christ all in all.
He is the Way, and the Truth, and the Life; no man
cometh unto the Father but by him.   Who but the
Son of God, can lie in the bosom of God?   From that
bosom he came to be our Surety in human flesh; to

that bosom he has returned, but with our flesh about him, to be our ever prevalent Advocate, and the accomplisher of our redemption ; for where he is glorified, our humanity is glorified ; and where the Son of God dwells, there dwells his body the Church, the fulness of him that filleth all in all.

LECTURE VII.

THE PROVISION OF A MEDIATOR.

SIXTH LORD'S DAY.

THE PROVISION OF A MEDIATOR.

HAVING ascertained the qualities necessary to a sufficient substitute or mediator for us with God, viz: That he be very man and very God in one person; we come to consider : —

FOURTHLY: *The provision of such a substitute or mediator in our Lord Jesus Christ, as we learn from the Holy Scriptures of the Old and New Testaments.*

" *Who, then,*" asks the 18th Question, " *is that mediator, that in one person is both very God and real righteous man ?* "

Ans. Our Lord Jesus Christ, " who of God is made unto us wisdom, and righteousness, and sanctification, and redemption."

" *Whence knowest thou this ?* " demands the Catechism, (Quest. 19th.)

Ans. " From the Holy Gospel, which God himself revealed first in Paradise, and afterwards published by the patriarchs and prophets, and was pleased to represent it by the shadows of sacrifices, and the other ceremonies of the law; and, lastly, has accomplished it by his only begotten Son."

The order in which these questions and answers occur is the most natural for the purpose of the Catechism; but for convenience of exposition we shall invert it,* and mark : —

* This Ursinus himself is forced to do. p. 128, Lond. fol. 1633.

I. The *Fact* of divine testimony to the Lord Jesus Christ as our Mediator (Quest. and Ans. 19th) ; and, II. The *Substance* of that testimony concerning him, (18th.)

I. The *Fact* of divine testimony to the Lord Jesus Christ as our Mediator.

" Whence knowest thou thy misery ? " asked the Catechism, when opening to us our ruin through sin ; and the answer given to us was : " Out of the law of God." From God only do we know our duty, our wickedness, and our condemnation ; so, from God only, can we learn the way of escape from guilt, and return to life. The revelation of such a merciful deliverance is, indeed, as it was called by the heavenly Messenger to the shepherds of Bethlehem, " glad tidings of great joy ; " which is more briefly expressed by our one Saxon word, *Gospel*, a contraction of *goodspell*, corresponding to the Greek, *Evangel*. This " glorious " and delightful term " Gospel," our Catechism applies to the whole doctrine of salvation as taught throughout the Scriptures of the Old and New Testaments ; for which there is the highest authority. The word Gospel, it is true, does not occur in our English translation of the Old Testament, but its synonyms are frequent there, and, in citations from the former Scriptures by the New Testament writers, it is freely employed : " Search the Scriptures," that is, of the Old Testament which only then were written, said our Lord to the skeptical Jews, " for in them ye think ye have eternal life ; and they are they which testify of me." So, also, in his memorable walk with the two disciples to Emmaus, he said : " O fools, and slow of heart to believe all that the prophets have spoken ! Ought not Christ to have suffered these things, and to enter into his glory? And, beginning at Moses and all the prophets, he expounded unto them in all the Scriptures, the things concerning himself." From these and many other texts, we learn, that the main purpose of all Scripture is to teach the doctrine of salvation by Jesus Christ, and whatever we find in them is contributive to the great theme.

A. "God himself revealed it first in Paradise." There, after their fall and before their expulsion from Eden, God himself, in the hearing of our first parents, said to the serpent-tempter: " I will put enmity between thee and the woman, and between thy seed and her seed; it shall bruise thy head and thou shalt bruise his heel." Christ, the son of a virgin, came emphatically as the seed of the woman; between him and " the old serpent the devil," there was battle to extremity; and though in the desperate struggle our Champion was sorely wounded, he crushed the head of our foe, " destroying death and him that had the power of death." Hence this prophecy, that the seed of the woman should bruise the head of the serpent, is properly regarded as the first promise and proclamation of the Gospel.

B. The sacrifice by Abel of the firstlings of his flock, the life of lambs substituted in typical expiation of sin, shows that he apprehended the future sacrifice of " the Lamb of God, which taketh away the sin of the world," for us, and told that in so doing he acted " by faith," and faith supposes a revelation of promise. The offering of the sacrifice was itself a publication of the Gospel by Abel, and so we find our Lord naming him as the first of the prophets, when, speaking of the prophets slain by wicked men he says : " The blood of all the prophets . . . . from the blood of Abel to the blood of Zacharias which perished between the altar and the temple."

The publication of the Gospel thus begun was, doubtless, continued by the patriarchs until the flood, though the record of their preaching and the range of it is but indistinct; for Jude speaks of Enoch prophesying concerning the coming of our Lord, and Peter expressly calls Noah " a preacher of righteousness," and that Christ preached by him " while the ark was a preparing," (2 Peter ii. 5; 1 Peter iii. 19, 20.) So Paul, in the Epistle to the Galatians, asserts plainly that God preached the Gospel unto Abraham, saying: " In thee shall all nations be blessed;" which revelation was repeated unto Isaac and Jacob, and by them all, and many of their distinguished descendants, " published " to the house of Israel.

The strain was taken up, and the publication continued, by prophet after prophet; their intimations becoming clearer and clearer, like the brightening dawn, until Jesus, of whom Moses and all of them did write, himself appeared, the Sun of righteousness, " with healing in his wings." Respecting this successive and unanimously concurrent testimony, the Apostle Peter has this remarkable language: " Of which salvation the prophets have inquired and searched diligently, who prophesied of the grace that should come unto you; searching what, or what manner of time the Spirit of Christ which was in them did signify, when it testified beforehand the sufferings of Christ and the glory that should follow. Unto whom it was revealed, that not unto themselves, but unto us they did minister the things, which are now reported unto you by them that have preached the Gospel unto you with the Holy Ghost sent down from heaven."

C. Nay, such was the condescending goodness of God, that, not content with " revealing it " himself, " first in Paradise," and " afterwards publishing it by the patriarchs and prophets," he " was pleased to represent it by the shadows of sacrifices and other ceremonies of the law." Under the former dispensation, the enlightening influences of the Holy Ghost were not granted so abundantly as they are to us under this which is emphatically " the ministration of the Spirit;" and our heavenly Father assisted the faith of his people by sensible signs and emblems. Such were the sacrifices of living victims taught to the worshipper, as we have seen, near the gates of Paradise ; the translation of Enoch, a testimony of God to the righteousness of faith ; the ark of Noah, an eloquent emblem of the covenant within which the Church is safe amidst the ruin of ungodly men ; the rescue of Isaac, the son of promise, from the death for which, at the command of God, the father of the faithful had prepared him ; the wrestling of Jacob with the Angel of the Covenant, until he obtained from the present Son of God the blessing he desired ; the deliverance of Israel from the destruction of Egypt by the blood of the Paschal lamb. But, after the formal constitution of the pilgrim tribes at the foot of Sinai, as a church or congregation of worshippers, God appointed the law of ordinances, that by a regular and complete system of types or shadows (so called because precursing the substance that was to come) all the great doctrines of the Gospel might be presented distinctly to the eyes of the people. All these representative cere-

monies typified Christ.   Every service and every officer
of that law pointed forward to Christ and his offices
for us.   The shedding of blood, the burning of the
victims, the sending of the scape-goat with the sins of
the people into the wilderness; the purification of the
sinner by the hyssop branch sprinkling the sacrificial
blood upon him; the shew-bread, the lights of the
sanctuary, the offering of incense, the Visible Glory
resting on the ark of the testimony; the ark itself
with its propitiatory and the memorials which the propitiatory covered; the officiating priesthood, especially
the high-priest, with the sanctifying mitre on his head,
the mystical Urim and Thummim on his breast and his
robes of ceremony; the intercession of the high-priest
once a year within the veil and the blessing which
followed it; all represented and preached Christ and
his Gospel, the provision made for our need, and the
glory consequent upon the grace.   All declared the
necessity and appointment of a Mediator for us, the
substitution of his person to bear the wrath of God on
our behalf, his acceptableness with God and his intercession, which the Father heareth always, and the gift
of the Holy Ghost through him.   The ceremonial law
was, in fact, the Gospel of the Old Testament.

D. All these promises, publications, prophecies, ceremonies, and officers had their anti-type or reality in
Christ. By his incarnation, his anointing from the
Holy Ghost, by his life of obedience, his bitter sorrows,
his unspeakable agony, his death in darkness on the
cross accursed of God, his burial, his uprising from the
dead, his ascension to heaven, his session at the right
hand of the Father, his pleading for us there as our
Advocate, and the outpouring of the Holy Spirit in

answer to his prayers, he has accomplished the truth of his Gospel and made clear as the light of day the doctrines dimly perceptible amidst the shadows of the law. " The law was given by Moses,"— the moral law which brings condemnation, and the ceremonial law, which shadowed forth the promises of life ; " " but grace and truth came by Jesus Christ "— *grace,* deliverance from the condemnation of the moral law, *truth,* the reality or actual fulfilment of the things before shadowed by the types of the ceremonial law.

It is, therefore, to this Gospel, the revelation of God concerning Jesus Christ, the foretellings and prefigurations of the Old Testament, with the histories and doctrinal expositions of the New, that we go for knowledge of the Mediator ; our faith is built on the foundation of apostles and prophets, Jesus Christ himself being the chief corner-stone." The truth on which we of the Reformed Churches rely is the word of God, the whole word of God, and the word of God alone. Nothing short of divine testimony do we credit ; all that is supported by divine testimony do we believe ; whatever has not the divine testimony we reject. From God alone we can derive our religious creed, for he is the object of all worship ; from him alone our rules of moral practice, for he is the object of all duty.

II. The *substance* of the divine testimony concerning the Lord Jesus Christ as our Mediator. This is given in the answer to the 18th Question, which has two parts — the first : a recital of the three principal names designating our Mediator ; the second : a comprehensive catalogue of the blessings which we have in him.

A. Our Mediator is " the Lord Jesus Christ." Of

these names we shall be required to treat fully in expounding the lessons of the Eleventh, Twelfth, and Thirteenth
Lord's Days, and need now note only a few things.

a. He is our *Lord.* This is an epithet of authority
and power, which belongs to him by delegated right as
appointed by the Father, in the plan of redemption, to
rule over the Church and over all things for the sake
of the Church ; and throughout the New Testament
(with but two or three not contradictory exceptions)
it is applied exclusively to him as the Son of God
incarnate, the Saviour. " Unto you," said the angel
to the shepherds, " is born this day in the city of
David a Saviour which is Christ the Lord ; " and the
Apostle to the Romans : " For to this end Christ both
died and rose and revived, that he might be Lord both
of the dead and the living." From which, and many
other passages, we see that he is called Lord, not
merely in virtue of his original divinity as the Second
Person of the Godhead, (Glory be to the Father, and
to the Son, and to the Holy Ghost !) but with special
reference to his mediatorial character ; nay, that it
was bestowed upon him in reward of his mediatorial
obedience. " All power," said he himself after his
resurrection, " is given unto me in heaven and in
earth ; " and the Apostle to the Philippians testifies of
the Immanuel : " Being found in fashion as a man, he
humbled himself, and became obedient unto death,
even the death of the cross. Wherefore God also hath
highly exalted him, and given him a name (or office)
which is above every name ; that at the name of Jesus
every knee should bow, of things in heaven, and things
in earth, and things under the earth ; and that every
tongue should confess that Jesus Christ is Lord to the

glory of God the Father." Yet does the delegation of such authority to him as the Saviour prove his divinity. To what mere creature could God the Father commit a viceroyship so great? Who, less than divine, could comprehend the divine counsels for the government of the Church? Who, less than divine, could sustain the weight of all power over all things in heaven, earth, and hell? Who, less than divine, could receive the homage of " every knee " and the ascriptions of "every tongue,"'as the " Lord," " whose right it is to reign ? "

b. " Our Lord *Jesus.*" This is the name which was given to him by the angel " before he was conceived in the womb," and when the announcement was made to the virgin that she should bring forth a son. It may be, therefore, considered as more peculiarly his human name, the name by which he was called by his mother and kindred and acquaintances. So Peter, preaching to the mixed multitude, says: " Jesus of Nazareth, a man approved of God among you ;" and Paul to Timothy : " There is one mediator between God and men, the man Christ Jesus." But the name was given to him because of its peculiar significance: " Thou shalt call his name JESUS, for he shall *save* his people from their sins." The word is an imitation of the Hebrew name Joshua, which means a saviour, or one who makes safe. As Joshua, the son of Nun, having succeeded Moses by the command of God, led the tribes in safety to a triumphant possession of the promised land ; so does our Jesus deliver his brethren of the true Israel, from the power of their sins, their worst enemies, and bring them through all difficulties to the secure enjoyment of their heavenly rest. For this he unites to his

infinitely divine attributes, the experience and full sense
of our humanity, assuring us of his sympathy, and encouraging us by his power.

    c. "The Lord Jesus *Christ.*" This is a verbal noun
from a word signifying *to anoint,*—anointing with oil in
solemn ceremony being the method by which prophets,
priests, and kings were consecrated under the Old Testament. It is properly neither a personal name, nor a title
descriptive of office, but being added to *Lord Jesus,* declares that he has been appointed and confirmed by God
as the Prophet, Priest, and King of his Church. "The
Spirit of the Lord God is upon me, for he hath anointed
me," is the language which was prophetically put into
the mouth of our Lord; and, accordingly, we read in
the Gospel that " Jesus, being baptized (by John), and
praying, the heaven was opened, and the Holy Ghost
descended in a bodily shape like a dove upon him, and
a voice came from heaven, which said: ' Thou art my
beloved Son ; in thee I am well pleased.' " This unction
of the Holy Ghost was the inauguration of our Lord
Jesus to his mediatorial office, by God the Father.
Hence, because of his infinite preëminence as an office-
bearer by divine appointment, he is called emphatically
"the Christ," or "the Messiah," which is the Hebrew
synonym. The doctrine which we should derive from
the word Christ, as applied to our Lord Jesus, is, that
the efficiency of our Saviour's atonement depended not
merely upon the dignity of his person, or the infinite
merit of his work, but also on the fact of his having
been called and set apart to his mediatorial office by
God himself. In the appointment of God the Son, by
God the Father, and his anointment by God the Holy
Ghost, we see the three Persons of the Godhead united
as the God of our redemption.

B. The Catechism adds a comprehensive catalogue
of the blessings which we have in our Lord Jesus Christ,
taken from 1 Cor. i. 30: "Of him (that is, by the
gracious will of God), are ye in Christ Jesus; who of
God (that is, by appointment of God) is made unto us
wisdom, and righteousness, and sanctification, and redemption;" to which the Apostle adds: "that, according as it is written, he that glorieth, let him glory in
the Lord;" the term "Lord," in this latter verse, with
"Christ Jesus" in the former, making the triple appellation by which we acknowledge and adore the Immanu-
uel as our Saviour, "the Author and Finisher of our
faith."

a. He is "made unto us wisdom." He is the wisdom of God unto our salvation, because it was infinite
wisdom which provided the method of our justification;
and the doctrine of Christ is the sum of all divine truth,
through which God makes himself known as our God.
He is made unto us wisdom, because by his Holy Spirit
the writers of the Old and New Testaments were moved
to prepare that only and sufficient treasury of divine
truth for our learning, comfort, patience, and hope;
and because, by the power of that same spirit within
us, we are enlightened to understand the truth, converted to love the truth, and strengthened to obey the truth.

All the knowledge which the Christian needs must
come to him through Christ the Mediator, as the Apostle says: "God, who at sundry times and in divers
manners, spake in time past unto the fathers by the
prophets, hath in these last days spoken unto us by his
Son;" and again: "God, who commanded the light to
shine out of darkness, hath shined in our hearts to give
the light of the knowledge of the glory of God in the

face of Jesus Christ." By Christ the Mediator, we
have infinite wisdom speaking to us with human lips.

b. "And righteousness." We have nothing of our own
that is fit to appear before him, but, covered with sin,
we could not stand in his presence ; and all the merit
of his expiatory death and obedient life is freely imputed to the believer as the perfectly sufficient ground
of his justification ; and, clothed in Christ's righteousness, he is accepted as a penitent and adopted as a child
by the reconciled Father.

c. " And sanctification." The blessing of sanctification is inseparable from the grace of justification.
" Jesus shall save his people from their sins." It is the
power of his Holy Spirit applying to our hearts the doctrine of his atoning and interceding love, which transforms our dispositions from enmity to the love of God,
purifies our affections from the contaminating grossness
of the flesh, and supplies to our faith those superior
motives which successfully oppose the temptations of
the world. This renovating change is gradual, and
never complete in this world, but it is begun with faith,
as the Evangelist says : " To as many as received him
. . . . gave he power to become the sons of God, even
to them that believe on his name." But the full perfection of his people is secured, for —

d. " He is made unto us . . . . redemption." Redemption most often, and certainly when following
sanctification, signifies the full and accomplished salvation of the believer, both body and soul ; his entire
deliverance from sin and guilt and death ; and his restoration complete to the favor, and presence, and enjoyment of God forever. This Christ undertakes, and this
he will perform. " He is able to save even to the

uttermost " extremity of this life, all that come unto God by him.   He is the Forerunner, who for us has entered and taken possession of heaven, the second Paradise; he is the Resurrection and Life, and all who believe in him, though they die, shall live; he is our life himself, and wherever he is formed in the heart, there he is the hope, the earnest, and the beginning of heavenly, immortal glory.   He is all our wisdom, all our righteousness, all our sanctification ; our all in all. Who then can pluck his people out of those pierced hands by which he holds them with an almighty love ! They are his own, purchased by his blood ; his own, the travail of his soul ; his own, the trophies of his grace ; and will he suffer himself to be robbed of his own ?   Beloved Master, our Elder Brother, Jehovah-Jesus, Lord our Righteousness, — thou art " the way, the truth, and the life ! "

Lessons.

First : Let us trust in Christ alone, fully, to the end ; for pardon, for strength, for glory.

Secondly : Let us rely upon his word ; for guidance, for instruction, for encouragement.

Thirdly : Let us live near to him, by prayer, by communion, by close following of his example.

LECTURE VIII.

SAVING FAITH.

SAVING FAITH.

QUEST. XX. *Are all men, then, as they perished in Adam, saved by Christ?*

ANS. No; only those who are ingrafted into him, and receive all his benefits by a true faith.

QUEST. XXI. *What is true faith?*

ANS. True faith is not only a certain knowledge, whereby I hold for truth all that God has revealed to us in his word, but also an assured confidence, which the Holy Ghost works by the Gospel in my heart, that, not only unto others, but to me also, remission of sin, everlasting righteousness and salvation, are freely given by God, merely of grace, only for the sake of Christ's merits.

QUEST. XXII. *What is, then, necessary for a Christian to believe?*

ANS. All things promised us in the Gospel; which the Articles of our Catholic, undoubted Christian faith briefly teach us.

QUEST. XXIII. *What are those Articles?*

1. I believe in God, the Father Almighty, maker of heaven and earth;
2. And in Jesus Christ, his only begotten Son our Lord;
3. Who was conceived by the Holy Ghost. born of the Virgin Mary;
4. Suffered under Pontius Pilate, was crucified, dead and buried; He descended into hell;
5. The third day he rose again from the dead;
6. He ascended into heaven, and sitteth on the right hand of God the Father Almighty,
7. From thence he shall come to judge the quick and the dead.
8. I believe in the Holy Ghost;
9. I believe in a holy Catholic Church; the communion of saints;
10. The forgiveness of sins;
11. The resurrection of the body;
12. And the life everlasting. Amen.

IT is the unspeakably precious privilege of the Christian preacher to declare that God hath no pleasure in the death of the wicked; but, on the contrary, hath himself provided by Jesus Christ, his only-begotten Son, our Lord incarnate as the seed of the woman, an aton-

ing righteousness infinitely sufficient to save all who go
unto him for pardon and life. This we have endeavored to do, briefly, in discoursing on the lessons of the
Fifth and Sixth Lord's Days, hoping for permission
from a good Providence to open the doctrines of redemption more fully in our comments on several articles of the creed. To-day, the Catechism teaches us
how we must go unto God that we may be received of
him in mercy; and the lesson before us shows: —

FIRST: *The necessity of Faith in Christ.*
(20th Question and Answer.)
SECONDLY: *The nature of true Faith.*
(21st Question and Answer.)
THIRDLY: *The Articles of true Christian Faith.*
(22d and 23d Questions and Answers.)
FIRST: *The necessity of Faith in Christ.*

The Catechism having taught us that all men, being
represented in Adam, came with him under condemnation; and that our Lord Jesus Christ, in his perfect
satisfaction to the justice of God, represented, as the
second Adam, all who are saved, an inquiry naturally arises: Is the representation of the Mediator commensurate with that of our first parent? *i. e.* " Are all
men, as they perished in Adam, saved by Christ?"
The answer given is, " No; " Christ's representation is
on another principle, and he saves " only those who
are ingrafted into him and receive all his benefits by a
true faith."

I. All men are not saved by Christ.

The Scriptures, while they conclude all under sin,
and set forth the infinite merits of the atonement provided for sinners, declare that there are those to whom
the benefits of the atonement are not applied.

The unregenerate are not saved:

" Except a man be born again, he cannot see the kingdom of God ; " said our Lord to Nicodemus.

The impenitent are not saved :

" Except ye repent, ye shall all likewise perish ; " said he to the Jews.

The unbelieving are not saved :

" He that believeth not shall be damned ; " said he to his apostles, when sending them forth to preach the Gospel.

The wilfully vicious are not saved.   Throughout the Scriptures, liars, adulterers, drunkards, thieves, murderers, and other gross criminals are denied the hope of heaven.

And, that there will be found such unreclaimed transgressors when Christ completes his mediatorial administration, we know from his own foreshowing of the final judgment : " When the Son of Man shall come in his glory . . . . before him shall be gathered all nations : and he shall separate them one from another, as a shepherd divideth his sheep from the goats ; and he shall set the sheep on his right hand and the goats on the left.   Then shall the King say unto them on his right hand : Come, ye blessed of my Father, inherit the kingdom prepared for you from the foundation of the world. . . . . Then shall he say also unto them on the left hand : Depart from me, ye cursed, into everlasting fire, prepared for the devil and his angels. . . . And these shall go away into everlasting punishment, but the righteous into life eternal."   Matt. xxv. 31–46.

All men, therefore, are not represented in Christ the Saviour.

II. Those, and those only, are saved, " who are ingrafted into him, and receive all his benefits by a true faith."

1. The representation of all men in Adam is on the principle of their natural descent from him, as the original man, and progenitor of the race. Between us and the Lord Jesus Christ there is no such natural or necessary connection. By his humanity he is our kinsman or brother, but not our parent, or, of birth-right, our sponsor. He represents his people of his free choice, according to the will of God in redemption; his people accept him as their representative, of their free choice, according to the same divine will. The relation is, therefore, not original, but appointed; not necessary, but gracious; not natural, but spiritual; ordained to deliver those whom Christ represents, from their condemnation with Adam; yet in no sense violating the justice which demanded the condemnation, but on the contrary, rendering a full satisfaction to the law of God for those who are delivered. In a word, Christ takes the place of Adam, to supply the righteousness which Adam failed to render, yet not on behalf of all whom Adam represented, but on behalf of those whom he represents as Redeemer. If this difference in the representation be not admitted, it must follow that as all men fell in Adam, all men are saved in Christ, which the Scriptures show is not the case; wherefore, when the Scripture says, that as in Adam all died, so in Christ shall all be made alive; and " as by the offence of one judgment came upon all men to condemnation; even so by the righteousness of one the free gift came upon all men unto justification of life," we must understand the Apostle as speaking of " all " represented in either; in Adam, the head of his race, in Christ the Head of his Church, which is his body and " his fulness."

The same rule of interpretation applies to many Scriptures, which the superficial or heterodox reader might quote, as proving that most inconsistent doctrine of universal redemption. It should also be remembered, that, under the former dispensation, salvation seemed confined to the Jews, whereas now it is preached to all people ; and when it is said that Christ is a propitiation for the sins of the whole world, it means for the sins of all (not of the Jews only but of all) nations, — or of all those in every nation who believe. Faith must always be supposed, for " he that believeth not (Jew or Gentile) shall be damned."

2. Such, then, being the character of the relation, there must be some method by which those who are saved are brought into a vital union with their representative, that they may receive the advantage of his mediation for them. This link, or bond, or method of the sinner's connection with Christ, the Catechism, according to the testimony of all Scripture, declares to be *faith*. It cannot be any merit, or anything that has merit, of our own ; because the representation of Christ presupposes that we are utterly guilty, and is intended to provide for us righteousness of which we are ourselves utterly incapable ; and, therefore, it must be some purely gracious process by which we are made Christ's, and Christ is made ours. Life, under the first covenant, was promised on a condition : " Do this and thou shalt live." Christ, the second Adam, assumed the condition in the room of his church, and by his perfect righteousness purchased, or merited for them, life. Our enjoyment of that life can, therefore, depend upon no condition, but is simply bestowment on Christ's part, and acceptance on ours. All this the answer of the Cate-

chism teaches : " Only those (are saved) who are ingrafted into Christ, and receive all his benefits by a true
faith."

Here is an act of God : They are grafted into Christ
by faith ; and an act of those who are saved : " They
receive all his benefits by a true faith." God brings
them into this union ; they receive (*embrace* or *lay hold*
of, is a better translation) all the benefits flowing from
the union. The act of God is first, for he is the giver ;
the act of the sinner follows, for he is the receiver.

The figure of ingrafting is taken from our Lord's
own parable of The Living Vine (John xv. 1–8), and
the Apostle Paul's of The Olive Trees (Rom. xi. 17–24);
but it is familiar to our own observation, and delight-
fully illustrative. By nature, we are branches of a condemned and pernicious vine, bearing only evil fruit,
and soon to be cast into the fire. Of ourselves, we
cannot separate ourselves from the accursed stem, much
less make ourselves part of the living vine, Christ Jesus.
God, by his Holy Spirit, takes us, cuts us off from the
ruined vine, and grafts us into the stem of Christ ; the
vital union is then formed, a new life flows into the
grafted branch, and it blossoms, buds, puts forth leaves,
and yields good fruit, not from itself, but by virtue of the
life it derives out of the stem. Christ is still the vine ;
the fruit is also all his, but he makes the once wild
branch a part of himself, and so makes it fruitful, and
himself fruitful. Or, to lay aside the figure : The sinner is joined to Christ by the free grace of God, and
derives spiritual life from Christ, and Christ works good
works through him. The glory is Christ's, the benefits are the believer's.

God, we have said, is the agent in the grafting, but

the method of engraftment which he uses is *faith*. Do you ask how this may be, since faith is the act of the Christian? We answer: Faith, though our personal act, is not of our own strength, but is the effect of the Holy Spirit's regenerating grace, and this grace comes to us from God, through Christ. Thus, the Heavenly Father provides in the Mediator the proper object of faith, and fills him with the Spirit of all grace ; he then brings the sinner nigh to the Saviour whom he has pierced, and, as he applies the sinner to the bleeding side, grace flows out to the soul, and the sinner, feeling within him the vivifying power, believes and clings to his embracing Saviour. Grace from the Saviour's side, and grace in the believer's apprehending soul, unite to bind in union close and sweet and vital, the sinner saved, to the Saviour of sinners. From that moment he becomes one with Christ; all the benefits which Christ, as his representative, has obtained for him, become his. Christ is, " of God made unto him, wisdom and righteousness and sanctification and redemption."

3. Do you ask again : Why faith is made the necessary method of union ? We answer briefly now, as we shall more at large hereafter. It is necessary that we return to our obedience ; and the great command of God in Christ is : " Believe on the Lord Jesus Christ." It is necessary that the sinner acknowledge Christ as his representative, and faith is such acknowledgment. It is necessary that the sinner should apply to Christ for his acceptance, and faith is such an application. It is necessary that the sinner receive the benefits of salvation, and faith is such an apprehending or laying hold of them. It is necessary that there be a channel of communication between Christ, the fountain, and the

sinner's soul, and faith is the golden conduit. As salvation is all of grace, so it is all through Christ; and as it is all through Christ, so it is all by faith.

How important, therefore, that our faith be true! Let us, then, learn:

Secondly: *The Nature of True Faith.*

We derive whatever knowledge we have of things beyond our immediate consciousness, either through our own perceptions or from the testimony of others; but, as both our range and power of personal observation are very limited, by far the greatest part of our knowledge is communicated to us by others. When such testimony is brought before us, we exercise our judgment respecting the witnesses, determining whether they can be relied on for veracity and intelligence; since a man may wish to state the truth, yet lack sufficient good sense or opportunity, or both, to know what is the truth; or he may have the sense and the information, yet lack honesty of purpose; but, when we consider him entitled to credit, we believe him, and add the facts which he states to our knowledge. Thus, I am certain that there is such a country as Japan, though I have never been there; and that Alexander was once king of Macedon, though he died two thousand years ago. This belief, or holding of testimony to be true, is the same as *faith; faith* being derived from a Latin word corresponding to our Saxon *belief.*

When, however, the testimony respects things in which we are personally concerned, and our belief of it is full, we rely upon it and act accordingly. Thus, a merchant has advices from a correspondent at a foreign port, that, by sending there a cargo of certain commodities, he will not fail to realize a larger profit

than he can by any other transaction ; and, if he relies
upon the testimony, he does not hesitate to make the
venture. Without such reliance upon others, how narrow would be the sphere of commerce ! Such a practical reliance is the same as *confidence* in testimony.

Now, the Scriptures contain the declarations of God
respecting all things which concern our everlasting
welfare ; and belief of God as the infallible witness,
and of the truths revealed in his testimony, is the *faith*
by which we are grafted into Christ and receive all his
benefits as our Saviour. But, at the same time, it must
be remembered that through the depraving effect of sin
upon our minds and hearts, we are unable, without
divine grace, either rightly to understand, or duly to
appreciate, spiritual (that is, religious) truths. Hence
the Catechism, in the 21st Question and Answer, teaches
us : I. The several essential parts of genuine faith ;
and, II. The divine source from which such faith is
derived.

I. The several essential parts of genuine faith.

These may be brought under three heads : Faith in
the *witness ;* faith in the *testimony ;* faith *in the application of the testimony to ourselves.*

a. Faith in the *witness.* The witness is none
other than God himself. The first act of religion is to
believe that God exists ; and to believe in the existence
of the true God, is to believe that he is the eternal,
self-subsisting Author and Sovereign of all things,
infinite as to his being, wisdom, power, holiness, justice,
goodness, and truth.* From him alone can come a
certain knowledge of whatever is requisite for us to
know, because only he who made and administers all

* See Westminster Assembly's Catechism.

things can know them aright; but especially is it necessary that he should make known to us the things of
religion, because he is the only and supreme Object of
all religion, and, therefore, has alone the right as well
as the knowledge to declare what is essential to true
religious belief, affection, and practice.   It is utterly
absurd to suppose for a moment, or on any plea, that
any man, or any creature, or any combination of creatures, can be authority to us on any matter between us
and God; for were we to receive their testimony, it
would be faith in creatures, not faith in God; and any
practice founded on such testimony would be obedience
to creatures, not obedience to God; and, consequently,
such faith and obedience would not be any part of true
religion.   Whatever faith it be that stops short of God,
is false, deceiving, and destructive.   Even our blessed
Lord, when incarnate as the servant-mediator, claimed
to be trusted only on the testimony of God the Father:
" If I bear witness of myself, my testimony is not true.
There is another that beareth witness of me. . . . .
But I receive not testimony from man. . . . . And
the Father himself, which hath sent me, hath borne
witness of me."   And, again, of God's people, " It is
written in the prophets: They shall be all taught of
God."

While, therefore, we utterly reject all dictates of
human reason or of any other creature, we should bow
unhesitatingly before God as the infinitely true and sufficient Teacher of all religion, receiving whatever he
declares to be truth, not because it coincides with our
reason, or because it has the stamp of ecclesiastical
authority, but simply because it is the declaration of
God.   Lay this at the foundation of your religious

principle, and you are safe from all the subtleties of men or devils. " He that believeth in him shall not be confounded." Attempt religion without this, and " the multitude of thoughts within " you will be dark and confused as chaos, before God said " Let there be light ! "

b. Faith in the *testimony* of God. This follows as a logical and moral necessity from faith in God as the witness. We are to ascertain whether or not God has made a revelation to us, and, if so, where that revelation is to be found ; after which there is no alternative but to believe whatever he has been pleased to reveal, all that he has revealed, and nothing beyond that he has revealed. It were preposterous for us, who have confessed that we can know nothing of religion except as God makes it known to us, to sit in judgment upon the matter of his teaching, receiving this and rejecting that portion of it, according as it seems consistent or not with our reason. In acknowledging God to be the only true and sufficient witness, we have bound ourselves to believe his testimony implicitly and unhesitatingly. Upon the same principle, we may not extend our religious opinions beyond what he has taught, for, besides our incompetence to make farther discoveries, we cannot allow ourselves, without gross irreverence, to suppose that God would teach us imperfectly, or keep back anything which is profitable or comforting.

God has given us a revelation, and that revelation is found in the sacred Scriptures of the Old and New Testaments. We may and should exercise our reason in judging of the evidences on which the claim of those Scriptures to be the Word of God is founded ; but, the moment that we admit their divine inspiration, right reason becomes faith in all they declare, and in their full declarations as utterly sufficient for our religious science and practice. Of the proofs that the Scriptures are the Word of God, this is not the place, nor have we the time, now to speak. It is enough, at present, to say, that we have historical testimony which puts beyond doubt the fact of their having been written by holy men of God, " as they were moved by the Holy Ghost ; " that such is the incomparable majesty of their style, the supernatural elevation of their truths, the admirable harmony of their parts, though published at intervals by different (secondary) authors, during a period of more than fifteen hundred years ; the purity and uncompromising sternness of their moral sentiments and precepts ; the vast and salutary control which they have had upon the lives of those who have believed them, and the nations through which they have been disseminated, as to render their ascription to any source less than divine a contradiction and absurdity. The Catechism does not argue, or even admit the question ; it is (as was shown in our remarks prefatory to the lesson of the First Lord's Day) addressed to Christians ; and every sincere Christian has in his own conscious experience a proof, divinely given him by the testimony of the Holy Spirit to his soul, stronger than all other proofs beside, and one which no arguments of infidelity can shake. " He that believeth hath the witness in himself," for none but he who made the heart could have promulged a scheme so adapted to its wants, its weaknesses, its temptations, and its immortality. The true Christian, therefore, has, in the language of the Catechism, " a certain knowledge, whereby he holds for truth all that God has revealed to us in his

Word." Not that a thorough knowledge of all that is taught in the Word is absolutely necessary to saving faith, for the Christian is born unto eternal life as a little child, and many are unfitted, for various reasons, to pursue the study necessary for a thorough science of divine religion; and such are the infinities of truth opened by the sacred writings, that no finite mind can fathom them in time, or even in eternity; but every true Christian, however simple or learned, believes the main fundamental principles on which the entire system is built up, and is ready, from his faith in God the witness, to receive with humble and glad faith all that he progressively ascertains " to be written in the Scriptures for our learning." He " grows in grace and in the knowledge of our Lord and Saviour, Jesus Christ."

c. Faith in *the application of the testimony to ourselves.* " True faith," says the Catechism, " is not only a certain knowledge, whereby I hold for truth all that God has revealed to us in his Word, but also an assured confidence, which the Holy Ghost works by the Gospel in my heart, that not only to others but to me also, remission of sin, everlasting righteousness, and salvation are freely given of God, merely of grace only, for the sake of Christ's merits."

The Catechism does not assert, as I understand it, that such " a certain knowledge whereby we hold for truth all that God has revealed to us in his word," can exist in our souls without an apprehension of that truth for ourselves, or that a sinner can believe in the grant of Christ's saving benefits to other sinners, while he does not believe in their grant to him; but, that a personal reliance on the Gospel with its promises is essentially necessary to a true faith, and that without such an application of the Gospel to his particular case, whatever semblance of belief in the Scriptures a man may have, it is but a semblance and not a genuine faith.   This will appear at once, if we consider the vast importance of the truths contained in the Scriptures to each sinner who knows the Gospel.   We are the sinners of whom the Scriptures speak ; upon us rests the wrathful curse of divine condemnation for time and eternity ; to us the only way of escape from death, the only way of life, is declared ; and salvation, though provided for many, is promised only to those who believe, and to them certainly.   " God so loved the world that he gave his only begotten Son, that whosoever believeth in him should not perish but have everlasting life."   Mark the change from the noun of multitude to the singular person, " whosoever."   Again : " If any man thirst, let him come unto me and drink."   The church is not saved in a mass, but individually.   Faith and repentance are personal acts ; pardon and life are given to persons ; and, therefore, except a man believe, and repent, and accept the grace for himself, he does not truly believe in the Gospel at all.   For a true belief in such momentous declarations must be something more than a mere acknowledgment that they are truths. Except we act upon them, except we are convinced of our own guilt, except we put our trust in Christ as our Saviour, except we forsake our sins and endeavor after new obedience, is it not clear that we have no genuine belief of the divine testimony ?   For who can believe in eternity and not make preparation for it ?   Who can believe in eternal punishment, and not strive to escape it ?   Who can believe in eternal blessedness, and not strive to attain it ?   Who can believe that Christ is able, willing, and ready to save every one that comes to him, and not go to him to be saved? I may be told that Julius Cæsar was murdered in the Roman capitol nearly nineteen hundred years ago, but whether I believe it or not, it will make no difference in my conduct, for his death has no perceptible bearing on my welfare; but, when God declares to me that a few years after Cæsar's death, his only begotten Son became incarnate, passed through a life of trial and righteousness, and died upon a cross, that by the merits of his substituted merits all who put their trust in him shall be saved, but all who reject him shall be damned; if I truly believe the testimony, I will trust and follow him as my Saviour; but if I profess to believe that he is the Saviour of other sinners, yet do not rely upon him as mine, my belief that he is willing to save all who believe must come fatally short of true faith in the divine Word. This personal application and apprehension of Christ's Gospel is the faith which unites us to Christ, grafts us in him, and makes the channel of his saving benefits to our souls. Thus the Apostle exultingly says: "I am crucified with Christ, nevertheless I live; yet not I, but Christ liveth in me; and the life which I now live in the flesh, I live by the faith of the Son of God who loved me and gave himself for me." Not that Christ died for him only, or in any exclusive sense, but that, because he believed in Christ, he knew the promise of salvation by Christ was applicable to him. A thousand other scriptural proofs might be added, for it is a doctrine running through the whole Gospel. So sings the sweetest singer of modern Israel: —

"O love divine, how sweet thou art!
When shall I find this longing heart

All taken up by thee ?
For thee I thirst, I die to prove
The sweetness of redeeming love,
The love of Christ for me."

II. The divine source from which this faith is derived.

" True faith," says the Catechism, is " an assured confidence, which the Holy Ghost works by the Gospel in my heart."

1. The Holy Ghost is the efficient agent, and works faith in the heart. Faith, as has been said, is a personal act, an exercise of a man's own judgment and will ; but sin has so disordered and impaired our moral faculties as to render us incapable of understanding or relishing the truths of the divine Word ; and as our hearts are by nature " enmity against God," so they are averse to all that he reveals. Ordinary observation shows that a criminal temper and conduct disinclines a man to hear whatever rebukes, condemns, or threatens him ; renders him insensible to argument or motive ; distorts his perceptions ; preoccupies his convictions ; stupefies his conscience ; and even enrages him against the reasoning and the reasoner on the opposite side ; so that we, without exaggeration, pronounce him to be incompetent to think truly, or decide justly ; but much more is this the case with our fallen nature in respect to the principles of religion, which are opposed to our innate dispositions, and the habits of an ungodly life. Man lost by the fall that spiritual likeness to God, which answered with echoing assent every declaration of the divine will. Hence there must be, in order to faith, a regeneration or re-creation of our natures ; an " enlightening of the eyes of our

understanding" that we "may know," a transformation by the renewing of our minds "that we may
prove (learn by investigation) what is that (the) good,
and acceptable, and perfect will of God." This repa-
ration of our moral faculties making us capable of
faith, is the operation of the Holy Ghost; and, so,
faith is said to be "wrought in us," though we exert
the faith, or believe. Thus: the "Lord opened the
heart" of Lydia, that she "attended unto the things
which were spoken of Paul:" and again: "No man
can say that Jesus is the Lord but by the Holy Ghost;"
which corresponds to our Lord's promise, that when
the Spirit of truth (before called by him the Holy
Ghost) is come, he will guide you into all truth;" and
the fact, that after the outpouring of the Holy Spirit
at the Pentecost, the triumphs of the Gospel over the
carnal prejudices of men began. The Apostle Paul
sums up the doctrine: "By grace are ye saved through
faith; and that not of yourselves, it is the gift of God;"
which means that the whole method of salvation through
faith is the gracious gift of God, by the operations of
the official agent in the communication of grace, — the
Holy Ghost. In fact, we can neither do or be what is
acceptable to God, but by the power of the Holy
Ghost.

2. The *instrument* which the Holy Ghost employs to
work faith in our hearts is "the Gospel," by which
the Catechism means the whole Word of God. The
truth of the Gospel is the testimony which we are to
believe; and, therefore, faith cannot be wrought until
the word is brought nigh to the soul by the Holy
Ghost. God might, certainly, fill the soul of a man at
once, and without any instrumentality, with all the

truths of religion, as he did the minds of prophets and
apostles ; but that would be inspiration by an act of
divine sovereignty, not faith, which is an act of our
our own. It is true, also, that there is a work of the
Holy Spirit in the soul of man, previous to his reception of the truth ; but that is rather a preparation of
the soul, a giving to it of a disposition to believe, than
faith itself. But we can hardly doubt that there is a
divine fitness in the Gospel to work this faith, when it
is wielded by the hand of the Holy Ghost. The truths
of the Gospel are precisely those which would, were
there no fatal defect in the reasoning of men, convince
them, and constrain their belief. Every Christian
knows, also, by experience, that the growth of his soul
in spiritual life is nourished by the Holy Ghost through
the doctrines of the Gospel, and that they are admi-
rably calculated for that end ; so that we may without
rashness believe the fitness of the same Gospel for the
conviction and conversion of the impenitent. The
manner, the arguments, the illustrations, the very language of the Scripture, have been arranged and adapted
by the only all-wise Metaphysician for the purpose of
working faith in the heart. Hence the main doctrine
of Scripture, " Jesus Christ and him Crucified," is
called, by the Apostle, " the wisdom of God, and the
power of God " unto salvation ; and, again, " the Word
of God is quick and powerful, and sharper than any
two-edged sword, piercing even to the dividing asunder
of soul and spirit, and of the joints and the marrow,
and is a discerner of the thoughts and intents of the
heart ; " that is, it dissects and probes the heart to the
quick. The Apostle Peter, also, makes the Word to be
the living seed by which God begets his spiritual chil-

dren to eternal life: " Being born again not of corruptible seed, but of incorruptible, by the Word of God,
which liveth and abideth forever." This ascription of
divine adaptedness to the Word as the chosen instrument, is not opposed to the efficiency of the Holy
Ghost as the agent. An instrument can produce effect
only when it is employed by an intelligent agent; and
oftentimes an instrument is of such a character that a
mighty and most skilful agent is required to wield it,
which is preëminently the case with the Word of God.
Because it is the Word of God, none but God can employ it effectually. It is a sword of exquisite keenness,
but it is the sword of the Spirit; impotent of itself, yet
powerful in his omnipotent hand.

The source of our faith is, therefore, the grace of
the Holy Ghost, who is the Spirit of Christ; and the
method of his operation is by the Gospel, which is the
doctrine of Christ. Hence we learn the wisdom of
looking to Christ for the Spirit of faith, its Author and
Finisher. " Lord, increase our faith!" was the prayer
of the disciples; let it be continually ours; until we
shall no more have need even of God's testimony, but
shall "see him as he is," "face to face!" And, also,
we learn to recognize as true faith, only that which is
wrought in our hearts by the Gospel. All dreams, or
visions, or supernatural intimations of any kind; all
impressions, sentiments, or impulses of our own; all
dictates of public opinion, ecclesiastical decrees, or tra-
ditions of men are unworthy of trust. These are not
instruments by which the Spirit works. The sword of
the Spirit is the Word of God alone. We believe God
and his testimony. We need no more; we will take
no less.

THIRDLY : *The articles of a true Christian faith.*

We learn from the 22d and 23d Questions and Answers, that these are stated in the admirable summary commonly called THE APOSTLES' CREED ; the study of which is, by divine permission, to occupy us for the next fifteen Lord's Days. We shall, therefore, reserve the opening of it until our next lesson, where it more properly belongs.

PRACTICAL INFERENCES. — *First* : The importance of ascertaining our union with Christ.

Secondly : The necessity of a personal faith in Christ.

Thirdly : The vital dependence of our souls for faith on the Holy Ghost.

Fourthly : The duty and privilege of studying the Word with prayer.

LECTURE IX.

THE BEING AND UNITY OF GOD.

EIGHTH LORD'S DAY.

THE BEING AND UNITY OF GOD.

QUEST. XXIV. *How are these articles divided?*
ANS. Into three parts: The first is of God the Father, and our creation; the second is of God the Son, and our redemption; the third is of God the Holy Ghost, and our sanctification.
QUEST. XXV. *Since there is only one divine essence, why speakest thou of Father, Son, and Holy Ghost?*
ANS. Because God hath so revealed himself in his Word, that these three distinct persons are the one only true and eternal God.

THE lesson of the last Lord's Day brought before us that compend of religious truth, commonly known as "The Apostles' Creed;" which, for at least thirteen centuries, has been acknowledged, formally or informally, by all bodies of men, not heretical, calling themselves Christians, as "a good confession." The lesson of to-day begins the commentary of our Church, in its Catechism, on its several articles; but, before entering upon the exposition, it is proper that some brief notice should be taken of the Creed itself, as a symbol or declaration of belief.

Here, and in the "Form for the administration of the Lord's Supper," it is denominated "our Catholic, undoubted Christian Faith," or summary confession of faith. *Christian*, because it distinguishes our only true religion from every false religion, the doctrine of salvation by Christ being its grand, peculiar characteristic; *undoubted*, because as a whole, and in its several particulars, it is derived from the sure and complete testimony of God's most holy word; *Catholic*, because it is

the faith of all true Christians of all ages, and throughout the world.

It takes its name of *Creed* or Belief from the Latin
verb *Credo*, at the beginning, the translation of which
is " I believe ; " and we do not refuse to call it " The
Apostles' Creed," because it sets forth the doctrine
which is authoritatively recorded for the faith of the
Church in the books of the apostles of our Lord Jesus
Christ.

The Church of Rome, however, misinterpreting
and misquoting the language of some eminent and
ancient doctors or fathers, and adding gross inventions
of its own, has claimed for the Creed that its very
form was actually the joint work of the apostles themselves ; and that, before separating on their different
missions, they determined to frame a common symbol
by which the disciples of each might be recognized by
the disciples of the others, and the unity of faith be
preserved, each apostle contributing an article, thus
making up the twelve as we find them ; or, if Paul
and Barnabas were among the compositors, fourteen,
as the division is sometimes made. This fable has
been incautiously received and reasserted by some
Protestants, but ought to be utterly repudiated as
unfounded and mischievous. For it is incredible that
so important a transaction as the provision of a Creed
for the whole Church, combining the inspiration of
the apostolical college, should receive no notice from
the historian Luke, or any other sacred writer ; yet no
mention of it is made anywhere in the New Testament,
nor does the document itself anywhere appear, there
being not the slightest allusion to it. All along down
to Augustine, himself included, the early doctors set

forth nothing else than the canonical books of Scripture as the rule of faith; nor can we find the Apostles' Creed, as we have it, earlier, at the earliest, than toward the end of the fourth century. Parts of it, indeed, did appear, and it was gradually increasing to its complete form; but its full consistency cannot be discovered until about the time just stated. Therefore do we believe the doctrines of the Creed, not because they are contained in the Creed, which, as to its form, is an uninspired and human document, but because they are the doctrines of the Word of God. At the same time that we deny divine inspiration to the Creed, we rejoice in receiving it as the most condensed, comprehensive, and scriptural digest, or abridgment, of Christian truth framed by human hands; and fully adopt the encomium pronounced on it by St. Augustine: " It is a perfect compend of our faith, simple, brief, full; its simplicity adapted to ordinary minds; its brevity to our memories; its fulness to the entire doctrine." May God make our belief of it clear, strong, and entire!

Let us now consider the lesson proper to this Lord's Day, which consists of: —

FIRST: *A Division of the Creed into three parts.*

Twenty-fourth Question and Answer.

SECONDLY: *The fundamental doctrine of One God in Three Persons, which is the substance of the whole.*

Twenty-fifth Question and Answer.

FIRST. *A Division of the Creed into three parts : —*

The *First*, of God the *Father*, and our *Creation ;*

The *Second*, of God the *Son*, and our *Redemption ;*

The *Third*, of God the *Holy Ghost*, and our *Sanctification.*

The mission of the Church of God to preach the

Gospel throughout the world required that it should be presented before the world in an outward, visible organization, for which was necessary some public ceremony of separation, and a distinct avowal of faith to distinguish its members from unbelieving men. It, therefore, might have been expected that the Head of the Church would himself prescribe both the ceremony and the form of the confession, which he did when, giving the apostles his parting injunction, he said : " Go ye, therefore, and teach all nations, baptizing them in the name of the Father, and of the Son, and of the Holy Ghost." Baptism, or the application of water to the person of the candidate, was the ceremony by which the Church acknowledged him as a believer, and admitted him to her fellowship. The doctrine which he professed, and which was set forth as the common belief of the whole Church, is stated in the formula accompanying the administration of the ordinance. It matters little whether the person to be baptized himself uttered the words: " I believe in the Father, and in the Son, and in the Holy Ghost ; " or the administrator, when pronouncing the formula, thereby openly signified that the confession had been given in to him more privately ; though it seems from several Scriptures probable that " confession " was made " with the mouth," publicly, at the time. The fact of his submitting to baptism administered to him with the formula, was a confession of his faith symbolized by those words. This, then, was the first form of the Christian Creed, and its three parts, the triple, yet united, foundation of all Christian belief. The instruction which he was to receive was not to be confined within the few words of the formula ; our Lord enjoined that all nations should be taught to " observe all things whatsoever he had commanded" the apostolical teachers; but the formula gives the three heads under which the more particular developments of the inspired scriptural doctrine should be arranged. Hence, the early churches, finding it necessary to guard against heretical misconceptions and unauthorized novelties, rendered their creeds more specific and nice, by parenthetical insertions, but preserved the order of the original symbol; and gradually the creed grew into the shape which it now has, and was adopted really, if not by express declaration, as the creed of the Church universal. Our Catechism, therefore, follows the organic division.

The supplementary titles of the three several parts, viz: Of our Creation, Of our Redemption, Of our Sanctification, are added, partly because that is the order of the Divine works concerning us, and especially because the Scriptures represent Creation as the official work of the Father, the First Person of the Godhead; Redemption as the official work of the Son, the Second Person; Sanctification as the official work of the Holy Ghost, the Third Person; but it must not be inferred that these divine adorable Persons operated each alone when performing their official works, since Creation is ascribed also to the Son as the eternal Word, and to the Holy Ghost as the efficient Agent; Redemption also to the Father, who sent the Son, and to the Holy Ghost who prepared and sealed the Immanuel for his mediatorship; and Sanctification also to the Father, who grants grace by the Holy Ghost, and to the Son, at whose intercession the grace is given; all which will be fully shown hereafter.

SECONDLY. *The fundamental doctrine underlying the*

whole Creed, which is : *The existence of one God in three Persons.*

An inquirer after truth might well put the question here suggested :

" Since there is but one only divine essence, why speakest thou of Father, Son, and Holy Ghost ? " But the answer is readily given on the best authority :

" Because God hath so revealed himself in his word that these three distinct Persons are the one only true and eternal God."

Here are three things stated : I. There is a God. II. There is only one God. III. There are three distinct Persons in the one only and true God.

I. There is a God. The word GOD is a radical found in several languages, (Persic, Goda ; Hindu, Choda ; Icelandic, Godi ; German, Gott ;) signifying One above all, or The Supreme. Many false or imaginary beings have been called and worshipped as gods by men ; but that is not a true belief in God, which is not belief in the true God. Hence the Apostle denominated the Gentiles of his day Atheists, or, as our translation has it, " without God " ; because, though they cultivated very many false gods, they had no knowledge of him who alone is God. It is requisite, therefore, that we understand what is meant by the word God ; and the best definition we can give of God is : The self-existent, intelligent FIRST CAUSE of all things. Our Church, in commanding us to lecture on this section, did not require an elaborate proof of its several propositions, as that would be far beyond the compass of a single Lord's Day ; but only that we should fairly present them preparatory to subsequent discussion. We must, then, be as succinct as possible. That there is a

God we know from his own declaration of himself; and from the existence of things constituting what is called nature.

A. From his own declaration of himself.   The fact that we have the idea of God demonstrates in the highest degree both that he is and that our knowledge of him is derived from himself.   The idea of God, according to the definition we have given, or, as set forth by the Scriptures, is infinitely above human imagination, and utterly beyond the scope of any argument human reason could frame.   It has never had place in men's minds, except where divine revelation has communicated it ; while the tendency of mankind, always and everywhere, except when restrained and enlightened by divine grace, has been to ignore and degrade it.   Men without revelation have worshipped false gods, and attempted to demonstrate their existence, but they have never reached the idea of the true God.   Therefore, since man could neither invent nor discover the grand idea, it must have been made known to us, and that by God himself.   " The world by wisdom," *i. e.*, by its unassisted reason, " knew not God," asserts the Apostle.   He cannot " by searching find out God," *i. e.*, " find out the Almighty unto perfection."   That men in all ages and countries have had some notion of a superior being or beings whom they called God or gods, does not impugn our position, because their vague belief may very well be, and we learn from Scripture is, a corrupted tradition from the fathers of the race to whom God made himself known. (Romans i. 19.)

To this revelation of himself, God has added the irresistible evidence of his works ; for

B. The existence of things can be accounted for only by the existence of God. We know that things do exist in that order and consistency which we call nature ; therefore, they must have always existed, or they must have come into existence by chance, or they must have been caused to exist by the great, self-existent, intelligent Being, whom it becomes us to acknowledge and worship as God.

That the present frame of things has existed always is disproved by all analogy. In all the processes of nature we see none occur but what follows some precedent which we call cause, but the effective power is not in that proximate cause, for that cause is itself an effect of a cause which is again an effect, and so link by link we trace the chain backward. There must be an original, uncaused energy working through all these causes all these effects ; for the first cause must be antecedent to nature, above nature, and independent of nature. Again : There is motion producing change in things as they exist. But matter of itself is inert ; it does not move except from some force applied to it from without itself. There must, therefore, be a cause of motion, a source of impulse, a power determining change, above and antecedent to all things that suffer change. Yet again : This motion and change are regulated by certain laws, many of which are discovered, and these laws coöperate in the nicest adjustment to each other ; this system of laws indicates design, there must, therefore, be a designer, or an intelligent cause, whose will is the supreme law antecedent to all these laws.

The supposition that things as they exist came into existence by chance, is as irrational as that they never had a beginning, and for the same reasons. We have no knowledge of such a thing as chance. Law is present always and everywhere, and he is a most ignorant fool who ascribes any change to chance. How then could the entire system originate by chance? There is evident design in all things; but design indicates purpose, and purpose supposes intelligence; and an intelligent directing will can tolerate no chance.

If a printer were to enter his office in the morning, and find that the types which he had left in confusion the night before were so arranged that an impression taken from them presented to the reader a clear, profound, metaphysical argument, he would laugh to scorn the supposition that it was the result of mere chance. How much less than folly is the notion that the wonderful system of nature, and above all of *man* able to set types and write metaphysics, have come into existence by chance?

We are thus compelled to acknowledge the cardinal truth on which the whole system set forth by the Scriptures is based, that in the beginning God created the heavens and the earth.

Let us, however, press the argument a little farther. Every one who reflects at all, must be conscious, that although in some sense, and to some extent, he is free, he is at the same time under a control from without himself which he cannot resist or escape. This consciousness, strongest in strongest minds, is so universal, that those so-called philosophers who have denied the being or government of God, substitute necessity or fate in his place; or, if they call it chance, it amounts to the same thing, for a blind chance over which we had no power, would be fate or necessity to us; but this necessity clearly works through laws; there must,

therefore, be a supreme intelligent will presiding over
our intelligent wills, regulating the issues of all human
agencies.   Besides, we cannot deny that there are
moral truths distinguishable from those which are natural, that is, which concern physical facts.   As beings
possessed of affections and reason, we are bound to each
other by certain relations; these relations are under
laws, conformity to which we denominate right; violation of which, wrong.   We have notions of right
and wrong, by which we approve ourselves when
we do right, and condemn ourselves when we do
wrong.   We also see a connection between right and
happiness, wrong and unhappiness.   There may be
differences of opinion on minor points, but in the essential, the sense of mankind is so general that there is no
community without laws to punish wrong in order that
the common welfare may be defended from the criminal
selfishness of individuals.   Whence, then, comes this
moral system, the fact of which we confess, and the
operation of which we imitate, if not from a moral
source original, independent, and sovereign?   The idea
of God is absolutely necessary to our satisfaction.   If
there be no God, the universe is without superintend-
ence, order, or government.   There is no guide for our
actions, no certainty, no right, no wrong, no truth, no
hope.   The soul of man is without security or satisfaction.   Matter reverts to chaos, humanity is fatherless,
and virtue with all her attendant train of blessings, a
vision fair but unsubstantial as a poet's dream.   God
has pervaded the universe with the divinity of its origin,
and planted in our very being the necessity of his own.

II. There is only one God.

"We know," writes the Apostle to his Corinthian

brethren, "that an idol is nothing in the world, and that there is none other God but one." Evident as this appears to us, it was then a new doctrine at Corinth and throughout the inhabited earth except in Judea. There is not in all Christian lands a single sceptic who would assert a plurality of gods, or regard such an hypothesis as less than absurd. Yet the overwhelming fact is indisputable that the very large majority of mankind, from the farthest times down to the present day, have been polytheists, worshippers of more gods than one. The gods of the classical nations were innumerable, as are now the gods of Asia and Africa. The unity of God has never been taught but by revelation, and is the belief which distinguishes Jews, Christians, and Mohammedans, from the heathen who fill the rest of the world. It should not, therefore, be considered useless for us to examine and declare the grounds of our belief, especially as we who hold the adorable mystery of the Trinity to be an essential part of the Christian system, (Glory be to the Father, and to the Son, and to the Holy Ghost, Amen !) have been accused of denying the unity of God by some who arrogate to themselves the name of Unitarian, which belongs as truly to us as does that of Trinitarian. Our exposition shall, however, be as brief as is consistent with clearness.

By the unity of God, we mean that there is one and one only Being, to whom the name of God should be given, the works of God ascribed, the perfections of God attributed, and the worship of God rendered. This we assert.

I. From the Scriptures, which, because they teach the original and only clear notion of the divine exist-

ence, are worthy of the highest credence in all that
relates to the nature of God.

a. God asserts it of himself. His first commandment is: " Thou shalt have no other gods before me."
The name by which he declared himself to Israel is
sublimely significant of both unity and eternal existence: " *I am that I am.*" He identifies himself as the
one God with the Creator: " Thus saith the Lord that
created the heavens, God himself that formed the earth
and made it; he hath established it, he created it not
in vain, he formed it to be inhabited: I am the Lord,
and there is none else;" also with the Judge and
Saviour of all men: " There is no God else beside me;
a just God and a Saviour; there is none beside me;
Look unto me, and be ye saved, all the ends of the
earth, for I am God and there is none else;" as
the Lord of providence: " I girded thee, though thou
hast not known me; that they may know from the
rising of the sun, and from the west, that there is none
beside me. I am the Lord, and there is none else;"
and so with regard to every distinct attribute and
operation of God.

b. His inspired worshippers throughout the Book,
adore him as the one only God. Moses says: " Hear,
O Israel, the Lord our God is one Lord;" David:
" Thou art God alone;" all the prophets of the Old,
and all the writers of the New Testament, combine in
declaring the oneness of God as the characteristic belief of Jews and Christians; but why should we multiply quotations when our divine Master sums up the
scriptural testimony, saying: " This is life eternal,
that they might know thee the only true God, and
Jesus Christ, whom thou hast sent."

II. We assert it from reason.

a. It is a rule of sound philosophy to rest satisfied with one sufficient cause for an effect; if, therefore, the God of the Bible with his boundless attributes be, as he is, infinitely sufficient for the causation of all things, it were absurd to inquire. further. The only objection to this having the shadow of plausibility is taken from the actual existence of evil within the dominion of the Supreme Good, which difficulty, felt by all reflecting minds, gave rise to the most ancient extra-scriptural philosophy, that which recognized two contending principles, the good and the evil. The answer to this is, that although the good cannot be supposed to have produced evil immediately, yet it sprung from the freedom necessarily given to his moral creatures. Besides, evil is so intermingled with the good, that it could not have existed but through the permission of the Divine good; since none can doubt that he who has ordained with such wisdom the economy of things might, had he chosen, have excluded evil; and, in fact, no advocate of the dualistic system (that of The Two Principles) from the early followers of the Persic Zoroaster, down to the Manichean heretics, ever doubted the ultimate triumph of good over the evil, or the real supremacy of the good.

b. The infinity of the perfections attributed to God, excludes the possibility of more than one God, since there cannot be more than one infinity. For instance, omnipotence excludes all other power not derived from and controlled by itself; omnipresence, all existence not within itself; omniscience, all knowledge without itself. To suppose anything external to the divine causation or comprehension, is to deny that

infinity to God which is essential to the very idea of
God.

c. The unity of the system of things, called for that
reason the universe, demands our faith in one supreme
will. Law is present everywhere, holding all the
smallest and the greatest, the nearest and the farthest,
in a grand harmonious whole. There is a countless
variety of operations, the invariable order of which we
call laws; but when we observe closely, we see these
laws coalescing into, or combined under, fewer laws,
those under still fewer, until we reach the necessity of
one highest law combining all, the will of that One
whom we adore as God.

d. Analogy confirms this reasoning; for in every
arrangement of things there must be some presiding
head; ultimate power must exist somewhere; government must be supreme. It is so in all human systems;
it must be in that system which comprehends all systems.

e. Moral duty (without which there is neither right
nor wrong, virtue nor vice) must have a supreme
object. No man can serve two masters; yet from the
multitude and variety of human relations, if we have
not one master in God, we cannot know what duty is.
Duties may clash with duties, and so cease to be duties;
there must be one highest duty comprehending all
duties, our duty to him who is the one Lord of all.

f. The wisest part of mankind, those who feel the
logical necessity of following premises to conclusion,
have been compelled, in effect, to acknowledge one Supreme. Even while dividing their worship among a
multitude of deities, there has been traceable in their
systems, popular or philosophical, a dependence from a

supreme original.   The leading theological problem
(of Proclus), " There is unity in all multiplicity," was
admitted by all the theistical sects.   Hence, though
shrinking from what they deemed the impiety of giving
a name or even a mode of being to the Head of all,
they called Him Tὸ 'Eν, or The One ; and he was the
ultimate truth of all their speculations and mysteries.
Even among the multitudinous idolatries of Hinduism,
the Brahminical books dimly but really acknowledge
an original source of all things, though they worship
him not, and his existence is rather an unavoidable
physical fact than a religious truth.   In fact, idolatry
has never been so much a denial of the One God, as
a perversion of his worship, and a profane subdivision
of his authoritative power under many names.   They
could not escape from the idea of the One God altogether ; but they put as many false shadows between them
and his all-seeing eye, as their sensual imaginations
could invent.   " They changed the truth of God into
a lie."

Let us, then, ever devoutly remember the great
goodness of God in giving us a clear revelation of
himself in his holy Scriptures, without which, left to
the imperfections of our own minds and the worse
seductions of our sensual hearts, we could never have
known him aright or offered him the worship that is his
due.   It is to the Bible that we owe that which distinguishes us from the heathen, who bow down to images
their own hands have made ; and only in the study of
those Scriptures can we approach that Light which is
the life of the soul.

Let us remember that the essence of idolatry is an
unwillingness to retain God in our imaginations ; and

that when we forget God, to place our trust, or to make the object of our conduct, other than in God alone, we are as really idolaters as the heathen who worship false gods, though far more guilty, because without their excuse.

And above all, let us remember that we cannot approach God or know him aright, but by faith in Jesus Christ, the only Mediator between God and man. " I am the Way, and the Truth, and the Life," saith the Lord; " No man cometh unto the Father but by me." " Lord Jesus Christ, to whom shall we go but unto thee?"

LECTURE X.

THE DOCTRINE OF THE TRINITY STATED.

THE DOCTRINE OF THE TRINITY STATED.

HAVING in our last discourse enforced the fundamental truths, I. That there is a God; II. That there is only one God; we now come to the third division of our subject, which embraces the all-important doctrine of the Trinity.

III. There are three distinct Persons, Father, Son, and Holy Ghost, in the one true and only God.

In the proper places, as we proceed with our exposition of the Catechism, we shall show out of Scripture, that the Father is God (Ninth Lord's Day); that the Son is God (Thirteenth Lord's Day); that the Holy Ghost is God (Twentieth Lord's Day); from which, since it has been demonstrated that there is only one God, it must follow irresistibly that these three, Father, Son, and Holy Ghost, coexist or subsist in the one God and as one God. Now, however, our aim, as required by the part of the Catechism under consideration, is to show what we mean by this subsistence of Father, Son, and Holy Ghost in One God; and this, not only for the confirmation of our faith, but also for the vindication of the doctrine from the false charges which ignorance or malice have brought against it.

Let no one turn away from this discussion, as though the doctrine were a mere technical mysticism, having no important bearing upon Christian belief, sentiment,

or practice.   Our Lord commands his disciples first to
" teach all nations," and then to baptize the converts
to his Gospel ; and the *formula* to be used in Baptism
(" In the name of the Father, and of the Son, and of
the Holy Ghost ") shows that the Gospel consists of
the true doctrine concerning the Father, and the Son,
and the Holy Ghost ; not of the Father only, but also
of the Son, and also of the Holy Ghost ; not of the
Three only as One, but also of each of the Three as
distinguished from the other two ; so that any error
respecting the doctrine of any one of the Three is fatal
to a Christian belief.   For example : If the Father
only be God, and we ascribe divine honors to the Son
or to the Holy Ghost, we are guilty of giving to others
the homage due to God only ; but, if the Son be God
and the Holy Ghost be God, and we worship not the
Son as God, and the Holy Ghost as God, we deny to
the Son and to the Holy Ghost the divine homage
which is their separate due.   On each side we run into
sin mortally offensive to God.   Again : If these three
names be only different titles of the same object, as
that the Father is the same as the Son and the Holy
Ghost, the Son the same as the Father and the Holy
Ghost, the Holy Ghost as the Father and the Son, each
of the Three not distinct from each of the other two,
and we worship each of the Three as God, we are verily
guilty of worshipping three gods, which is a blasphe-
mous folly ; but, if God has revealed himself as distinct in
Three, — Father, Son, and Holy Ghost, — and demands
that homage be rendered to Father, to Son, and to
Holy Ghost, as distinct in some real not nominal sense,
then, by refusing this distinct homage to each or any
one of the divine Three, we refuse to worship him in

the manner he requires, confounding what he declares is distinct in his divine nature.

Besides, the Scriptures clearly show that this distinction of Three, — Father, Son, and Holy Ghost, — in One God, is not a mere technical mysticism, but that it underlies all the doctrines of salvation, pervading them with a divine energy, which, if they lacked, they would lose all warrant for our trust ; since not only would many scriptural statements respecting the processes of redemption be utterly inexplicable, but also without the divinity of the Son there can be no sufficient ground for a vicarious atonement, and without the divinity of the Holy Ghost there would be no efficient agent for our new birth and internal sanctification ; and we should revert to a faith, if faith it could be called, in a God without a Mediator, through whom the sinner may approach him and a quickening Power by whose help we may ascend the living way to life eternal.   Experience confirms this in a most melancholy manner; for those who are so unhappy as to deny the proper divinity of the Son and of the Holy Ghost, have with scarcely an exception rejected the doctrine of salvation by the blood of Jesus, and of a spiritual regeneration by the divine inworking. They may use the terms, but, if so, in a sense utterly apart from that of the evangelical Scriptures ; nor will they deny that an error here on either side must go through all the Christian system.

Let it also be kept in mind from the outset that this distinction of Three,—Father, Son, and Holy Ghost,—one God, is purely a doctrine of Scripture, and especially of the New Testament, as only from the interpreting light of the later books are we able to see any traces of it under the older covenant.   We make no

argument in favor of it from reason or the light of
nature ; what some students, more enthusiastic than
wise, have thought to be corroborations of it in the
trinities of Platonism and eastern mythologies, though
startling at first sight, we are compelled to reject as
unworthy of parallelism with this article of our Christian faith.   If we cannot find it in Scripture it is to be
found nowhere.   It is above the discovery of reason,
though not contrary to reason when discovered, and
could have been taught only by God himself, even by
the Spirit which searcheth the deep things of God.
He, therefore, who rejects the Scriptures as the only
infallible rule of faith, need go no farther with us, as
we shall not leave their sacred platform to contend on
meaner ground.

Nor will it do for any to object in advance, that God
would reveal nothing which is beyond the comprehension of human reason, and, therefore, that anything
in the Scriptures which seems to teach this doctrine
should be either torn out of the Book as spurious, or
so interpreted as to be deprived of such meaning.
That would be to make finite man the judge of divine
truth ; a monstrous assumption which limits the wisdom of the infinite God by our little capacity.   Yet
we freely admit that God would reveal nothing contradictory to human reason, for then he would be so inconsistent with himself as to demand from us a faith he
had unfitted us to exercise ; but at the same time we
know that human reason is finite, cannot go beyond its
sphere, and is very weak even within its proper limits ;
so that it is one thing for a doctrine to be above our
comprehension, and another to be contrary to our understanding.   A doctrine contrary to our reason is

false ; as that a thing may be and not be at the same moment ; but it does not follow that a doctrine above our reason is false, as any mystery of the divine nature. As well might I deny that nothing exists beyond what I can hold in the hollow of my hand, as that nothing is true beyond what I am able to comprehend by my mind ; else ignorance would be the annihilation of truth, and the stupidity of the dunce who cannot understand the *Principia* of Newton would put aside the planetary system. There are many scientific truths certainly demonstrated that are utterly beyond the perception of uneducated men, nay, which seem to what they call common sense necessarily absurd ; yet are they not the less true or the less conformable to right reason ; and if this be the difference between the philosopher and a savage with regard to material things, what must be the difference between the best cultivated human mind and the mind of God respecting the mode of his infinite adorable existence ? If he condescend to give us the highest proof of a doctrine, which is his own direct testimony, it is, then, the part of reason to receive it implicitly, however mysterious it may be.

Besides ; it is one thing to know a fact, and another to know the mode of a fact. We know the fact of the needle's tendency to the pole ; but who, as yet, has fully explained the reason of that phenomenon ? There is no fact of which all men are more fully convinced than that we can control our muscles by a mere effort of will ; yet what physiologist can explain how this control is put within the power of our will ? A man who should deny either fact is a fool, and not a philosopher ; but what is he who denies a fact in the divine nature, because he cannot measure God by his foot-rule? If reason is at fault in its searches of our own mode of being, how may it judge absolutely of the divine? Let those follow the dim lamp of reason which they have lighted from the sun, — we will pursue no such dim glimmer; it goes out amidst the damps of death; it has never shone a foot beyond the grave; be it ours, my brethren, to uplift our souls to the Sun of Righteousness whose universal splendor so illustrates heaven and earth, that the believer, from the promises of time, gazes with realizing sense on the certain glories of his immortality.

Let us, then, who are convinced that the Scriptures are the testimony of God, study the doctrine of God by them revealed; and receive it as true because God teaches it. In other discussions we have premises from which to argue, and analogies with which to compare; but in this we have neither, for God is himself first of all, and infinitely above all parallel. The doctrine before us is one purely of faith in the testimony of the Holy Scriptures.

After this preface, we go on to state in as precise language as we can the belief of the Reformed Churches respecting the subsistence of Father, Son, and Holy Ghost, in one God; termed by Theologians the doctrine of the Trinity in Unity, — Latin terms signifying Threeness in Oneness; or, more shortly, since all are agreed as to the unity of God, the Trinity, — by which is meant the coexistence of Three distinct Persons in one God.

The term Trinity is not found in the Scriptures, yet should not on that account be objected to, as it is used not to convey any new or extra-scriptural doctrine, but only to express in one word what would otherwise require many. The advocates of the doctrine have been compelled to adopt this and some other terms by the subtle cavils and mischievous sophistries of its opponents ; as Dr. Waterland says : " The early Christians easily believed that the Father, the Son, and the Holy Ghost, in whose name they were baptized, and whom they worshipped, were equally divine, without troubling themselves about the manner of it, or of reconciling it with their belief in one God ; as men generally believe that God foreknows everything, and that man, notwithstanding, is a free agent, scarcely one, perhaps, in a thousand, concerning himself how to reconcile these two positions, or being at all apprehensive of any difficulty ; so, probably, these plain honest Christians believed each of the Three to be God, and yet but one God, and troubled not their heads with any nice speculation about the mode of it. This seems to have been the artless simplicity of the primitive Christians till prying and pretending men came to start difficulties and to raise scruples and to make disturbances, and then it was necessary to guard the faith of the Church against such cavils and impertinences as began to threaten it. Philosophy and metaphysics were called in to its assistance, but not till heretics had shown the way, and made it, in a manner, necessary for the Catholics (orthodox) to encounter them with their own weapons. Some new terms and particular applications came in by this means, that such as had a mind to corrupt or destroy the faith might be defeated in their purposes." For the same reason, the language of some early writers who were firm believers in the true doctrine, differs from, and at first sight seems to contradict that of the later Church, but the discrepancy lies in the meaning attached to these added terms in subsequent centuries.

1.   We do not differ except from those who deny that God is one, or that the Father is God, that the Son is God, or that the Holy Ghost is God; and if we are not able to prove each of these propositions from Scripture we yield the controversy.

2. When we say that there is this distinction of Three in the Godhead, we mean that this distinction is real and not merely nominal; that is, these names are not several names of the Godhead, as Caius Julius Cæsar, are names of one man; nor are they used separately of the Godhead in reference to the several operations of the Divine will, as that God is called the Father, in reference to the Creation; the Son, in reference to the Redemption; the Holy Ghost, in reference to the Sanctification of man; but that, as the Scriptures teach, these three are so distinct from each other as to have relations to each other.   It is absurd to speak of a being having relations to himself, because relativeness implies distinctiveness between those spoken of as related.   Thus God cannot be said to send himself, or to be sent by himself, or to go forth from himself; yet the Father, in Scripture, is declared to send the Son, the Son to be sent of the Father, and the Holy Ghost to be sent from both.   The Son and the Holy Ghost are said by the Scriptures to have coexisted with the Father at the time of the creation; for if it be said that the Father created the heavens and the earth, it is also said that he created the world by his Son, and that the Spirit of God moved on the face of the waters; whence also God speaks as if there were more than one in council, when he said: " Let us make man;" *i. e.*, Let us,

Father and Son and Spirit, unite in making man. Us is plural though God is one; yet God said: " Let us," which indicates more than the Father. Hence it cannot be that Father means only God as Creator, since the Son and the Holy Spirit were also engaged in the work of creation. So also the Father is said to have coexisted and coöperated with the Son and the Holy Ghost in the work of Redemption: " God so loved the world as to send his only begotten Son; " the Son himself took part of flesh and blood ; the Holy Ghost overshadowed the Virgin Mary, and she conceived that holy Thing which she brought forth of the Holy Ghost. Here are three separate acts imputed to three separate agents. Hence it cannot be that *Son* only means God as Saviour, since the Father and the Holy Ghost were also engaged in the work of salvation. So also the Father and the Son are said to coexist and coöperate with the Holy Ghost in the work of Sanctification: " When the Comforter (whom he declares in another place to be the Holy Ghost) is come," saith our Lord, " whom I will send unto you from the Father, even the Spirit of truth which proceedeth from the Father, he shall testify of me." The Apostle Jude speaks of those that are sanctified of God the Father; the writer to the Hebrews attributes sanctification to the Son, when he says: " Both he that sanctifieth and they who are sanctified are all of one ; for which cause he is not ashamed to call them brethren ; " the Apostle Paul declares the converted Gentiles to be " sanctified by the Holy Ghost." Here are then several agents in the one work ; and in the first-cited text three separate acts in this one work ; the Son praying the Father to send the Holy Spirit, the Father sending the Holy

Spirit, the Holy Spirit proceeding from the Father and testifying of the Son. Hence it cannot be that Holy Ghost is only the title of God as Sanctifier, since the Father and the Son are also engaged in the work of sanctification. The same council of Three which said: " Let us make man," said also, " Let us redeem man," and, " Let us sanctify him." To mark the error we are contending against, let us put the simple name of God in the place of the three personal names which it is asserted mean only God acting in each of his three great works, and it will strike you at once as absurd: God prays to God that he would send forth God ; or again : God sanctifies through God by God ; or again : through God we have access by one God to God. But how clear, and in accordance with Scripture, it is when we say : God the Father sanctifies through God the Son, by God the Holy Ghost.

3. When we assert that the Father then is God, the Son is God, the Holy Ghost is God, we do not mean that there are three Gods, but that each is divine. For when we speak of one God, we mean by God one divine Being ; but when we speak of each of the three as God, we do not mean the divine substance, but that each is divine or subsisting in, or partaking of, this divine Being or Essence, which is but the Latin synonym for Being. Thus the syllogism by which the Unitarian would drive us to absurdity, fails : " There is one God ; but the Father and the Son and the Holy Ghost are each God ; therefore there are three Gods ; " for God in the minor is not of the same sense as God in the major. The true form of the syllogism is: There is one divine essence ; but there are three that are divine ; therefore there are Three in the one divine

essence; or, as the Catechism states it, " There are three distinct Persons in the one only true and eternal God ; " by which is meant that each Person is divine, — God, but not the Godhead, — and that the Godhead is one but three Persons. Do any start from this as though it were impossible that three should be as one, and one as three ; we bid them remember that God is infinite, and, therefore, as we cannot comprehend infinite, we cannot comprehend the mode in which the infinite God exists. Each man has in him a trinity : his body, his soul, and his animal life ; yet is he one person. Even material substances may be composed of two, three, or many constituent elements, yet each substance so composed is, as respects its aggregation, one thing. Shall we then dare to deny that there may be three in the divine being of one substance ?

4. But as we have employed the term *Person*, we must define what we understand by it, when the truth of the doctrine will be yet more apparent.

The term person is employed somewhat in an arbitrary sense, as it is not possible for the human mind to understand, or for any language to declare the distinguishing properties of the Three in the adorable Godhead. It assists, however, better than any other.

a. By person, we mean one possessed of a distinct understanding and will. Thus the Scriptures distinguish between the understanding of the Father, and that of the Son, and that of the Holy Ghost. " No man knoweth the Son," saith our Lord, " but the Father, neither knoweth any man the Father save the Son, and he to whomsoever the Son will reveal him." Again : " He that searcheth the hearts knoweth what is the mind of the Spirit ; " again : " God hath revealed them (the

things of the Gospel) unto us by his Spirit; for the
Spirit searcheth all things, yea, the deep things of God."
Again, the Saviour saith: "He (the Holy Ghost) shall
glorify me; for he shall receive of mine and shall show
it unto you. All things that the Father hath are mine,
therefore said I, he shall take of mine and shall show
it unto you." It is clear that in these texts, not one
but three are spoken of. So, also, is the will of the
Father distinguished from the will of the Son, and that
of the Holy Spirit from either. " I came down from
heaven," saith the Saviour, " not to do mine own will,
but the will of him that sent me." Again : " Father,
not as I will, but as thou wilt;" and in some afore-
cited text, we read of God " knowing the will of the
Spirit," and of the Spirit acting from his own will separately from the Father and from the Son. The will
of each is ever in accordance with the will of the other
two, so that the will of God is one; but as they each
exercise will, they are distinct Persons.

b. We use *person*, to signify relative distinction.
Hence we call I, thou, he, we, you, they, personal pro-
nouns. Such personal relations the Scriptures declare
exist in the Godhead. Thus, the Saviour saith; " I
will pray the Father and he will send you another
Comforter." Here the Son speaks, the Father is spoken
to, and the Spirit is spoken of. We need not multiply
passages though we might.

c. So, also, we use the word person, because we find
distinct personal acts and offices attributed to each of
the adorable Three. Thus the Father accepts, the Son
redeems, the Spirit quickens.

d. But let it be carefully remembered that when we
speak of Three Persons in the Godhead, we do not

mean that they are separate as three human or created persons are separate. This we deny; for they are of one essence or nature, not of the same common nature as three men are of a common humanity, but actually of one being, not three beings. Such a distinction is, we admit, incompatible with oneness in any finite being; but it is not incompatible with the Oneness of the infinite, because finiteness has parts, infinity must be ever one. We are not ashamed to confess that we cannot explain, for we do not know how these three Persons coexist as one Being, but we believe that they do, because the Scripture says that they do. If God could be understood by us, he would cease to be God; as an eminent thinker (Daniel Webster) is reported to have said: "The arithmetic of infinity is not for us to cipher."

Nor shall we attempt as some have done to illustrate these truths by other examples, because there can be no analogy; yet we might show the inconsistency of men who consider the Trinity of the Godhead contrary to reason, yet believe greater difficulties every day of their lives. Thus: A, B, and C, may be distinct from each other in a property, D, yet be one in a relation to E. The three sides of a triangle are distinct from each other and may be equal, yet they constitute one triangle. We do not contend that these cases are analogous to the Divine Trinity, yet, if there may be tri-unity in an algebraic formula, or a mathematical figure, who dare deny that it may in the Godhead? Again: The sovereign authority of an Italian city was once vested in a council, known by one name; that council was composed of three equal members; as respects the action *ad extra* (externally) of the council,

it was one ; as respects the action of the three *ad infra*
(or in their relation to each other) they were distinct.
The illustration, we admit, is not complete, because the
Supreme God is infinitely above any human authority ;
but does it not fully meet the objection that a tri-unity
is impossible ?

5. The Three Persons in the Godhead are equal
each to each.   On this we need not enlarge, for if our
previous reasoning be received, the co-equality of the
Father, and of the Son, and of the Holy Ghost, must
follow.

a. If each of the Three Persons be divine, each
must be possessed of divine attributes ; but the divine
attributes are infinite, and infinity is not separable into
parts ; therefore the Father, the Son, and the Holy
Ghost must be equal, else one infinity would be greater
than another infinity, which is impossible.

b. Divine worship is homage to the Supreme authority ; and such worship is demanded for each of the
Three divine Persons ; therefore they must be equal,
else they could not receive each the homage due to the
Supreme.

c. If it be objected that the Scriptures of the New
Testament often represent the Father as superior to the
Son, and the Holy Ghost subordinate to both ; we
answer that all such passages will be, on examination,
found to refer to the working out of the redemption,
and describe not the original or natural relations of the
Three to each other, but the official distinctions they
have voluntarily assumed to each other in the remedial
scheme : The Father, as the Representative of the
Godhead ; The Son, as the incarnate representation of
man ; and, therefore, in the form of servant to the

Father; the Holy Ghost as the efficient agent of both. In the essential constitution of the Godhead, they are, and have been from all eternity, and will be to all eternity, equal. Is it rejoined that the relation of a son to a father necessarily implies inferiority? We answer: Those names cannot be applied to the first two persons of the Godhead in the same sense as in the human relation, since the Son is eternally existent with the Father; but are used to indicate that the Son is of the same nature with the Father, as the begotten is of the same nature with the begetter. Neither is it true, that a son is necessarily inferior to the father, but only while under age; in adult years, a son takes his place by the side of his father, nay, comes to be, from the decrepitude of the aged parent, in every way besides that of affectionate reverence, superior to his father. The divine Father and the divine Son have no such changes, and therefore there is nothing in the terms Father and Son which supposes the one to be greater in authority than the other.

Here, for the present, we rest our exposition, the nice technicalities of which have been required to guard our faith from the uncandid attacks of its opponents.

PRACTICAL INFERENCES.

First: In all our studies of God, we should humble our reason at the feet of Divine Wisdom. What know we of God beyond what he has revealed of himself?

Secondly: We should confidently trust the great Three in One for our whole salvation; the Spirit for his sanctifying grace; the Son for his prevalent mediation ; the Father for his adopting love ; God the Spirit within us ; God the Father above us ; God the Son between us and God the Father.

Thirdly : We should ever thankfully adore with equal praises, The Father, The Son, and the Holy Ghost, — the One God, the God of our salvation.

LECTURE XI.

FAITH IN GOD THE FATHER.

NINTH LORD'S DAY.

FAITH IN GOD THE FATHER.

QUEST. XXVI. *What believest thou, when thou sayest: " I believe in God, the Father Almighty, Maker of heaven and earth " ?*

ANS. That the eternal Father of our Lord Jesus Christ (who of nothing made heaven and earth and all that is in them; who likewise upholds and governs the same by his eternal counsel and providence) is for the sake of Christ his Son, my God and Father, on whom I rely so entirely that I have no doubt but he will provide me with all things neces- sary for soul and body; and that he will make whatever evils he sends upon me in this valley of tears turn out for my advantage; for he is able to do it, being Almighty God, and willing, being a faithful Father.

IT is necessary here, and, indeed, throughout our study of the Catechism, to be mindful of what was stated at the beginning of our exposition, that the answers given are supposed to come from the mouth of a true Christian; and, therefore, not only is very strong language used, but, also, the order is rather that of Christian experience than of systematic theology. We shall not, however, err, if, in opening the truths taught by the section for this (Ninth) Lord's Day, and the one following, we do not confine ourselves to the course suggested by the words; but unite, as far as we can, the theoretical with the experimental, the doctrinal with the practical. You will also please to note, that the lesson for the Tenth Lord's Day is an expansion of this for the Ninth, and that the edifying inferences are from the whole, allowing us to reserve until our next Lecture several important things, which ought, other- wise, to be treated of to-day.

We are now to inquire (Quest. and Ans. 26th):

What a Christian professes when he says : "*I believe in God, the Father Almighty, Maker of heaven and earth*"?

If we ascertain,

First : *What is to be understood by the divine title : God, the Father Almighty, Maker of heaven and earth,*" we shall know,

Secondly : *What is the doctrine held by us when we assert this first article of the Creed.*

First : *What is to be understood by the divine title : God, the Father Almighty, Maker of heaven and earth?*

In our last Lecture we took pains to show from the Scriptures, that there is One Divine Essence, and in the One Divine Essence three distinct Persons, Father, Son, and Holy Ghost. Upon this distinction and order of Three Persons in the Godhead, as set forth in the formula for Christian baptism, our Christian Creed is founded. Hence the holy and reverend name of God is used to signify the one divine Being in Three Persons, and also each of the Three Persons as divine. Therefore, this first article of the Creed relates to God the Father, the First Person in the ever-adorable Godhead.

It was also shown that, while the distinction of Three in the one God is eternal, the mode of their coexistence is utterly beyond our comprehension ; but when the names, Father, Son, and Holy Ghost, are used with reference to the plan of redemption, they have a significance which we can better understand ; and, as the Christian Creed is meant to set forth specially God in our redemption, it is of the First Person that we here speak of as God, the Father, and of him as engaged with God the Son and God the Holy Ghost in the economy of saving grace. In that economy, according to the eternal counsel and covenant of the Three

Divine Persons, each assumes his peculiar office; and while the Son executes the work necessary for our redemption, and the Holy Ghost applies the benefits of that work to the believer, the Father is constituted the representative of the Godhead and vindicator of its honors; and, therefore, *officially* the source and end of the scheme, to whom we must go for acceptance through the Son by the Holy Ghost; as the Apostle says: " Through him (*i. e.* Christ) we have access by one Spirit to the Father."

You will observe, however, that, by a difference in punctuation, this article may read: I believe in God; the Father Almighty, etc., *i. e.* I believe in God, viz: *in* " the Father, ... and in . . his only begotten Son, . . . and in the Holy Ghost." According to this reading, the Creed asserts first the unity of God, in opposition to those heretics who contended for more gods than one, and in refutation of those who reproach believers in the Trinity with believing in three Gods. There is in the history and comparison of the Creed, as adopted by different portions of the earlier church,* some little ground for this view; but as the difference is not essential, and as we have already proved the unity of the true God, we shall adopt the ordinary acceptation.

With this preface we proceed. *God, the Father Almighty, Maker of heaven and earth.*

Here are several titles of the First Person in the Godhead combined: The I. absolute, God; the II. relative, The Father; the III. characteristic, Almighty; the IV. executive, Maker of heaven and earth.

* See King and others on The Creed.

I. *God.* — This is an absolute term for that ineffable
mode of being in which God exists alone, independently
of all his creatures, offices, and acts.   For although,
because of his authority over us, and of our derivation
of all we are and have from him, we are accustomed
to consider God in connection with his infinite sovereignty, and the effects of his will; he would be not
the less God if there were no being animate or inanimate
in the universe but he.   We can, therefore, attempt
no definition of the word God, used thus absolutely.
He himself has given us none.   " I am that I am," said
he to Moses; and again by the prophet: " I am Jehovah (THE LORD), and besides me there is none else."
The composition of the name Jehovah has the same
meaning, — being of two words signifying existence, —
existing; which ought not to be considered as implying his eternity, but the mode of being in which he is
eternal.   Josephus calls Jehovah " the shudder-causing
name of God; " and the Jews never pronounced it, such
was their awful reverence for its inscrutable meaning.

We need not stay to prove this essential Divinity or
Godship of the Father, seeing that it is disputed by none,
— Jew, Mohammedan, Arian, Socinian, or Sabellian, —
who contend against us only because we impute personal divinity also to the Son and to the Holy Ghost,
but all are united with us in calling the Father God.

II. God, the *Father.* — Father is a relative term, implying that there is one or more of whom, or to whom,
a father is father.   We use it to signify the author of
life in a conscious being, as a man is of the child he
has begotten, or the Creator of men and angels.   This
is its first and radical sense.

From this it comes to signify one who extends **over**

another or others such care as a father has for his off-spring.   So Job was "a father to the poor," because he felt for their wants and supplied them.   Often it implies instruction, as followers of an eminent teacher (Socrates, for example) address him as their father ; and as the apostles Paul and John call those whom they instruct their children.   It also may include gov-ernment and protection, as kings are spoken to by their subjects by the name of Sire ; and as our Indian tribes call our President their Great Father.

It may, therefore, designate a natural relation, an affectionate relation, or an authoritative relation ; and these three senses may be combined by the word.

When we speak of God the Father, we may use the phrase with one of two references.   1. We may speak of the First Person of the Trinity in his relation to the other two Persons, but particularly in his peculiar re-lation to the Second ; as when it is said : " God sent forth his Son ; " and Christ says : " I go unto my Father."   Or, 2. We may speak of God the Father in the relation which he, with merciful condescension, sustains to his intelligent creatures, and especially through Christ to the new creatures of his grace.   Thus the Catechism here : " I believe that the eternal Father of our Lord Jesus Christ, ... is, for the sake of Christ his Son, my God and Father."

1. We speak of the First Person in the Trinity in his relation to the other two, but particularly his pecul-iar relation to the Second, who is called the Son.

The Three Persons in the Godhead are, as we took pains in a former discourse to show, originally and essentially equal.   They are divine ; and, as Deity is essentially supreme, there can be no natural superiority

of one over another. They are divine ; and, as Deity
is essentially self-existent, therefore eternal, no one
could be before another ; they must have coexisted
from all eternity. As the Father is eternal, so is the
Son eternal, and the Holy Ghost eternal. But in the
Scriptures the First Person is called the Father ; the
Second, the Son ; the Third, the Holy Ghost, is spoken
of as sent from both.

Yet, as we have seen, these relations cannot, from
the essential properties of the Holy and Divine Persons, imply any difference in rank or order of being.
They are relations we cannot understand, the mystery
arising from the incomprehensibility of God by our
finite minds. The terms employed by theologians, as
" eternal generation" and " procession," and the like,
though useful as technicalities of science, really throw no
light on the subject ; nor can they themselves be farther
explained, although the offices which the several Persons hold in the redemption are clearly distinguishable.

It is, however, to the Second Person that the First
bears, peculiarly, the relation of Father. As Jehovah
said unto David, the royal type of Christ, and, therefore, according to the writer of the Epistle to the
Hebrews, prophetically of Christ himself: " I will be
his Father, and he shall be my Son ; " and again in the
Second Psalm, which we know on the same authority
(and from the strain of the Psalm itself) refers also to
Christ, God says by solemn decree: " Thou art my
Son, this day have I begotten thee." " This day " —
that is in eternity ; — from all eternity he is the only
begotten Son of God the Father.

a. He is his Father, because of that ineffable relation subsisting between them in the Godhead.

b. He is his Father, because the Begotten is of the same nature with the Begetter.

c. He is his Father, because the Son is appointed to appear acknowledged as the representative to receive honor in his Father's name.

d. He is his Father, because, by the Holy Ghost, he begat his human nature in a miraculous manner.

e. He is his Father, because he raised him up from the dead, so giving him a renewed life.

f. He is his Father, because he constitutes him the head of that spiritual family which he has adopted for the sake of the Son, from among the fallen race of men.

For all these reasons, the Catechism speaks of God the Father as the eternal Father of our Lord Jesus Christ; eternal, because himself eternal; eternal, because from all eternity the Father of the Second Person, who, at the fulness of time, became incarnate for us.

2. In using the title God the Father, we may speak of the First Person in the relation he sustains to his intelligent creatures.

a. God the Father is our Father, because he is the author of our being. He created us as he created all things. We came into existence only through the efficient *fiat* of his will. The Son and the Holy Ghost coöperated with him in the divine work; for the Son is the Eternal Word by whom the worlds were made, and " without whom there was not anything made that was made; " and the Holy Ghost was the Spirit that moved on the face of the chaotic deep, and that breathed into man's nostrils the breath of life; yet, as we are taught to recognize in the First Person the representative of the combined honors of the Godhead, we ascribe to him the official work of creation through the Word by the Holy Spirit.

b. He is our Father, because he is our Teacher, having given us intelligent souls, and instructing us by his works, his Word, and his Spirit.

c. He is our Father, because, knowing the wants of our nature, physical and moral, he feels for us, watches over us, and supplies us with that which we need.

d. He is our Father, because he is, in the same manner, our Protector, so that nothing can affect us but by his order or permission ; while, as our Sovereign Ruler, he insists upon our entire obedience, chastening us when we stray, and punishing us if we be obstinately impenitent.

In these senses God is a Father to all his intelligent creatures, though his chastening of those who err belongs more properly to the dispensation of grace.

But, as the First Person is peculiarly the Father of the Second Person, who became incarnate as the Lord Jesus Christ, so is he in a peculiar manner the Father of penitent sinners among men, who, believing on Christ, the appointed Saviour, are represented by Christ the Son of God. We have by our sins forfeited our original right and natural claim to our Maker's regard, and, having lost the image of God, there is in us nothing correspondent to the divine holiness. Before we can be restored to our primeval estate of favor, our sins must be expiated ; we must have a new righteousness which may recommend us to his approval ; we must have a new nature in which we can hold communion with him. That expiation he has provided for us by the death of Christ ; that righteousness has been wrought out for us by the active obedience of Christ ;

that new nature is created in us by the Spirit of Christ, the divine image being renewed in our souls. These benefits become ours the moment that we receive them and apply them to ourselves by faith in Christ, which is an acceptance of him as our atoning Mediator with the Father, and a reliance on his merits alone for our justification in the sight of God. This faith unites us to Christ; he becomes our Head, we become members of his body. We are then found in him; we in him look to God; God looks upon us in him; and, as Christ is the Son of God, we become by him children of God.

We are his children, because we are begotten again by his power; because we have the right (a right through grace, but still a right) of children; and because God formally, absolutely adopts us as his children, making us objects of his affectionate care, instruction, and discipline, reflections of his image, and heirs of his kingdom above. "To as many as received him (i. e. Christ), to them gave he power (prerogative) to become the sons of God, even to them that believe on his name."

III. God, the Father *Almighty*. — This title, characteristic of his power, is in some versions of the Creed joined to "Father," in others to "Maker of heaven and earth;" but the difference is little whether we speak of God as the Father Almighty or as the Almighty Creator, since our Father and the Creator are one and the same, — our gracious and faithful Lord God. He could not be the Creator were he not almighty; nor could he be our Father were he not the Creator. It is his boundless power which warrants and demands our sole and entire trust in him, according to his promises of merciful love through Jesus Christ his Son and Lord.

When we say that He is *almighty*, we mean that he
can do what it pleases him to do, and prevent what it
pleases him to prevent, and overrule what any of his
creatures may do in disregard of his authority, for his
own ends and his own glory. It is worse than idle and
impertinent to ask if God can do anything inconsistent
with his holiness, or anything not conformed to the
nature of things which he has ordained. It pleases
him to do nothing of the sort ; it is morally impossible
that anything inconsistent can occur in his acts; but
his power is limited only by his will. How great his
power is we cannot know, for it is infinitely above our
thoughts ; yet, that it is unbounded, we easily discover
in his acts. He who can make the least thing out of
nothing, must be able to make what he pleases out of
nothing ; and he who has thus made all things must
be able to control all things. Think what power there
is in that will which at once brought all things into
existence ; which since maintains them in existence, and
repeats or multiplies many of them by such nice, gradual, wonderfully adapted laws and instrumentalities.
What power there is in the wind, the fluxes of the
waters, the expansion of heat, the contraction of cold,
the electric fire, and the magnetic attraction ! What
power there is in the motion of all the radiant worlds
throughout all space, and their restraint to their harmonious orbits by the centrifugal and centripetal forces !
What power there is in the upheaving from the soil of
the vegetating seeds that cover the earth with verdure,
and the vital sap that nourishes and perfects plant and
shrub and vine and tree ! What power there is in the
strength put forth by all animated beings ! Think,
also, that this power is irresistibly exerted and felt at

once, constantly, everywhere! Yet is all this power his. Nay, these are parts of his works; and we know but a small portion of the vast effects which result from his will; nor can we deny that he who has done, or is doing, what we now must ascribe to God, may, if it pleases him, accomplish infinitely more. In a word, his power has no bounds; he is almighty.

IV. *Maker of heaven and earth.* — This we have called an executive title, because it represents God the Father not merely possessed of infinite power, but as exerting it in the first great work of his will, which is the basis or beginning of all his system of operations, at least of all that concern our race.

The making of heaven and earth by God the Father Almighty, is so vast a subject that to discuss or even speak of all the things which closely relate to it, would exhaust the longest lifetime; and, if the pen were employed, " I suppose that even the world itself could not contain the books that should be written." We must, therefore, confine ourselves to a statement of a few general heads, under which all may be arranged, with such brief comments as are required for our practical use of the matter, and shall treat 1st, Of the making; 2d, Of what was made; 3d, Of the time of the making.

1st. Of the making. The translators of the Creed into our vernacular have evidently endeavored to use, as far as possible, purely English words, for the better understanding of the common people; and, here, have chosen the verb *to make* as the only Saxon one by which the idea can be at all expressed. Yet *making* does not give the whole sense implied; for a man may make various things out of material supplied to his hand, while here is intended an act of sovereign omnipotence. Nor is it true that either the Latin, Greek, or even the Hebrew words rendered here by " made," signify, radically, any more. Still, our word " create," formed from the Latin, is universally used by us, especially by theologians, to convey the sense of entire origination, or, when applied to the great fact before us, of *making out of nothing;* and so we shall use it. The insufficiency of the terms of the other languages should not, however, prejudice us against the idea of the origination by God, because the Romans and Greeks, being heathen, had no notion of what we mean by creation, and thought that matter was eternal; while the Hebrew has few radicals, and Moses took the one nearest to the full sense. The Jews, however, universally understood the making to be out of nothing; indeed, such belief in the divine origination of all things, distinguishes those who enjoy the benefits of a written revelation from all others. The writer to the Hebrews puts beyond doubt the belief of both Jews and Christians on the subject, when he says : " Through faith (*i. e.* reliance on divine testimony), we understand that the worlds were framed by the word of God, (or speech of God, ῥήματι, not λόγῳ,) so that things which are seen (visible) were not made of things which do appear (*i. e.* are distinguishable) ;" meaning, as Chrysostom observes, things that are were made of things which are not (see 1 Cor. i. 28 ; τὰ μὴ ὄντα . . . τὰ ὄντα), that is, of nothing. Besides the notion that matter itself has not originated from God's supreme will, would impeach the divine almightiness, since that which had existence without his will must continue to be, in some degree, beyond his power. When, therefore, we read that " in the beginning God created the heaven and the earth," we understand that he made them out of nothing.

2d. What was made. The verse just cited tells us, " The heaven and earth." The only question arising here is respecting what is meant by " heaven ;" [*] whether it signifies the heaven of the divine Presence, with the various orders of angelic spirits whose abode is there, — or what we call heaven, intending the sky and the starry worlds which we call the heavenly bodies. The Rabbinical opinion is that it means the former, and this is followed by most divines ; but the latter idea, confining it to the visible heaven, has, at least, a strong probability for several reasons. In the first place, the scriptural history throughout relates to this world, or rather to the Church in this world ; and what concerns other worlds, which are the abodes of happy or lost spirits, is spoken of with great reserve, and only when necessary to the development of facts bearing on the Church and the future state of men. Then, again, the account is everywhere else of the physical creation, except where the spiritual nature of man and his moral condition (in the image of God) are stated. So the writer to the Hebrews, speaking of what we know by faith respecting the creation, says : " the things that are seen." Besides which, the Jews (and the sacred language is conformable) believed that there were three heavens : the earth's atmosphere (as we say the fowls of heaven) ; the supernal atmosphere, or what we should call the space beyond ; and the third heavens, or heaven of heavens, which last is rarely, if ever, without some distinguishing epithet, alluded to by the sacred writers. Certainly, this view of the subject relieves us from many embarrassments ; as we believe firmly that all creatures in heaven as well as on earth,

---

[*] Or heavens; the word is plural.

came forth from the almighty will; and only confine
the sense of the word heaven or heavens in the text
before us.

3d. The time of the making. The present theories of geologists and others have introduced large
discussions on this point; and Christian inquirers
have sometimes ventured dangerously far through
anxiety to reconcile the inspired account with scientific opinion. There can be no doubt that, if our
knowledge of facts were sufficient, revelation and science would be, in every respect, agreed; but, as firm
believers in the Divine testimony, we should never
consent to try the truth of Moses by the deductions of
philosophers. Science is progressive, and, therefore,
imperfect, and, therefore, fallible. The present hypothesis of geologists is scarcely half a century old, being
based on facts until then undiscovered; it is itself contradictory to the hypothesis of the same science in the
centuries before; so that they who insist upon modern
views would themselves laugh at us were we to attempt
the trial of the sacred story by what was once science,
but now is exploded. Yet, since such changes have
been made in science by facts discovered lately, who
can assert that no new facts shall be discovered to-mor-
row, or fifty or a hundred years hence, which will
change as entirely the scientific opinion as it has been
before? We do not doubt the accuracy of the facts
which the geologists state; but we doubt their theoretical deductions, because we doubt the sufficiency of
their facts to warrant an absolute conclusion, as one
new fact may change the whole combination. We
shall, therefore, adhere to the Word of God, let other
men argue as they please. Still, as the Mosaic account

does not enter into questions of science, but is meant for the general mind of men, our interpretation of its language should be correspondently liberal, though not licentious to a degree that would impeach its fundamental accuracy.

Thus we read that " in the beginning God created the heavens and the earth." When " the beginning" was, is not stated ; and it may very well be a general comprehensive statement of an original fact, viz : the creation of the substance out of which the present order of things was framed ; and not necessarily included by the first day. Nay, this might seem to be intimated by the statement that the earth was without form and void until the subsequent mandates of Jehovah were issued. If this interpretation be received, we can consistently allow the possibility of the substance of things having existed long before ; and that, antecedent to the present constitution, other forms had been given to such substance ; a supposition, not forbidden, which would go far to meet the main objections derived from facts discovered in the deeper parts of the earth ; while the fluxes and changes of the waters of which Moses speaks are confirmed by the facts of science.

Again ; some, from motives stated a little while ago, have contended that " the day " in six of which " all things were made," does not mean a day of twenty-four hours, but a period of time including, it may be, centuries or thousands of years ; but, when we read closely, such an assumption is unwarranted ; for Moses expressly limits by night and day, as we do our day — " the evening and the morning were the first day," and so with the other five ; and, besides, on the seventh day he rested, and from that fact he ordained then, and on Mount Sinai, the sacredness of the Sabbath to his honor. It will not, therefore, do to make "the day" indefinite when reading one verse, and confine it to twenty-four hours when reading another. The same rule must measure each and all of the seven.

In few words, then, we understand by the account given in Genesis, just so much, no more, no less, as an ordinary yet cautious and reverent reader would understand by it; that God in the beginning made all things out of nothing, and that in six days he gave to matter the form which it now has, and created man body and soul to be the inhabitant of the world, and the vicegerent of God over all things that are in the earth.

We now know,

SECONDLY: *The doctrine held by us when we assert this first article of the creed: I believe in God, the Father Almighty, Maker of heaven and earth.*

The catechumen is made to speak in the first person (I believe), because he is addressed personally and required to state his own personal faith and convictions; yet in adopting the creed of the true Catholic Church, he declares his adherence to the principles of faith held by the whole Church, and, therefore, that what the creed teaches concerning himself is equally applicable to all genuine Christians.

Some commentators are unnecessarily anxious to insist upon the difference between "believing" and " believing in," as if " believing" were simply recognizing a truth to be true, and " believing in " implied trusting in or relying upon that truth. Such a distinction is, however, by no means universal when these terms are employed; yet, as was shown in our discourse on Saving Faith (21st Question and Answer), sincere belief in the blessed truths here set forth, must be accompanied by a cordial reliance upon them.

The answer of the catechist (to the 26th Quest.) declares the main Christian doctrine here professed: " I believe " " *that the eternal Father of our Lord Jesus Christ . . . is, for the sake of Christ his Son, my God and my Father.*" This is the doctrine of *Adoption;* which includes two things: —

I. The relation which God, represented by the First Person of the Godhead, the Father, graciously bears to all, who through faith are represented by the Second Person, the Son, incarnate as the Saviour of sinners; and,

II. The spirit or disposition, which all those thus adopted bear to God as his children.

I. The relation which God, represented by the Father, the First Person of the Godhead, graciously bears to all, who through faith are represented by the Second Person, the Son, incarnate as the Saviour of sinners.

All that God was to man before he fell, he is now graciously, and in a more eminent degree, toward sinners through Christ his Son. The reconciliation, by the infinite merits of the Saviour is complete; and in honor of his Son, he advances the believer to far higher honors than man, though he had continued holy, could ever have won by his own righteousness. God renews the sinner whom he calls to a new life, by begetting in him a new nature through the word of his Gospel which the Holy Ghost applies. But this life, though, like the life given in his first creation, it bears the image of God, yet, unlike that, is not liable to be lost, but is derived from God through the divine Son to whom he is vitally joined by faith, as a member of the body of which Christ is the Head; and is maintained in him by the constant power of the Holy Spirit. Hence the Master says: "I am come that ye might have life, and that ye might have it more abundantly;" again: "My sheep hear my voice, and I know them, and they follow me; and I give unto them eternal life; and they shall never perish, neither shall any man (*i. e.* any one) pluck* them out of my hand;" and again, addressing his Father: "Glorify thy Son that thy Son also may glorify thee; as thou hast given him power over all flesh, that he should give eternal life to as many as thou hast given him." The new life is as infallible and incorruptible, therefore eternal, as is the union of the believer to the Son, and as is the favor of the Son with the Father. As the Son by the power of the Holy Ghost partakes of our human nature, so the believer, by the Holy Ghost dwelling in him, is (using the strong language of the Apostle Peter) "partaker of the divine nature."

For the same reasons, and in the same manner, is the fellowship between God and the believer more intimate and full. The Son is near to the Father; the believer to the Son. The word of truth is enlarged for his benefit; the communications of divine knowledge far greater, things hidden from the foundation of the world, and things of the world to come, are revealed; and, especially, does the Holy Spirit, the Illuminator, dwell in him, enabling him to hear and understand the language of the Father's love to his soul; while the privilege of prayer based on the merits of Christ, and inspired by the Spirit of Christ, is equally enlarged, so that he has access with the affectionate boldness of a dear child to the throne of grace.

So, also, with his inheritance. It is as superior to God's original bestowal on innocent man, as Christ's mediatorial righteousness is to any possible righteousness of man. The eternal life which Christ gives, and the communion which God allows, demand for their full consummation, a higher, purer, more glorious and enduring sphere than this world will permit. God first gave man the earth ; now he gives him heaven. Christ came from heaven to dwell with the believer, and he returns to heaven that the believer may dwell with him there. Christ's home as the Son of God is in heaven ; there is the place of his highest dignity and honor ; and there is the believer's home as the child of God in Christ, and there will he share in all the dignity and honor of his Elder Brother forever.

But as sin yet lingers in the believer's soul, and the effects of sin are in his body, there is a necessity of a purifying process before he is fit to enter upon the perfection of his bliss. Hence, the salutary discipline which God by affliction, exerts upon the believer's soul. Even Christ, though sinless, yet as the Head of a sinful Church, and partaker of all our infirmities except sin, yet " as a Son, learned obedience by the things which he suffered ; " and as the Apostle says : " If children, then heirs ; heirs of God and joint-heirs with Christ ; if so be that we suffer with him that we may be glorified together." Thus, even trial is a most blessed proof of God our Father's love, " that the trial of our faith being much more precious than of gold which perisheth, though it be tried with fire, might be found unto praise and honor and glory at the appearing of Jesus Christ."

II. The spirit or disposition of the adopted ones to

God as their Father, is correspondent to the privileges
of the adoption. It is stated in the answer before us.
He believes and asserts, " that the eternal Father of
our Lord Jesus Christ, (who of nothing made heaven
and earth, with all that in them is) who likewise upholds and governs the same by his eternal counsel and
providence, is, for the sake of Christ his Son, my God
and my Father; on whom I rely so entirely that I have
no doubt but that he will make whatever evils he sends
upon me in this valley of tears, turn out for my advantage; for he is able to do it, being Almighty God; and
willing, being a faithful Father."

1. Here is a spirit of reverence, for who can so approach the holy and infinitely majestic God without deep
awe! An affectionate, yet humble fear, is a necessary
characteristic of a child of God. It includes, also,
a spirit of obedience, for now there is a double claim
upon his service; the claim of God as his Creator, and
the claim of God as his loving Father in Christ. He
belongs wholly to God his owner, and now his Redeemer
in Christ, the author of his natural life, and the author of
his spiritual eternal life. How can he hesitate to believe
the commands of such a Father to be wise and kind?
How can he hesitate to obey that divine Father who is
so merciful to him in this life, and has provided for him
such a glorious bliss in the life to come? For the same
reason it includes submission and resignation to all
God's dispensations, since God has a right to do what
he will with his own, and the heavenly Father will do
nothing hurtful to his child.

2. But here is, also, the spirit of confidence. God,
the Almighty Maker of all things, must be the Disposer
of all things; therefore, all things are his to order as

he pleases. Thus assured of his power, the believer is, also, sure of the willingness of God to do all things necessary and profitable for his best good, because God is his faithful Father. Therefore, he is "not afraid of evil tidings, his heart is fixed trusting in God." He dreads no want, for all things are in his Father's hand. He quails before no enemy; his Father is stronger than all that can be against him. He shrinks from no trial in the path of his duty, for he knows that the angel of the covenant is in the midst of the flame; and, when called to die he is triumphant, for he can say: "Now, O Father, I come to thee." "All things are yours," says the holy Paul, . . . "the world, or life, or death, or things present, or things to come; all are yours; and ye are Christ's, and Christ is God's."

Thanks to thee, O blessed Father, for such an adoption! Thanks to thee, O blessed Son, for thy merits, which commend us to God! Thanks to thee, O blessed Holy Spirit, by whose grace we draw nigh to God's embrace! Thanks! Thanks! Thanks eternal, O blessed Trinity, God of our life, God of our mercies, God of our hope!

And O, grant when all thy children are brought. home safely to thy heavenly house, there may be wanting not one of all these before thee this day!

Amen.

LECTURE XII.

THE PROVIDENCE OF GOD.

TENTH LORD'S DAY.

THE PROVIDENCE OF GOD.

QUEST. XXVII. *What dost thou mean by the Providence of God?*

ANS. The almighty and everywhere present power of God, whereby as it were by his hand, he upholds and governs heaven, earth, and all creatures; so that herbs and grass, rain and drought, fruitful and barren years, meat and drink, health and sickness, riches and poverty, yea, and all things come, not by chance, but by his fatherly hand.

QUEST. XXVIII. *What advantage is it for us to know that God has created, and by his Providence doth still uphold all things?*

ANS. That we may be patient in adversity, thankful in prosperity; and that in all things which may hereafter befall us, we place our firm trust in our faithful God and Father, that nothing shall separate us from his love; since all creatures are so in his hand, that without his will they cannot so much as move.

THE lesson of the Ninth Lord's Day sets forth two principal things which must be kept in mind for a better understanding of the lesson before us : 1. That God, the Creator of all things, is the eternal Father of our Lord Jesus Christ ; and 2. That he is, for the sake of his Son, the God and Father of all who believe in the Lord Jesus Christ as their Saviour ; from which truths we were taught to infer the duty and privilege of relying confidently and entirely on his almighty and gracious will, as the certain source of all things requisite for body and soul, for time and eternity. But that this eminent comfort of the believer might be fully assured, there must be added to the fact of creation by God alone, the consequential fact of his all-wise, supreme, and unceasing government over all he has made. This constant and universal government, the Catechism, agreeably to general usage, has in the 26th Question and Answer called *Providence*, and

The doctrine of Divine Providence, with the Practical Lessons which it suggests, is the subject for our study to-day.

The doctrine is stated in the answer to the 27th Question ; the lessons are given in that to the 28th.

First : *The doctrine of Divine Providence.*

We unhesitatingly and thankfully adopt the statement of it supplied by our Church :

" What dost thou mean by the Providence of God ? "

" The almighty and everywhere present power of God, whereby as it were by his hand, he upholds and governs heaven, earth, and all creatures ; so that herbs and grass, rain and drought, fruitful and barren years, meat and drink, health and sickness, riches and poverty, yea, and all things come, not by chance, but by his fatherly hand."

Following this our guide, we are to consider : I. The signification of the phrase ; Providence of God. II. The fact of such Providence. III. The extent of Divine Providence. IV. The particularity of Divine Providence.

I. The signification of the phrase: Providence of God.

1. The word *providence* occurs only once in the Scriptures, where Tertullus, opening his action against Paul, and addressing Felix, says : " Very worthy deeds are done unto this nation by thy providence," that is, by the vigor and skill of his administration ; but Christians have universally adopted it, or its equivalent, in their several languages, as aptly descriptive of the great work here ascribed to God.

It is taken from the Latin, and by its etymology

means foresight, not merely in the sense of seeing before (as then it would be *pre*vidence or *pre*science) but
in the sense of taking care * for the future, or rather
an ordering of things and events after a predetermined
intelligent plan ; which supposes wisdom to devise and
power to execute.

2. In the divine mind there is, properly speaking,
neither past nor future, hence by the Providence of
God we understand his supreme disposition of his creatures according to the infinitely wise counsel of his own
will.   Thus it is not only an operation but an economy ;
and when the Catechism here speaks of " the almighty
and everywhere present power of God," it means the
sovereignty of God systematically, constantly, and universally active, " whereby (as it were by his hand) he
upholds and governs heaven, earth, and all creatures ; "
or as the Westminster Assembly's Catechism has it:
" His most holy, wise, and powerful preserving and
governing all his creatures, and all their actions."

II. The fact of such a Providence.

1. The testimony of Scripture to Providence is so
general, explicit, and strong, that the citation of particular texts is hardly necessary.   It is the joy of all believers to know that the Lord reigneth, and that "he
doeth according to his will in the army of heaven and
among the inhabitants of the earth ; " that his doings
are neither capricious nor uncertain, but that " known
unto the Lord are all his works from the beginning,"
because he " worketh all things after the counsel of his
own will," " according to the eternal purpose which he
purposed in Christ Jesus our Lord."

But for his Providence, where would be the govern-

* Such is the classical force of *pro* in composition.

ment everywhere ascribed to him? Where the truth of the prophecies he inspired holy men to utter? Where the faithfulness of his promises on which he encourages us to rely? Where the certainty of his rewards proposed to the obedient, or of his penalties threatened against the trangressor? All his declarations are based upon his efficiency to carry out his determinations; so that without Providence there can be no order, no confidence, no justice, no hope.

2. Reason abundantly confirms the testimony of Scripture; from

A. (*à priori*.) The being, perfections, and creation of God.

a. When we admit the existence of God, we admit his sovereignty. It enters into our definition of God. Take away the idea of supreme rule from him, and you have denied what is meant, what all understand, by God.

b. It is necessary to his power; for latent power in a being, whom we can know only by his manifestations of himself, is, for us, all the same as inertness. It is necessary to his wisdom; for without application in the exercise of his power, it is equally undiscoverable. It is necessary to his moral attributes of holiness and goodness; for how can we conceive of a being worthy of adoration, service, and trust, who gives no evidence of regard for justice, or affection for his subjects?

c. And this the more since we know the fact of his creation. Was the construction from nothing of this vast, complicated, harmonious system of things, a mere passing amusement for its Maker, a mere caprice, an idle, purposeless stroke of his hand, that he should cast it aside when done, as unworthy of his farther care?

Has he called into conscious being so many intelligent creatures, dependent for knowledge and happiness upon circumstances utterly above their management, to leave them in their weakness, blindness, and yearning anxieties, the sport of chance, the prey of necessity, the victims of ignorance? Will the divine Father abandon his children? Will the Author of all things despise the works of his own hands?

B. (*à posteriori.*) The frame and order of the universe, physical and moral.

a. When we observe, though superficially, the nature of things around us, and with which we have necessarily more or less to do, we cannot fail to see that there is a systematic arrangement by which very many things, each having its peculiar characteristics, are combined as a harmonious whole; and that, though there are continual changes and successions, the original organization is maintained by an all-pervading energy, operating uniformly through what are popularly denominated causes, or as we prefer to say, according to certain laws. These great facts, though at once obvious, are more fully apparent, the farther and more closely we investigate. It is, in fact, the whole object and business of science, through all its departments, to discover these laws and bring them within the reach of our uses; for it is upon our conformity to these laws that our welfare depends. These laws, being applied by special adaptations to the many various things in their various purposes, seem, at first sight, to be almost innumerable; each (so called) kingdom of nature, animal, mineral, and vegetable, nay, each thing in each of those kingdoms, being under a peculiar regulation, yet when followed out, coalesce into fewer, as we see them pervading all, until we reach a point where they converge, compelling the logical conviction, that there is one law supreme over all, one grand centre from which they all radiate. What is that grand source, that sovereign law, but the will of the Creator? For nothing is more clear than that no one of those phenomena (or appearances) which are styled causes, has in itself the force to produce what is called its effect, since it is itself an effect of a cause preceding it, and so backward as far as we can trace the succession. There must be, therefore, an original single force operating through all these coöperating, never conflicting causes. But is it not equally clear that these laws of operation proceed from an intelligent will? — And as these laws are operative throughout all things, combining them as a consistent whole, that that intelligent will is imperial, supreme, and one? If no one thing, or change of a thing, occurs by chance, or produces itself, or is independent of the rest, or can be separated from the whole, but all are subject as parts or as combination, to law, how could the entire system have come by chance, or produced itself, or in any way exist, but from the energy of an almighty, all-wise Will? If so, is not the same almighty, all-wise Will which was necessary to create, yet more necessary to maintain the organization, since the act of creation was an instant exercise of omnipotence, while in the continuance of the moving system the impelling force is constant? And, if so, are there not stronger reasons for the Divine will to maintain it than there were for its creation; since not to maintain would be to destroy the wonderful structure which has been called into existence out of nothing? The skilful arrangements, everywhere seen, for the continuance of the economy, prove the design of the Creator that it shall be continued until the purpose of the creation is reached ; and the equally certain fact that these arrangements are *not* themselves causes, or of themselves efficient, but simply methods through which the almighty will operates, proves that the Divine power is and shall be constantly put forth in its continuance.   To sum up our brief argument : The order of natural things demonstrates their having been created by the almighty all-wise God ; therefore, the active continuance of that order must be maintained and governed by God alone.

b. A similar course of reasoning proves the providence of God over moral beings and events.   That there is a distinction between right and wrong, that God has created conscious intelligent beings, whose conduct must be either right or wrong, and that their welfare individually and collectively is inseparably connected with such, their moral conduct, no one will soberly pretend to deny.   The inference, however, is irresistible that there is a system of moral things as there is a system of things physical ; and that, as there can be no such thing as chance, the order of moral events is presided over by the same almighty, all-wise will which has ordained the connection between moral actions and their retributory consequences.   God, by his creation of moral beings, has put himself at the head of the moral economy ; and no moral event can occur outside of his will, that is without his determination, except through his indifference or impotence.   That he is indifferent to what so intimately concerns the welfare of his creatures, it were impious denial of his character to assert ; that he is unable to exercise such control, is as inconsistent with his essential almightiness; but, as the moral events which concern his moral creatures are intimately and systematically connected with their moral conduct, so their moral actions must as certainly be within the control of his sovereignty. This we argue farther from the fact that men, for the most part, if not always, immediately or more remotely, make use of physical things in carrying out their moral purposes; and, therefore, if uncontrolled, would interfere with the physical order which God has established; yet farther, from the fact that the moral acts of an individual affect necessarily more or less the welfare of other moral creatures with whom he is systematically connected. The denial of moral providence would be, therefore, to put the order of physical things, and the welfare of other moral beings, at the disposal of any individual moral agent. Where then would be the Creator's right to his own? Where the paternal government of God over his moral children? Where his power to punish or reward? Where the knowledge of distinction between right and wrong? There would be an end of truth, of certainty, and of hope; and the universe would be abandoned to a self-destructive anarchy, until it became worse than hell, over which the power of God is dominant, — a chaos of desires and passions and furious actions, where the vile would rage and torment without check, and the good suffer without a possibility of escape. There is no avoiding one or the other of these conclusions; the divine government must be supreme, or there is no divine government; every moral being except God must be in all respects his subject, or there is no God; and any, even the least, limitation of the divine control, is a denial of divine control altogether. God, I speak with deep rever-

ence, must be over 'all, through all, all in all, or nothing.

If it be asked: How this can be consistent with that
moral freedom of the creature which makes him a
responsible agent? we answer, That the free agency
of the moral being, the fact of which every one knows
by his own consciousness (and there can be no higher
proof), must be the freedom of a *creature*, and, therefore, limited by his nature and the circumstances of the
economy under which he has his being. His being a
creature, supposes his being to have been derived and
to be maintained; so that he must act only within the
limits the creative will has set to his agency. A bird is
not without freedom as a bird, because he cannot live
the life of a fish; or a fish because he cannot live the
life of a bird. An angel is not without freedom as an
angel, because he cannot perform the corporeal actions
of a man: or a man because his spirit here is incorpo-
rated. Neither are without freedom, because the organization of our natures makes us dependent for physical
life and comforts on the economy of physical things
around us; because we must have food and shelter and
healthful air, or we die. God never intended that we
should be independent of him; though he did intend
for us the opportunity of that happiness which springs
from personal choice and correspondent action; and,
therefore, with our freedom he ordained the system of
things in which we may choose and act for our own
good by a conformity with the laws which he has established; yet is our freedom within law; and by the operation of the laws of the economy in which he has placed
us, and to which he has adapted our natures, he holds
us, notwithstanding our freedom, under perfect control.

He never forces us to harm ourselves by doing wrong, but provides methods in using which we may advantage ourselves by doing right ; yet we may harm ourselves by doing contrary to the very laws which he has appointed for our good.   That which he prevents us from, he reserves within his own action ; that only in which he allows us to act is within our freedom, and consequently within our moral responsibility.   He may slacken the reins, but never lets them drop from his hands.

Now, we do not say that the methods of his moral providence can be always as distinctly traced as those of his physical rule ; natural things are merely passive, and their changes being from his power alone are more obvious ; yet it cannot be that his moral administration is less systematic, and could we trace it out as distinctly, we should perceive it to be equally uniform.   As it is, the history of individual men and of nations clearly proves that wrong is punished and right rewarded ; or, if present inequalities occur, they are yet to be compensated beyond this sphere.   This last fact could not, it is true, be discovered by our unassisted reason, but divine revelation relieves us of all doubt.   If you ask again, how it is that evil exists and that men do wrong when God could have prevented it ?   We answer, that it is not for us to accuse or defend the sovereign will of God ; he has permitted and does permit evil, therefore, he must have the best reasons for such permission, and in the end his glory will be manifest through all ; but it must be acknowledged that there is a wide difference between permitting evil to occur through the unforced action of his moral creatures, and causing it to occur by his own immediate power ;

nor can we see how a creature could be free to choose virtue or the right, and not be free to choose sin or the wrong ; as in such case, all morality would be lost in a necessity.   As it is, no man, let him dispute as he will, can put himself outside of the moral system in which God has placed him ; while he is as certainly conscious that, though the issues of his actions are beyond his control, his actions themselves spring from his own choice.   Depraved habit may superinduce a force of tendency, which we have not force enough of will to resist ; but the tendency is acquired, not original, and has come from the will of God only so far as the depraving nature of sin is part of its inevitable punishment.   The common sense of mankind will not allow the force of such habit to avail a transgressor of human laws ; nor will it be tolerated in the judgment of God. Philosophy, falsely so called, has sometimes argued for such a necessity in men ; and a mawkish sensibility over criminal suicides of their own well-being, has pleaded it in their excuse ; but the doctrine in either case is as contrary to the practical reasoning of the world as it is to the declarations of inspired Scripture ; for according to both it is subversive of all morality, of human responsibility, and of divine government, reducing men below the brute.

III. The extent of Divine Providence.

It is, says the Catechism, " The almighty and everywhere present power of God, whereby, as it were by his hand, he upholds and governs heaven, earth, and all creatures."   This is in accordance with our argument, for if there be any force in our previous reasoning, Providence must be commensurate with creation, and continuous as its continuance.   The up-

holding or maintenance of things as they exist is as
necessarily an act of divine power, as the calling of
them into existence out of nothing ; and, as the entire
universe is the creation of one almighty, all-wise will,
so it must all be comprehended by the purpose of that
divine will, and, therefore, constitute one grand system
of active laws ; for the preservation of which economy
a constant government by its Divine Author is both
morally and physically essential.

Such is the extent assigned to the government of
God in innumerable passages of Holy Scripture ; and
many corroboratory evidences of the fact are discoverable by an observant reason. Science has demonstrated
that the various parts of the universe, within its ken,
are held together in harmonious motion by the two
grand laws of attraction and repulsion ; that there
is nothing so minute as to be beneath them, nothing
so vast as to be beyond them ; nay, that there could
not be a suspension or violation of either law in
any part without producing confusion and destruction
throughout all, such is the exactness of the balance
with which the apparently opposing forces are harmo-
nized by the divine rule. The doctrine of the New
Testament is, that all providence is committed to the
hands of Christ, the Mediator, for the accomplishment
of his covenant purpose toward the Church ; and,
therefore, in their nearer or more remote relations,
" all things " work together under his kingly directions,
that God " according to his good pleasure which he
hath purposed in himself . . . in the dispensation of the
fulness of times . . . might gather together in one all
things in Christ, both which are in heaven, and which
are in earth ; even in him." Hence the doxology of the

four and twenty elders before the throne : " Thou art
worthy, O Lord, to receive glory and honor and power;
for thou hast created all things and for thy pleasure
they are and were created ; " hence also John the rev-
elator heard " every creature which is in heaven, and
on the earth, and under the earth, and such as are in
the sea and all that are in them . . . saying : Blessing
and honor and glory and power be unto him that sitteth upon the throne, and unto the Lamb forever and
ever."   From this, and many other passages of Scripture, it would appear that a universal providence is
necessary to the carrying on, and completion of the
plan ordained for the redemption by Christ of the
Church, ' which is his body, the fulness of him that
filleth all in all."

IV. The particularity of Divine Providence.

Our Church, ever mindful of its design to put the
answers of the Catechism into the mouth of each pious
believer, specifies some of those things which more immediately affect his experience here : " Herbs and grass
(or all vegetation,) rain and drought, fruitful and barren years, meat (food) and drink, health and sickness,
riches and poverty, yea, and all things, come not by
chance, but by his fatherly hand."   But for the same
reason that some events are particularly ordered by
God all must be ; and the whole of our previous argument goes to show the fact and the necessity of such
particular action on the part of God in his providence.

The order and arrangement of laws under which all
things are placed by the almighty will, because it proves
an all-wise design, proves a universal providence ; but,
also, as the economy is 'a combination of parts, each
under its own laws consistent with the general laws, it

proves a particular attention of Providence to each part or process, and to the operation of the laws which concern it. In fact, it is upon the divine regulation of each and every part, that the continuance of the whole system depends. As in a vast complication of machinery, if you take away a single wheel, or connection between the wheels, the whole is checked, or made to work wrongly, or even to destroy itself by its own disarranged forces ; so it would be with the movements of the providential economy. They mutually depend on each other. If you balance a pair of scales on either side by portions of sand, it is, indeed, the aggregate weight on each scale that maintains the equilibrium, yet, were the beam adjusted with sufficient delicacy, the taking away of a single grain from either would give the preponderance ; so it is with the system of worlds, which worlds are made up of atoms. Each atom has its weight, as well as the vastest orb that rolls along its circuit singing of its Maker's power. Again : we see that though there are processes common to different departments of nature animate and inanimate, yet that each individual of the class has its own peculiar place and history. You look over a meadow field ; it is all waving in green except where it is sprinkled with wild flowers ; but examine more closely and you see that the mass of verdure is not one and single ; but that it is made up of separate individual plants, each of which has sprung from its own seed, and has its own life subject to accidents peculiar to itself. So it is with the animal creation. Each conscious being has his own experience, differing from that of all others in some discoverable particulars, while it is with all the others subject to the laws which preside over the family

to which it belongs. So it is with intelligent commu-
nities. Take our own nation under its admirable system of government. One grand law of the constitution presides over it as a whole ; yet each State of the
confederacy has its distinctly recognized individuality,
each county in the State, each town in the county, each
subdivision of the town, nay, each individual citizen
has peculiar rights and a peculiar action. The Executive President at the head of all is one ; but he represents the constitutional will of the nation, yet the
nation not as a single mass, but every individual citizen
who contributes his individuality to make up the aggregate people. So, though with infinitely greater right
and power and wisdom, doth the Supreme Lord, the
Creator, rule, through the operation of his own divinely
appointed laws, the universe he has made, by ruling
over each individual creature, event, and process. The
tallest angel before his throne, and the least insect that
lives its little life and dies in an hour, are equally dependent upon his constant care. The history of mankind under his controlling will, is the aggregate of the
history of each individual of the race. We may not
be able to trace the connection, but could we see as he
sees, it would be all manifest ; and as the weaver forms
the long, wide web by adding thread to thread in the
woof and warp, so does he by his constant, unerring
control of each and all, accomplish the result of his
infinite design.

Is it objected to this, that it deprives men's actions
of their freedom ? We answered the cavil in a former
part of our argument. He does not force our actions.
We are free to act within the limits of the constitution
of law he has ordained, — but he does control the con-

sequences of our actions, else would he cease to be God, and each man cease to be his subject. Wise and good laws, so far from endangering freedom, are essentially necessary to its preservation ; and all the laws of God are infinitely wise, infinitely good ; if we conform to them, we live ; if we dash ourselves against them, we perish.

Is it objected again, that such particularity is beneath the infinite God ? We answer, that as it was not beneath him to create particular things, it cannot be to take care of particular things ; as it was not beneath him to ordain particular laws, it is not beneath him to execute them ; it is not beneath him to know each thing, for he is omniscient ; it is not beneath him to do or control each thing, for he is omnipotent ; it is not beneath him to be everywhere, and, therefore, it is not beneath him to be everywhere the all-wise, almighty Ruler of each and of all things which he has made.

Is it further objected, that, as God has been pleased to create things in a perfect system, a sufficient impulse may have been given to the universe as a whole as well as in its parts, and it is not necessary that he should continue to exercise his power, but might leave the system to evolve itself from the force originally given. We answer, (as once before,) that that would be to make the organized universe a machine, such as men construct to assist their weakness. God sends no such contrivance, and it is far more in accordance with his infinite excellence to believe that his power is everywhere, and continually, directly active. The almighty God has neither difficulty nor weariness in his works.

Is it asked, why, then, are we commanded to pray, since God acts in everything, even the least, according to a plan which he will not alter to suit our wish ? We answer, certainly prayer will not so control the divine plan as to make it vary from his purpose, for then the events would be as contradictory as are the wishes of men ; but, at the same time, he carries on his plan by operating through laws he has seen fit to impose ; and it is one of those laws, that prayer founded upon the promises he has revealed shall be answered, a law as certain in its operation as any other, though we cannot see as distinctly the connection between the prayer and its fulfilment ; and, therefore, prayer must be used to obtain our desires from God as much as any physical law regulating what is called cause and effect. Thus the grand law of his evangelical system, prescribed to Christ himself its mediatorial head, is : " Ask and I will give thee." For observe, that God does not engage to answer all prayer, but prayers offered in faith, or prayer based upon the promises he has revealed, and, therefore, prayer for things agreeably to his will. " This," says the Apostle John, " is the confidence that we have in him, that if we ask anything according to his will he heareth us ; it must be according to his directions as to what we should pray for, and our prayer is the method through which his will is accomplished. By prayer we put ourselves in harmony of purpose with himself, and in his answer to our prayer, he performs his own will ; still the prayer is the method of our obtaining what we desire, without which the blessing would not occur. Various good reasons might be given, if we had the time, for this ordained connection between prayer and the event sought for ; but the principal are, the spiritual benefit it is of to the petitioner, and the stimulus it gives him to personal exertion, according to the divine direction, to secure the things we pray for ; because the blessing is not vouch-safed to those who only pray, but to those who work as well as pray. It might as well be asked why, since the will of God must be done, we must work, as why should we pray? The will of God must be done, but it is done by answering our prayer, and blessing our zeal ; or, equally, in withholding from us what we desire because we do not pray and work. The law is not for any necessity on the part of God, since he is supremely independent of second causes ; but it is for our benefit that we may be brought in will and effort to a cordial concurrence with God. In a word, prayer with correspondent action, is a right use of that free agency which God allows us under the laws of his kingdom ; and not the least evidence of his fatherly care for his human children.

Secondly : *The Practical Lessons* which the doctrine of divine Providence suggests.

What advantage is it for us to know that God has created, and by his providence doth still uphold all things ?

" That we may be patient in adversity, thankful in prosperity, and that in all things which may hereafter befall us, we place our firm trust in our faithful God and Father, that nothing shall separate us from his love ; since all creatures are so in his hand, that without his will they cannot so much as move."

I. To adore God, the Creator and Lord of Providence, as our Father in Christ.

The faith which unites us to Christ, the Son of God, makes us the children of God. Represented by Christ, we are made partakers of all the blessings which he enjoys as the Son of God, and of all the rewards which he has earned by his mediatorial righteousness. With him the Father is well pleased, and for his sake he is well pleased with us, unworthy and guilty as we are by nature, because washed from our guilt by Christ's blood and covered by his merits. It is, therefore, not with slavish fear, but a reverent, filial boldness that we are to approach God through Christ, rejoicing in his love, and making our refuge under the very shadow of his throne.

All providence has been committed by the Father to the hands of his Son Jesus Christ; and he administers it for the advantage of the adopted family, whose Elder Brother he is, as a Son over his Father's house. All things belong to God, and the Father hath given them all to the Son, and the Son shares them all with us. It is, therefore, as heirs of God, because joint heirs with Christ, that we are to worship him whose all things are, assured of his faithfulness because of the covenant which God has made with us in Christ our Lord.

This spirit of adoption, springs from no imagination or pretension of our own, but from the Spirit of Christ, the Son of God, sent of the Father through the Intercessor to dwell in us; and is, therefore, the voice of God in our hearts calling us to him as children to a Father. It is the Spirit witnessing with our spirits that we are children of God; nor will he refuse to answer the filial reliance which he has himself inspired. Such in general, is the affectionate sentiment of adoring homage which we should offer to God.

II. This filial adoration will cultivate in us an entire confidence that all things will work, and are working, for our good, if we love God. Nothing can harm us, for all things are under his control; everything is for us, because all things are directed by his hand. The end of providence is "for the praise of the glory of his grace" in Christ Jesus, wherein he hath made us accepted in the Beloved. He has ordained that his glory shall be in the full salvation of his Church, and he has so linked our blessedness with his own, that his power and wisdom and truth in all his operations are as certainly for his people as they are for himself.

How patient then should we be in adversity! We call many trials which come upon us here adversity, for such is the common phraseology of the world; but they are only adversity in seeming; they cannot be really so since they are dispensed by our Father's hand. The ways of providence may be to us mysterious, for how can we enter into the wisdom of God? They may seem dilatory; for we cannot see, as God sees, the end with the beginning. The ways of providence may seem hard; but their hardness is only the merciful severity of a wise Father's faithful love, disciplining us to a fitness for a higher bliss.

How thankful should we be in prosperity! When we consider how tenderly mindful he is of our wants, how rich in bounty to our desires, when, as a Father rejoicing among his children, he crowns us with blessing. What wisdom, what power, what riches are exerted for our good! Surrounded by God, upheld by his hand, watched by his eye, cherished by his love, defended by his sovereignty, how precious should be all the proof of his kindness, — kindness purchased for us by the infinite price of Christ's atonement, obtained for us by Christ's intercession, and ordered for us by Christ's authority as head over all things.

How trustful should we be for all time to come! He,

who has been at such cost to redeem us to himself, —
who has taken us out of our guilt and misery and rebellion, to make us children, — who has predestined all
things for our eternal happiness, — will never desert us,
never leave us to our own folly, never suffer any to pluck
us out of his hand ! His word is passed, and he will
keep his covenant as long as his power shall last.

III. But how sad is their condition, who, because
they believe not in Christ, have no part in the love of
God ! If all things work together for the good of those
who love God, all things must work against those who
love him not. Now they are under his displeasure ; but
what will be their terrible fate, when God, long-suffering no longer, arms his omnipotence for their defeat,
and eternity shall cumulate upon them the fierceness
of his wrath ! O my people, let us escape while we
may, and cling to the cross of him who sitteth upon
the throne !

LECTURE XIII.

THE NAME OF JESUS.

APPENDIX XIII.

THE NAME OF JESUS,

ELEVENTH LORD'S DAY.

THE NAME OF JESUS.

QUEST. XXIX. *Why is the Son of God called* JESUS, *that is, a Saviour?*

ANS. Because he saveth us, and delivereth us from our sins; and likewise because we ought not to seek, neither can find salvation in any other.

QUEST. XXX. *Do such then believe in Jesus, the only Saviour, who seek salvation and happiness of saints, of themselves, or anywhere else?*

ANS. They do not; for, though they boast of him in words, yet in deeds they deny Jesus, the only deliverer and Saviour; for one of these two things must be true: that either Jesus is not a complete Saviour, or that they, who by a true faith receive this Saviour must find all things in him necessary to salvation.

HAVING exhibited the doctrine of "God the Father," as professed by us in the first article of the creed, we are now to enter upon the doctrine we hold concerning God the Son, as set forth in the next six articles, which it will be our duty to discuss in the order of their occurrence. Following this arrangement, our first inquiry is respecting the meaning of the several names, or rather appellations by which he is revealed to our faith, as our Mediator with God:

Jesus Christ, His only begotten Son, our Lord.

The first only of these is properly a *name*, designating personal individuality, though significant of the great work which he undertook for our salvation: "Thou shalt," said the annunciating angel to Joseph and Mary the blessed Virgin, speaking of the child she should bear from her conception by the Holy Ghost,

"call his name JESUS, for he shall save his people from
their sins."

The other appellations are descriptive epithets:
"Christ," of his anointment, or divine consecration
to his office; "the only begotten Son of God," of his
essentially divine nature; and "Lord," of his mediatorial authority over his Church, and over all things
for his Church.

Our lesson, to-day, is on the name JESUS.

Jesus! How does the very word overflow with exceeding sweetness, and light, and joy, and love, and
life! Filling the air with odors, like precious ointment
poured forth, irradiating the mind with a glory of
truth in which no fear can live, soothing the wounds of
the heart with a balm that turns its sharpest anguish
into delicious peace; shedding through the soul a cordial of immortal strength! Jesus! the answer to all
our doubts, the spring of all our courage, the earnest
of all our hopes, the charm omnipotent against all our
foes, the remedy for all our sicknesses, the supply of
all our wants, the fulness of all our desires! Jesus,
melody to our ears, altogether lovely to our sight,
manna to our taste, living water to our thirst! Jesus,
our shadow from the heat, our refuge from the storm,
our cloud by night, our morning star, our sun of righteousness! Jesus, at the mention of whose name
"every knee shall bow and every tongue confess!"
Jesus our power, Jesus our righteousness, Jesus our
sanctification, Jesus our redemption! Jesus our Elder
Brother, Jesus our Jehovah, Jesus our Immanuel!
Thy name is the most transporting theme of the Church,
as they sing going up from the valley of tears to their
home on the mount of God — thy name shall ever be

the richest chord in the harmony of heaven, where the angels and the redeemed unite their exulting, adoring songs around the throne of God and the Lamb. Jesus, thou only canst interpret thy own name, and thou hast done it by thy work on earth, and thy glory at the right hand of the Father; Jesus, SAVIOUR!

In pursuing our meditations on this most delightful subject, and for our edification through a better knowledge of the truth it contains, let us consider : —

FIRST : *The name Jesus.*

SECONDLY : *The reason of it.*

THIRDLY : *The practical inferences.*

FIRST : *The name Jesus.*

I. It is a *name*. Every person has a name which distinguishes, or is intended to distinguish him from every other person, and stands as the sign or verbal representative of his individual self. Thus JESUS was the personal, and, eminently, the peculiar name of the Son of God incarnate, the name to which all his other appellations are added and attributive; not assumed by him after he had reached manhood, but given to him when a babe; not imposed on him accidentally or by the will of man, but appointed for him by God, through a special revelation which an angel communicated, before he was born, to those who were to have the legal charge of his tender years; and so appointed, as we are divinely taught, because in its etymology significant of the gracious design of God which he should accomplish.

II. It becomes us, therefore, as devout and deeply interested students of unerring Scripture, to search out the remarkable significance of this name JESUS.

The revelation by the angel to Joseph, and, because

recorded, to us, was: " Fear not to take unto thee Mary thy wife, for that which is conceived in her, is of the Holy Ghost ; and she shall bring forth a son ; and thou shalt call his name JESUS, for he shall save his people from their sins." Here the appropriateness of the name is asserted from its radical meaning.

1. The word JESUS, though exactly transferred to our language from the Greek original of the text, where it is written in Greek letters, is not Greek either in form or derivation. Some have erroneously supposed that it is a verbal noun from a Greek verb signifying to *heal* or to *cure ;* and, certainly, he, in whom we trust, had been prophetically called, " the Lord that healeth," " who healeth all our diseases," and his blood described as a balm of sovereign efficacy ; and we are warranted in honoring as the Great Physician ; still the rule of the Greek language will not allow us to admit that such is the etymology of JESUS.

2. It is the Hebrew name Joshua, imitated, as nearly as difference of language would permit, in Greek.

Joshua, from its remarkable meaning and historical associations, was a rather common name among the Jews, who, like other orientals, were fond of such pretentious ostentation ; though first given by Moses under divine inspiration to the son of Nun, his pious, heroic successor in command of Israel ; and wherever there was occasion to record it in Greek, it is written Jesus, as when Stephen the Martyr, speaking of the tabernacle, says: " which our fathers that came after (Moses) brought in with Jesus into the possession of the Gentiles, whom God drave out before the face of our fathers ;" and as the writer of the Epistle to the Hebrews, speaking of that Canaan as only a type, says : " If Jesus had given them rest, then would not he (the Psalmist from whom he had been quoting) not afterwards have spoken of another day." It is, therefore, to the original bestowal of the name on the victorious leader of the Tribes that we must turn for its proper etymology. This we find in Numbers xiii. 16 : " Moses called Oshea, the son of Nun, Jehoshua," or, as it is afterwards written in our English Vulgate, Joshua. Now, as in Hebrew the consonants only are the radical letters of a word, this was easily turned to Jeshua, which by substituting the Greek termination *s* for the Hebrew *a*, and by throwing out the aspirate *h*, which the Greeks never used except in the beginning of a word, we have : JESUS.

It is at once seen that this change from Oshea to Joshua, was significant of some great prophetic truth. Oshea and Jehoshua are derivatives from the same verb ; but Oshea is from the present, probably the imperative, and signifies simply *Save,* or *Saviour :* the prefix of the letter we represent by J, shows Jehoshua to be from the future, and it signifies : *He shall save.* This is not, however, all. The letter prefixed is the initial letter of the peculiar name of God, Jehovah, or Jah ; and, according to the constant symbolical habit of revealed language, conveys a certain divine emphasis and dignified sense ; so that Jehoshua may be interpreted *The* LORD (Jah) *shall save,* or more freely : *The* LORD *shall save through or in or by Oshea.*

Let us compare with this what the LORD says in Exodus xxiii. 20 – 23 : " Behold, I send an Angel before thee, to keep thee in the way, and to bring thee into the place which I have prepared. Beware of him, and obey his voice ; provoke him not, for he will not pardon your transgressions; for my name is in him. But if thou shalt indeed obey his voice, and do all that I speak; then I will be an enemy unto thine enemies, and an adversary unto thine adversaries. For mine Angel shall go before thee, and bring thee in unto the Amorites, and the Hittites, and the Perizzites, and the Canaanites, the Hivites, and the Jebusites; and I will cut them off." Now, doubtless, the angel here spoken of is the great Angel of the covenant, or of the presence, who dwelling in the Shekinah, the pillar of cloud and fire, led the tribes to their conquest of the promised land; and by the name of God in him we are to understand the authority or power which the divine name represents. But it is as certain that Joshua was the human, visible instrument through whose personal agency the work of the divine Angel was done. Hence the sacred propriety of changing his name to one which should have the Divine name in it: Oshea into Jehoshua.

Yet further: The Angel of the covenant, we have strong reason to believe, was none other than the Second Person of the ever-adorable Godhead, and the Saviour of the typical Israel; he who in the fulness of time would come, — blessed be his name! has come — to be in human form the Saviour of the true Israel, the church. Hence Joshua was a double type, of the then present, though unseen, Saviour, the Angel of the covenant, and of the Saviour, who, according to covenant and promise, was to bring his people into their heavenly rest. The divine name was in the name of the human Saviour by whom God gave the triumph to Israel of old, as a typical prophecy that Jehovah, the Angel of the everlasting covenant, would be incarnate as the Saviour of his people. This is established by the testimony of the Evangelist Matthew, following his record of the annunciation to Joseph : " Now all this was done that it might be fulfilled which was spoken of the Lord by the prophet, saying : Behold a virgin shall be with child and shall bring forth a son, and they shall call his name EMMANUEL, which being interpreted is, God with us." The prophecy was fulfilled not only in the birth of Christ as the son of a virgin, but also in the import of his name, the interpretation of which corresponds with that which we have given of the word JESUS. Such, we believe, is the majestic import of the most precious name JESUS — JEHOVAH-JESUS ; for in him who received it at his circumcision, and now bears it on his throne of highest glory, our Elder Brother, the born of woman, we recognize, adore, and trust the EMMANUEL, God with us.

We are now, in answer to the 29th Question of the Catechism : " *Why* is the Son of God called JESUS, that is, Saviour ? " to declare,

SECONDLY : *The reason on account of which the name of Jesus belongs by divine appointment to the Son of God incarnate.*

This is stated by the Catechism : —

" Because he saveth us and delivereth us from our sins ; and, likewise, because we ought not to seek neither can find salvation in any other."

If the first part of the answer be proved, the doctrine of the second follows necessarily ; and, therefore, will come appropriately under our third head. For the present, we occupy ourselves with the first clause : " Because he saveth us and delivereth us from all our sins ; " the thought in which is taken from the annunciation of the angel to Joseph, Matthew i. 21 : " Thou shalt call his name JESUS; for he shall save his people from their sins." This brings before us three questions: I. From what doth JESUS save? II. How doth he save? III. Whom doth he save? Or, the Nature, the Manner, and the Objects of his salvation.

I. The *nature* of the salvation by JESUS. " He shall save his people *from their sins.*"

All men are sinners; the people of Christ are sinners, for he " came into the world to save " — not the righteous, but " sinners." Now, because sin is a violation of the law of God, who denounces the most terrible consequences upon all who shall be guilty of so offending his holy majesty, all sinners are in a state of ruin, or, as the Scripture strongly expresses it, " lost," except they be saved from their sins; which, the Gospel everywhere asserts, can be accomplished only by the mediatorial work of JESUS CHRIST. Thus, " Cursed is every one that continueth not in all things which are written in the book of the law, to do them." " Christ hath redeemed us from the curse of the law, being made a curse for us." Again: " By one man sin entered into the world, and death by sin; and so death passed upon all men for that all have sinned." " Where sin abounded, grace did much more abound; that as sin hath reigned unto death, even so might grace reign unto eternal life, by Jesus Christ our Lord." From these, and many other synonymous passages, we see, that the salvation which sinners need, and which Christ accomplishes for his people, is twofold: From the wrath of God, and from our sins themselves; or from the penalty of sin, and the power of sin.

1. From the wrath of God, the penalty of sin. Sin is the very opposite of the divine holiness, and a direct

violation of that moral order, which, after the pattern
of his own blessed character, he has ordained for the
happiness of his human creatures, in conformity with
the general laws of his moral universe. It must,
therefore, be that sin is ever to God an object of his
infinite disgust and hate ; but, as he is the moral Governor of the world, it becomes necessary to his truth,
his justice, and even to his sovereignty, that he should
punish sin by whomsoever and howsoever committed.
The laws which he has established are the rules of his
administration as well as of our conduct, and extend in
their exceeding breadth over every possible particular
of our moral action. His sovereignty is so complete
that at no moment we can in thought, word, or deed,
put ourselves beyond our responsibility. But the penalty he denounces is equally explicit : " The soul that
sinneth, it shall die." Every soul that sins, by the
very fact of his sin, comes under the divine displeasure
not only, but under the penalty of the divine law, and
a penalty which is extreme ; for it is death, which from
its very nature is perpetual, there being no escape out
of death or any return from it. A sentence to impris-
onment or any other form of punishment for a term of
years, short of the natural life, may be served out and
the convict recover his freedom ; even should it be for
the whole of his natural life, he may have the sentence
reversed after he has suffered some time ; but an infliction of death as a penalty is final, and once that it has
been executed, nothing but the power of God in giving
a new life can restore from it. The ruin of the sinner
is, therefore, utter, perpetual, irremediable, except by
the intervention of some divine method which shall
justify God who ordained and has inflicted the penalty,

in pardoning the sinner, and in recovering him from under its power by quickening him with a new life.

Farther : The penalty of death, though perpetual like death, is not annihilation or insensibility. The soul, though it dies, ceases not to be, nor loses its consciousness or sensitiveness. It is a moral death. As the favor of God is life, and he, who has that favor is conscious of the divine love, enjoying with keen delight the holy pleasures which flow from that love ; so death is the divine wrath on the soul, and he, who is under its power, is conscious of the terrible doom, suffering with keenest anguish the infamous tortures which pour forth from that wrath. We can measure the ruin of the sinner only by the eternity, the inexorableness, the fierceness of the divine anger against sin. " Even according to thy fear, so is thy wrath." " Tell me," said one whom faith, not genius, made eloquent, " tell me what the wrath of God is, and I can tell you the sweetness of the name he bears who delivers me from it ; Jesus, my Saviour."

2. From our sins themselves, or their power over us. It is clear that our salvation must be more radical than from the penalty. The penalty is consequent upon the evil in us that is behind it. God is angry with us because of our sins, so that our sins are the procuring cause of our death — they would bring death on our souls, even if there were (what it is impossible to suppose) no judicial infliction of death as a legal penalty. The whole nature of things, the very character of the ever-blessed God must be changed, before a soul can sin and not die. The first act of sin puts us in opposition to the law of life. It is like a taint of leprosy, a fatal, infectious plague which mortifies all our moral

spiritual being, corrupting our powers, depraving our perceptions, and, not only incapacitating us to recover ourselves, but tending surely, constantly, rapidly to greater disease, loathsome decay, deformity, and anguish. Its power over us is not the less, but greater, because a marked symptom of it is an insane love of the mortal cause, a wilful determination to persevere in courting the contagion.   Our death is not less certain, because our moral practice is a continued suicide.

Nay, even were it possible that, our moral nature continuing as it is, God should remit the penalty of our past transgressions, the suspension of his wrath would be but for a moment ; because, instantly sinning again, we should incur fresh guilt ; and, again, yet more guilt ; so that the pardon would need to be repeated as often as sin would be committed ; a course utterly irreconcilable with the faintest sense of justice. What mockery would it be, if human laws were so neutralized, if immediately on sentence being passed upon him for one crime, a pardon would set the criminal free to commit new offences, the penalty of each successively remitted as often as he was sentenced ? What authority would there be in such a government ? What security would there be for the subjects it claimed to protect ?   What hope even for the reform of the transgressor, thus encouraged by impunity to laugh at the cobweb restraint, and to harden himself by habitual crime ?   Can such weak, false lenity be tolerated in the government of God ?

Salvation must, therefore, be radical as the cause of the ruin.   The sinfulness of the sinner which is the occasion of the divine wrath, the very cause of hell, nay, in its own workings, itself hell, must be eradicated.

A new virtue of life must be infused, to meet in our corrupted system the fatal *virus*, to counteract its corruption, to overcome and to drive it out by a returning vigor and health, from a divine power. In a word and without a figure, we need to be set free from sin, to be delivered from the power it has over us, to have the bent of our inclinations changed upward toward God and holiness, to receive strength for the conquest of evil habits and the resistance of temptations; nay, in the strong language of Scripture, to be " born again," that we may come out into the world as thoroughly changed in our principles, purposes, desires, and motives, as if we had been created anew with a nature morally the opposite of that which we have had and manifested from our first birth.

Ah! my brethren, now we see the reason of the divine name being in the name of JESUS. Who but God can deliver from the wrath of God? Who but he who created man at first in the image of God, can create us anew and re-stamp the divine likeness on our souls!

II. The *method* of salvation.

How doth JESUS save his people from their sins? Like the nature of salvation, the method of it must be twofold: By his atoning merits, and by his sanctifying grace; the first of which delivers his people from the wrath of God, the penalty of sin; the second, from the power of their sins over them.

1. His *atoning merits*.

The word lost, or ruined, supposes not only present calamity, but a loss of former prosperity, the ruin of a former happiness. Hence, also, we speak of man as *fallen*, and of the act, which occasioned our present misery, as the *fall*. The Scripture teaches us that our race, as represented by our first parent, was created with a likeness to God and originally enjoyed the divine favor, which the Scripture, as has been stated, denominates life. The condition on which this favor was to be continued could be no other than his conformity to his divine pattern by obedience to the divine commandments; the penalty of his disobedience was, necessarily, death, the entire withdrawal of divine likeness, the infliction of divine wrath, and consequent misery. In order, therefore, to our full restoration, there must be a reconcilement to God. This is what is meant, properly, by atonement. God and sinful man have been divided; it is necessary for our salvation that we be at-*one* again with God. Atonement is often used to signify the basis of the reconciliation, as the procuring cause of the effect; but radically, it is the reconciliation, the at*one*ment itself.

Now to this reconciliation, the full restoration from the misery into which we are fallen because of the divine wrath, it is necessary that the law which we have broken should be so satisfied as to justify our holy, divine Sovereign in removing from our souls the curse of his wrath and taking us again into his approving favor. This justification of his mercy it pleased God, out of the riches of the glory of his grace, to provide in the vicarious merits of Christ, who took our place under the law, that all who believe in him might be admitted to his place in the divine regard; and, hence, we call them his atoning merits. The infinite propriety, wisdom, and mercy of the sinner's salvation through the righteousness of a sufficient substitute, the necessity of both a divine and human nature for the personal constitution of such a substitute, and the divine appointment of JESUS, the only begotten Son of God, and the miraculously conceived Son of the blessed Virgin Mary, the EMMANUEL, to be that substitute, — were all demonstrated at length in our lectures on the lessons for the Fifth and Sixth Lord's Days. It is now requisite only that we refresh our memories and our hearts with a mention of what Christ, as our atoning substitute, did on behalf of his people. His work was twofold: Expiation of our sins, and obedience to the divine law.

For the law of God, unlike most human laws, not only threatened the transgressor of it with punishment, but also proposed reward for our obedience. We are, therefore, because of our sin, not only exposed to the wrath of God, but without any possible claims to his favor. Even were the penalty remitted, no blessing could be justly bestowed upon us, because we are not entitled to the reward of obedience. Before God can, consistently with his own word, receive us back to his love, not only must the *guilt* of our sins (by which we mean our liability to punishment) be taken from us, but there must also be provided a perfect obedience, the reward of which may be bestowed upon us. Thus JESUS took upon him the guilt of his people's sins, and satisfied the penalty which they had incurred, by his death on the cross ; but he also, by his previous active obedience, purchased, or earned, or became entitled to the reward of divine favor, which, according to his covenant with the Father, is transferred to those who accept his substitution for them by believing on his name. This is what theologians technically call *imputation* — the imputation of our sins to Christ, and the imputation of his righteous obedience to us; by which we are to understand, not that our sins become his sins, for that is impossible as personal acts are not transferable, or that his righteousness becomes our personal obedience, which is alike impossible, but that the legal consequence of our sins, which is death, is inflicted on him, and the legal consequences of his obedience, which is life, is conferred on us. Even as the apostle says : " All things are of God, who hath reconciled us to himself by Jesus Christ, and hath given to us the ministry of reconciliation : to wit, that God was in Christ, reconciling the world unto himself, not imputing their trespasses unto them ; and hath committed unto us the word of reconciliation. Now, then, we are ambassadors for Christ, as though God did beseech you by us ; we pray you in Christ's stead, be ye reconciled to God. For he hath made him to be sin for us, who knew no sin, that we might be made the righteousness of God in him." JESUS is our Saviour in both ways : his expiatory death, and his active obedience, constituting the ground on which the sinner that believes in him is reconciled to God ; and not only relieved from the penalty of death, but also restored to the full enjoyment of divine favor. His death saves us from hell ; his obedience entitles us to heaven ; but in both the merit is all his, and to him be the glory !

2. His sanctifying grace, by which he delivers us from the power of our sins. We have seen under our former head, what, alas ! we know by sad experience, that sin corrupts our whole nature, giving us such an inclination to sin more and more that even pardon itself cannot deliver us from the misery which is its inevitable consequence. The Scripture represents this depravity as a bondage to sin. Such is its power over us that

though its chains are willingly worn, we have not moral strength to break them; and the bondage is aggravated by bringing us under the power of the devil, the great tempter, and of his two principal instruments of temptation, — the world and the flesh. Thus, our sins are denominated our enemies, who oppose our entrance to heavenly rest, as the Canaanites did the entrance of Israel to the promised land; and from them our Joshua must deliver us by a victory which we cannot accomplish of ourselves. So the father of the Baptist speaks of Jesus as " a horn (or strength) of salvation " sent to fulfil the promise which God " sware unto Abraham, that he would grant unto us that we, being delivered out of the hand of our enemies, might serve in holiness and righteousness before him all the days of our life." For, if we be free from the power of our sins, we are safe from all enemies, because none " can harm us if we be followers of that which is good." This deliverance from sin is called, theologically, *sanctification*, is begun in the conversion of the sinner, and carried on until he is made perfect in glory. It is gradual for wise reasons; and among them, obviously, because the divine process is conducted through the operation of the sinner's own faculties. The immediate agent in this sanctification to whose power the several steps in the process is attributed by the Scriptures, is the Holy Ghost. He it is that begets us again in regeneration, dwells as a new life in our hearts, enlightens our understanding, turns our affections upward to God, invigorates our faltering will to determine good, and by faith in the gospel transforms us from rebels to children of God. But, as we shall consider at large this sanctifying work of the Holy Ghost, when we come to the lesson for the

Twentieth Lord's Day, we shall now briefly note the
sense in which our deliverance from the power of sin is
ascribed to JESUS.

a. He obtains for us by the prayers of his intercession, based on the merits of his life and death, the
influences of the Holy Ghost.   When he had accomplished a righteousness of infinite value, and the Father,
well pleased with his work, said: "Ask, and I will
give thee," the Mediator asked that the various graces
of the Holy Ghost might be given him for his people.
Accordingly, we find that immediately on the Saviour's
beginning his intercession at the right hand of God, the
Spirit was sent down on the multitudes of the Pentecost, and has never ceased to dwell with his true church
or in the heart of every true believer.   So says the
prophetic Psalmist: "Thou hast ascended on high;
thou hast led captivity captive; thou hast received gifts
for men; yea, for the rebellious also, that the Lord
God might dwell among them.   Blessed be the Lord,
who daily loadeth us with benefits, even the God of
our salvation;" and our Lord at the Last Supper: "I
will pray the Father, and he shall give you another
Comforter, that he may abide with you forever, even
the Spirit of truth."   All the effects of the Holy
Ghost, without whose grace we can do nothing, — faith,
repentance, love, hope, peace, holy desires, and all good
works, — thus come from JESUS, because of his merits.
The Holy Ghost is emphatically *His* Spirit; the Spirit
of the Son of God, our Saviour.   We have nothing of
our own; all that is good in us, all the good we
ever shall or can have in us, is the result of his
work and the answer of his prayers.   "It pleased
the Father that in him should all fulness dwell;"

" and of his fulness have all we received, and grace
for grace."

b. The instrument by which the Holy Spirit accomplishes the work of sanctification is the Word of God,
which, from its beginning to its end, testifies of Christ.
The legitimate effect of the Gospel when applied to the
soul of the sinner by the Holy Ghost, is to " work by
love," to " purify the heart, and to give victory over
the world." The love of JESUS is the great converting, animating, sanctifying argument and motive over
all that is evil in our natures, and corrupting in the
world around us. It is the divine story of his condescension which brought him to earth, his incarnation as
the Babe of Bethlehem that he might be very man ;
his sorrowful experience of human griefs and human
temptations, that he might assure his people of his
sympathy ; his pure example of human virtue that he
might mark the way to heaven ; his bitter death on the
cross that he might pluck the sting from the last enemy ;
his resurrection in his crucified body, and his ascension
with that human body scarred by the thorns, and nails,
and spear, to the right hand of the Father, that as the
second Adam he might be head over all things to his
Church ; and the blessed conviction, which the Holy
Ghost bears home on the penitent soul that all this love,
and humiliation, and suffering, and righteousness and
death, and power and glory, were for every one who
believes, which melts the obdurate, encourages the fearful, strengthens the weak, and keeps the unstable.
No one can have a heartfelt conviction of a love so great
without an answering affection ; and the sentiment of
every Christian soul must be that of the glowing Apostle when he says : " The love of Christ constraineth us,

because we thus judge that if one died for all, then were all dead, and that he died for all, that they which live should not henceforth live unto themselves, but unto him which died for them and rose again." The transformation is not immediate, but, for wise reasons, gradual; yet it is certain, because every one "that hath this hope in him purifieth himself even as he is pure;" and because it is written, "He shall save his people from their sins." The sanctifying process which is begun in the regeneration of the penitent will be carried on until it is complete in his celestial life; and the sinner whom JESUS saves, is lifted from the depths of corruption to the height of holiness.

III. The objects of the salvation by JESUS.

Here we need but little argument. The text decides at once who they are whom JESUS saves, and the nature of the salvation confirms the text.

1. "He shall save his *people*."

It is our high privilege to believe that the merits of Christ, substantially considered, are infinite. His human nature, however pure, his human righteousness, however perfect, his human sufferings, however great, must, like all that pertains to the human creature, be finite. Had our JESUS been only man, he could, at best, have saved only himself, because he could not have transcended the obligations which every man is personally under to God. But our JESUS was not, is not, a mere man. Even his humanity was miraculously engendered and sanctified, though real. He was JESUS, the EMMANUEL, God with us; the only begotten Son of God in the Son of the Blessed Virgin. He, existing from all eternity in the form of God, took to his divinity the nature of humanity; and it is from this union of his infinite divinity with our finite humanity, that the obedience and expiation of the man Christ Jesus derive their value, and, therefore, their value must be infinite.

It is not, however, of their absolute value that we now speak, but of their application. Had the Father, Son, and Holy Ghost been pleased so to apply the saving merits of JESUS, they would be sufficient for the salvation of all men, though the race were millions of times more numerous than it is ; but we know that all men are not saved, because those who do not believe are lost. The salvation of JESUS cannot, therefore, be applied to all men. Yet it is equally clear that JESUS cannot have failed in his purpose or any part of it; and, therefore, that his people whom he came to save are not all men, but those among men who are his in some peculiar sense.

It is, also, undoubtedly true that the provisions for the pardon of sin in the merits of Christ are so great, so infinitely great, as to assure every sinner who will believe on his name of acceptance and everlasting life; but it is as true that no sinner will believe except under the constraining influence of the Holy Spirit. If then the salvation of Christ's people depended on the contingency of their unassisted faith, or faith not wrought in them by divine grace, none would be saved, and the purpose of JESUS has failed. The language of the text, however, is not that JESUS will offer salvation to all men, which, blessed be his name! he does ; but that he *shall*, positively, certainly " *shall* save his people; " and as the grace of the Holy Spirit by which faith is wrought in the soul, has been purchased by his merit and is given by him, the inference is irresistible that

JESUS not only offers his salvation to all men, but actually and infallibly secures and will accomplish the salvation of his people. Therefore, the Master himself says : " I am the good shepherd, and know my sheep, and am known of mine ; . . . and I lay down my life for the sheep." Again : " All that the Father giveth me shall come to me ; and him that cometh to me, I will in no wise cast out." This is no discouragement to the seeking soul, for all who come are sure of being received ; but it is the highest encouragement for us to be assured that our salvation is in no sense dependent on our own strength, because all who are willing to be his people, he will certainly save.

2. The nature of the salvation confirms this : " He shall save his people *from their sins*." Not only did Christ by his death pay the penalty due to them on account of their sins for all who believe ; and by his righteousness purchase for them an eternal happiness of which they are personally utterly undeserving ; but it was a principal object of his purpose, and is the main benefit which they receive through him, that his people shall be saved by the grace of his Holy Spirit from their sins themselves, that is, from the power of their sins, their sinfulness of nature, tendency, and habit. Deliverance from punishment is the least part of salvation ; for salvation is complete only in sanctification. Sin is the cause of hell, and our sinfulness constitutes our danger of eternal death ; until our sins are taken from us, or we are assured that they will be, we are in danger. But this is the work of Christ's spirit through Christ's gospel. Hence, only those are saved who are Christ's people, his " peculiar people, zealous of good works ; " and all those whom he came

certainly to save, he sanctifies that they may be saved. It is all of grace. "We love him," says the Apostle, "because he first loved us." It is grace to the end, as it is grace from the beginning. He ordained his people, not because he foresaw that they would be holy of themselves ; but because he purposed that they should be holy by his power. "For whom he did foreknow, he also did predestinate to be conformed to the image of his Son. . . . Moreover, whom he did predestinate, them he also called ; and whom he called, them he also justified; and whom he justified, them he also glorified," which is the height of sanctification. It is all of grace, therefore, all of Christ. This is the truth of the Gospel. Our Church teaches no other. They who think that they can save themselves will reject it as a hard saying ; but to all who cling to Christ as their only Saviour, it is their only comfort in life and death.

THIRDLY : *The Practical Inferences.*

These flow so easily from our previous exposition, and are so clearly stated in the Questions and Answers for this Lord's Day, that they need only to be set forth, and may then be left to our personal meditations.

I. "We ought not to seek, neither can we find salvation in any other," but JESUS.

1. We ought not to seek salvation in any other.

a. For it is God whom we have offended, God whose wrath we deserve, God who alone can save us. It is not for us to dictate how he shall save us ; but since he has revealed the Gospel of JESUS as the only way in which he is willing to save us, and freely offers salvation to all who believe, we should gratefully, gladly and at once believe on Christ for our salvation.

b. He has also declared that his highest glory, the glory of his justice and mercy, of his wisdom and his power, is in saving all who come to him through JESUS; and, therefore, should we most reverently and devoutly turn from our sins, by which we so greatly dishonor him, and offer ourselves to him through faith in Christ, that he may have his glory yet more manifest in our salvation.

c. And, when we contemplate all he has done for us in the humiliation, obedience, and death of Christ, with all he is willing to do for us on earth and in heaven by the power and grace of Christ, how should his love constrain us to become the followers of the Good Shepherd, who laid down his life for us that he might lead us, through green pastures and beside still waters, to his heavenly fold.

2. But we cannot find salvation in any other.

a. " There is none other name under heaven given among men, whereby we must be saved," but the name of Jesus.   God has said it ; and since our salvation can come only from God, there can be no other. What folly for us to think of finding another way than that which the wisdom of God devised ; or of trusting another way than that which his power has executed !

b. If there could have been any other way, God would never have put his only begotten Son to such humiliation, or that Son incarnate to such shame and suffering.   That no method less would have sufficed, is shown in the sorrow and death of JESUS ; that there could be none greater is shown in the divine merit of the vicarious sufferer.

c. So far from there being any other way, God in many Scriptures denounces a fearful aggravation of punishment upon all those who reject Christ. " He that believeth not is condemned already, because he hath not believed on the name of the only begotten Son of God." " He that despised Moses' law died without mercy under two or three witnesses. Of how much sorer punishment, suppose ye, shall he be thought worthy who hath trodden under foot the Son of God, and hath counted the blood of the covenant wherewith he was sanctified, an unholy thing, and hath done despite unto the spirit of grace ? " O my hearers, " how shall we escape if we neglect so great salvation ? "

II. Those do not believe in JESUS " who seek salvation and happiness of saints, of themselves, or anywhere else."

" They may boast of him in words,"—call themselves Christians, — " but in deeds deny him to be the only deliverer and Saviour. For one of these two things must be true: either Jesus is not a complete Saviour, or they who by a true faith receive this Saviour, must find in him all things necessary to salvation."

We can add nothing to this reasoning. Jesus saves his people from their sins. If he cannot do it, none can help him, for his power is infinite. If he undertakes to do it, he will accomplish it. To look elsewhere is to doubt his power to save, or to refuse his grace. There is not a saint in glory who does not ascribe all his salvation to JESUS; and how can they save others who themselves were saved ?

If we be not lost, utterly lost, we have no part in

Christ, for he came to save only the lost; and how can a lost sinner help to save himself?

No, blessed JESUS! Thou art the Way, and the Truth, and the Life! No man can go unto the Father but by thee. Save us for thy name's sake, O blessed JESUS!

...

LECTURE XIV.

THE TITLE, CHRIST.

TWELFTH LORD'S DAY.

THE TITLE, CHRIST.

QUEST. XXXI. *Why is he called Christ, that is, anointed?*

ANS. Because he is ordained of God the Father, and anointed with the Holy Ghost to be our Chief Prophet and Teacher, who has fully revealed to us the secret counsel and will of God concerning our redemption; and to be our only High Priest, who, by the one sacrifice of his body, has redeemed us and makes continual intercession with the Father for us; and also to be our eternal King, who governs us by his word and Spirit, and also defends and preserves us in the enjoyment of that salvation he hath purchased for us.

QUEST. XXXII. *But why art thou called a Christian?*

ANS. Because I am a member of Christ by faith, and thus am partaker of his anointing, that so I may confess his name, and present myself a living sacrifice of thankfulness to him; and, also, that, with a free and good conscience, I may fight against sin and Satan in this life, and afterwards reign with him eternally over all creatures.

IN our last lesson we were taught the meaning of that most precious word JESUS, the personal name of our divine Redeemer, given him because he is the Joshua of the new covenant, who " saves his people from their sins." But there is another word habitually associated in our faith and praise with the name JESUS ; which, if understood, greatly confirms our trust and excites our thankfulness. Dear brethren, you anticipate my utterance, and your hearts, burning within you, know that it is CHRIST.

" I believe," says every true confessor of our holy religion, " in JESUS CHRIST." The name Jesus, being as has been shown sacredly personal, and from its signification, applicable only to him who alone can save, ought never to be used with any other reference, nor should any epithet be derived from it; though some, under the shadow of a deplorable superstition, have so abused it, especially that infamous band of conspirators against the peace of the world, who cloak a systematic falsehood, opposed to every rule of the gospel, by denominating themselves The Society of Jesus Christ, is not a personal name, however, but a descriptive appellation; and all who, by their union to JESUS as their Head, share in the honorable blessings which it represents, may, whatever was the first occasion of the title, profess and call themselves CHRISTIANS.

We are, therefore, now following the order of the Creed under the guidance of the Catechism, to learn,

FIRST: *Why Jesus is called Christ?*
And

SECONDLY: *Why those who acknowledge Him as their Saviour are called Christians?*

The former inquiry is met by the 31st Question and Answer; the latter by the 32d.

FIRST: *Why is Jesus called Christ?*

I. The word itself is Greek, and an adjective derived from a verb signifying to apply oil; it translates exactly the Hebrew word which we pronounce *Messiah*, and is translated by the Latin *unctus*, participle of *unguo*, from which we make *unguent, unction*, and, through the French, *ointment, anoint;* so you perceive that both Messiah and Christ mean, as the Catechism says, *anointed.*

2. Yet, although, radically, anointment signified the application of oil in any way, it came to have, among the Hebrews, a particular and dignified sense; because God had ordained that persons designated to the high functions of prophet, priest, or king, should be conse-

crated or ceremoniously confirmed in their several offices by the pouring of oil on their heads.

a. Thus the word of Jehovah was: " Touch not mine *anointed ;* and do my *prophets* no harm ; " using the two terms, in poetical parallelism, as synonymous, and expounding each other.   It does not appear from express Scripture that prophets generally received such external unction, but, from the fact of Elijah being commanded to anoint Elisha as his successor in the prophetical authority, we may suppose that in more eminent cases the rite was performed.   Certainly it is to his office as prophet, that the language of Messiah in Isaiah lxi. 1, refers, where he says: " The Spirit of the Lord God is upon me, because the Lord hath anointed me to preach glad tidings."

b. As to *priests*, the testimony is explicit.   Thus, the Lord, having directed Moses how to compound of olive oil and many precious spices "an holy anointing oil," said, " Thou shalt anoint Aaron and his sons, and consecrate them, that they may minister unto me in the priest's office. (Ex. xxx. 30.)   By comparing this with correspondent passages in Ex. xxxix. and Lev. viii., we learn that the anointing oil, mingled with the blood of sacrifice, was sprinkled upon the sacerdotal garments of both Aaron and his sons, their right ear, right thumb, and right great toe being also touched with it ; but the fragrant oil, unmingled with the blood, was poured upon the head of Aaron alone.   Hence the Psalmist: " Behold, how good and how pleasant it is for brethren to dwell together in unity !   It is like the precious ointment upon the head, that ran down upon the beard, even Aaron's beard ; that (the beard) went down to the skirts of his garments."   It has been supposed by some, though perhaps not correctly, that, after this first recognition of an inferior priesthood, they were not publicly anointed ; but to the consecration of a high priest the unction was essential.

c. Samuel anointed, by divine command, first Saul, afterwards David, to be king over Israel ; Zadok the priest and Nathan the prophet, anointed Solomon ; Elijah anointed Hazael to be king over Syria, and Jehu to be king over Israel. So we may believe the custom was perpetuated, at least until the confusion which ensued on the degeneracy of the circumcised people. In Psalm ii. 6, Jehovah declares : " Yet have I set (literally, anointed) my king upon my holy hill of Zion ; " in Isaiah xlv. he calls Cyrus " his anointed," and many other Scriptures show that the term was applied to those gifted by the special revelation or providence of God, with kingly power.

3. The Jews, from the covenant of God with their father Abraham, and some older promises, expected that at a divinely appointed time a great personage would appear, under whose administration their people were to attain the summit of heavenly favor and an unparalleled prosperity. That he would be a mighty king was more than intimated by the declaration of the dying Jacob concerning Judah : " The sceptre shall not depart from Judah, nor a lawgiver from between his feet (*i. e.* from among his descendants), until Shiloh (or The Pacificator) come, and unto him shall the gathering of the people (or the Gentiles) be. That, while a priest and a king, he was to be a prophet, they knew from the inspired testimony of Moses : " The Lord thy God will raise up unto thee a prophet from the midst of thee, of thy brethren, like unto me ; unto him shalt

thou hearken." That he was to be a Priest, they naturally inferred from the eminently sacerdotal character
of their national constitution, and the unchangeable rule
by which all approaches to God and blessings from him
were through the mediation of the high priest; which
inference was fully justified by David.   The Lord hath
sworn and will not repent.   " Thou art a priest forever
after the order of Melchisedek;" and Zechariah:
" Thus saith the Lord of Hosts, Behold the man whose
name is The Branch, . . . he shall build the temple
of the Lord, and he shall bear the glory, and shall sit
and rule upon his throne; and he shall be a priest upon
his throne, and the counsel of peace shall be between
them both " (*i. e.* God and Israel).   These passages,
and at least seventy more, were interpreted by their
most able doctors (as seen in Chaldee Paraphrase) as
referring to Him who was " the expectation of Israel."
Hence, though we find the word retained by our translators only in one chapter of the Old Testament (9th
of Daniel), they habitually called this promised personage, who was to unite in himself their three greatest
offices, — prophet, priest, and king, — the Messiah, or
the anointed.   Thus, Andrew, after his first meeting
with Jesus, told Simon: " We have found the Messias,
which is," adds the Evangelist, " being interpreted, the
Christ."   So, also, the woman of Samaria said to
Jesus: " I know that Messias cometh, which is called
Christ (again interpolates the Evangelist) ; when he is
come, he will tell us all things; " and Simon, when he
answered his Lord's question by the clear acknowledgment, " Thou art the Christ," must, in his native
speech, have said, " Thou art the *Messiah*."

II. Our Lord Jesus is called, throughout the New

Testament, Christ, for two reasons: first, because He
was the true Messiah of whom Moses in the law and
all the prophets did write; secondly: " Because he is
ordained of God the Father, and anointed with the
Holy Ghost, to be our *Chief Prophet,* . . . . our only
High Priest, ... and our *Eternal King.*"

1. That our Lord Jesus is the true Messiah, need
not now to be further demonstrated than it is in the
New Testament; for we are not Jews but Christians,
and believe the testimony of the evangelists and apostles who have shown us in Jesus of Nazareth all the
signs and characteristics which the prophets had foretold of Christ.   Whatever discussion on this point may
yet be necessary, will be found as we follow the Catechism in the answer to the 31st Question.

2. Our Lord Jesus is Christ, because he is ordained
of God the Father and anointed with the Holy Ghost
to be our Prophet, and Priest, and King.

A. Ordained of the Father, anointed with the Spirit,
Himself the Son of God incarnate.   Thus are the
three persons of the ever-adorable Godhead united in
the provision of a Saviour for us guilty sinners; the
Father ordaining, the Son accepting, the Holy Ghost
anointing.   Glory be to the Father, and to the Son,
and to the Holy Ghost, Amen.

a. According to the plan of redemption in which the
Son, as the representative of servants, takes officially
the place of a servant, he could not assume the mediatorship without the appointment, or, as the word in the
Catechism is, ordination of the Father, who represents
the majesty of the Godhead.   As the writer to the
Hebrews argues: " No man taketh this honor (the
high priesthood) unto himself, but he that is called of

God, as was Aaron. So also Christ glorified not himself to be made an high priest, but he that said unto him, Thou art my Son, to-day have I begotten thee. As he saith also in another place, Thou art a priest forever after the order of Melchisedek," — Melchisedek, the Priest of the most high God, and also king of Salem or peace, and also, we may add, a Prophet, for he blessed Abram. From this appointment or ordination of God, the Saviour's office derived its validity, and on its validity depended its efficacy. The Emmanuel is mighty to save, not merely because of his righteousness, but because the Father sent him to save, and covenanted to accept him as the surety of his people. His works were not his own exclusively, but the works which his Father had given him to do; and hence when he had accomplished them his *right* to save.

b. His ordination from all eternity was known to the Godhead, but it was necessary that it should be confirmed and assured to us, since we could not rely upon him until we knew his appointment by the Father. Hence, the necessity of his public inauguration with the anointing of the Holy Ghost, which the sacred perfumed oil typified. Accordingly, we find that after he had reached the proper age, and by accepting baptism from his forerunner he had fulfilled all preliminary righteousness, it came to pass, as he went up from the water, praying or asking for the consecration, in the sight of a vast multitude, the heaven was opened, and the Holy Ghost, in a bodily shape like a dove, descended upon him, and a voice came from heaven which said, " Thou art my beloved Son; in thee I am well pleased." It should not be overlooked that the dove-like glory did not reascend, but (John i. 33) remained upon him, as the oil on the prophet, priest, and king. This unction of the Holy Ghost was his anointing, and, with the proclamation from heaven, constituted his inauguration to the Messiahship. Here we have a direct fulfilment of that afore-cited prophecy which the ancient Jewish doctors unanimously referred to the Messiah : " The Spirit of the Lord God is upon me ; because the Lord hath anointed me to preach good tidings unto the meek ; he hath sent me to bind up the broken-hearted, to proclaim liberty to the captives, and the opening of the prison to them that are bound; to proclaim the acceptable year of the Lord, and the day of vengeance of our God ; to comfort all that mourn," etc. (Is. lxi. 1 – 3.) As the sacred anointing oil was ever accompanied with the promise of divine qualifications, and as its spices diffused around the consecrated one a ravishing perfume, so did the Holy Spirit remaining on him strengthen his human nature, body and soul, for his work, and render all his righteousness a sweet-smelling savor to God, acceptable because the perfect merits of the Saviour, ordained of God the Father.

B. The office of the Saviour was threefold, uniting those of prophet, priest, and king, to each of which he was consecrated by the unction of the Holy Ghost. The Catechism directs us to examine them severally, that we may learn their gracious meaning.

a. He is " our Chief PROPHET and Teacher, who has fully revealed to us the secret counsel and will of God concerning our redemption."

The Catechism adds " Teacher " by way of definition, for, though people now understand a prophet to

be one who foretells, such was not the full sense of the
term among the ancients, Hebrew or Greek; but they
meant by it one who declares the truth of God to men.
Our Lord did, indeed, foretell many things, but he was
and is the great Teacher of his people, from whom we
learn all that God would reveal to us. So he declares
of himself, " I am . . . the Truth; " and Peter at
the Beautiful Gate says : " Moses truly said unto the
fathers, a prophet shall the Lord your God raise up
unto you of your brethren, like unto me; him shall ye
hear in all things whatsoever he shall say unto you ; "
and when the Catechism asserts that he has fully revealed to us the secret counsel and will of God, by
" secret " is meant the " counsel and will " which, but
for his teaching, would be unknown.

The learned Jews found it necessary for the understanding of the Scriptures, to believe that God revealed
himself and uttered his will by a personal word or
voice, and never immediately, or without such intervention, communicated to men ; but their doctrine on
this point was painfully obscure. John, in the first
chapter of his Gospel, makes the fact clear, by showing
that the Word which was in the beginning with God,
was also himself God, even the only begotten Son of
the Father, who, in the person of our Lord Jesus,
" became flesh, and dwelt among us." " No man
(rather no one) hath seen God at any time ; the only
begotten Son which is in the bosom of the Father, he
hath declared him ; " that is, has made his being and
will known to us. Thus our Lord Jesus, who is our
Prophet or Teacher, is none else than God the Son,
the second Person of the ever-blessed Trinity, incarnate
as the Son of man. The epistle to the Hebrews sets

forth the same truth : " God, who at sundry times and
in divers manners spake unto the fathers by the prophets, hath in these last days, spoken unto us by his Son,
whom he hath appointed heir of all things, by whom
also he made the worlds ; who, being the brightness,"
that is, the shining forth, " of his glory, and the express
image (or manifest counterpart, as the impression is of
a seal), and upholding all things by the word (utterance) of his power, when he had by himself purged
our sins, sat down on the right hand of the Majesty on
high." Here our Saviour Jesus Christ is identified
with the Son of God, who alone reveals the glory of
God and his excellent nature ; and the Father now in
the Gospel speaks to us by the same Word by whom
" the worlds were made." The Son, whose divine office
it ever has been to declare the truth of his Father's
will, now becomes incarnate, that he may by his Gospel
make a nearer and fuller revelation of his grace.

The Scriptures of both the Old and the New Testaments were written by men whom the Holy Ghost inspired for the work ; but as, according to the plan of
redemption, the Holy Ghost is the Spirit of Christ, our
Lord Jesus teaches us by the whole Book of God. He
is the great Prophet who speaks through all the prophets ; he is the great Apostle who speaks through all
the apostles ; the Prophet of prophets, the Apostle of
apostles. And as it is the Holy Ghost, whose illuminating and transforming influences, accompanying the
various means of instruction ordained for us of God,
make them effectual, and the Holy Ghost is the spirit
of Christ ; so all the knowledge we gain from the blessing of the Spirit of God without, and the blessing of
that divine Spirit within us, is derived from the Lord

Jesus, our Prophet and Teacher. To him alone are we to look, from him alone we are to learn. The eternal Word made flesh, our Lord Jesus Christ is " the True Light which lighteth every man that cometh into the world."

b. He, who is " the Apostle," is also the " High Priest of our profession." Our Lord Jesus is " our only HIGH PRIEST, who, by the one sacrifice of his body, has redeemed us, and makes continual intercession with the Father for us." That our Lord Jesus has been ordained and anointed to be our High Priest, is sufficiently established by the Epistle to the Hebrews, and other Scriptures. " For such a High Priest became us, who is holy, harmless, undefiled, separate from sinners, and made higher than the heavens."

Like the typical high priests, his office is twofold: To make an atonement by sacrifice for those whom he represents ; and to make intercession with God for them.

a. a. In our study of several previous sections of the Catechism, and particularly the last, we learned how the Lord Jesus has redeemed his people from the curse of death, due to them for their sins, by taking their place and suffering the penalty of the law in their stead. This vicarious suffering is represented as a sacrifice. The victim was himself, his divinely begotten and sinless humanity, body and soul ; the altar was his own indwelling divinity which sanctified the offering, making its merits, of itself finite, infinitely meritorious ; and as he was both Sacrifice and Altar, so he is also the Priest ; and, as none but the High Priest could make an atoning sacrifice, he is our only High Priest. The typical sacrifices being mere figures, utterly in-

sufficient, needed to be repeated; but our great High
Priest, " after he had offered one sacrifice for sins forever," a sacrifice infinitely sufficient, and therefore of
eternal efficacy, sat down on the right hand of God,
from henceforth expecting till his enemies be made his
footstool; his offering accepted, his work as a Sacrificer
was done, and he now waits for his promised reward;
" for by one offering he hath perfected forever them
that are sanctified." " There remaineth no more sacrifice for sins;" none other is needed, none other can
be offered; nor can that one sacrifice be repeated, as
the Papists in their deplorable superstition pretend by
the Mass, nor need we nor can we have any High
Priest but he, as the Papists blasphemously pretend by
calling the head of their superstition the Chief Pontiff.
The work of atonement is finished, finished for us,
finished for all who believe: whereof God has given
assurance in raising our Lord Jesus from the dead, and
setting him at his own right hand in the heavenly
places.   O blessed Lord Jesus Christ, our hope of
pardon is alone in thee, and in thy death upon the
cross !

b. b. When the typical high priest had offered the
sacrifice of atonement without, he entered within the
vail, and there, having sprinkled the blood of the victim over the cover of the ark that contained the broken
law, he made intercession by fervent prayer for the
people. So our true High Priest, after finishing his
work of satisfaction, passed into the heavens; and
there, not for a little while but constantly, he abides,
making intercession for us; not as a suppliant, at the
foot of the throne, but as the Son of God seated on
the throne itself, and asking of his willing Father the

fulfilment of the covenant, whose condition on his part he had fulfilled : even eternal life for all who believe in his name. Through him, therefore, unworthy as we are in ourselves, we may have access with boldness " unto the throne of grace, that we may obtain mercy and find grace to help in time of need." All our prayers must go up to the Father through him, and, as he has been accepted for a sacrifice, his advocacy of our cause will be prevalent ; and the Father through him will grant us pardon and life eternal. All our services, with our hearts, must be presented through him, and, having washed them from their sinfulness, he, with the perfume of his anointment, will make them acceptable ; and he, receiving the reward of his own righteousness, will bestow in return for our poor services blessings far more abundant " than we can ask or think." Unto him be glory in the Church throughout all ages, world without end, Amen.

c. He is " our eternal King, who governs us by his word and spirit ; and who defends and preserves us in (the enjoyment of) that salvation he has purchased."

God, because he is the only Creator, is the only Sovereign of all creatures intelligent or material, and any authority or control over them exerted by any other than himself immediately, must be derived from his ordination or providence. Our blessed Saviour, when he condescended to be our representative, and associated our humanity with his divinity, took a position necessarily inferior to the Sovereign, though, as to his original nature, the Second Person of the Godhead ; and accordingly, that he might be fully qualified to accomplish all the divine purposes of his mission, he received

from the Father, representing the Godhead, all authority and power.   This kingship or lordship is delegated;
and must not be confounded with the infinite right to
reign which is his, coequally with the Father and the
Holy Ghost, as the Second Person of the ever-blessed
Godhead. " All power is given to me in heaven and in
earth," said he to his apostles just before his ascension;
and it was granted to him in acknowledgment of his
perfect righteousness, passive and active, during his
humiliation on earth.   " Let this mind be in you, which
was also in Christ Jesus; who, being in the form of
God, thought it not robbery to be equal with God : but
made himself of no reputation, and took upon him the
form of a servant, and was made in the likeness of
men : and being found in fashion as a man, he humbled
himself and became obedient unto (*until*) death, even the
death of the cross. WHEREFORE, God also hath highly
exalted him, and given him a name (*authority*) which
is above every name : that at the name of Jesus every
knee should bow, of things in heaven, and things in
earth, and things under the earth ; and that every
tongue should confess that Jesus Christ is LORD, to the
glory of God the Father."   Here you see that this universal dominion is given to JESUS, the Son of God incarnate, as a servant, — to Jesus *Christ*, or the anointed
Jesus, after he had been obedient until death, and
because of his obedience, and the result will be " the
glory of God the Father."   Hence, as this authority
was delegated to Jesus as the Mediator, we are accustomed to distinguish it from his original authority as
the Son of God by calling it his mediatorial kingdom;
by which we mean all the power necessary for the full
salvation of those he has redeemed by his righteous-

ness, and for the vindication of the divine honor in the redemption of his people.

This kingdom has two parts, as the Catechism teaches. One, a kingdom over his people ; the other, a kingdom over all things for the benefit of his people ; " He saves us ; " " He defends and preserves us in that salvation he has purchased for us."

a. a. His kingdom over his church.

Thus the annunciating angel to the blessed virgin : " The Lord God shall give unto him the throne of his father David, and he shall reign over the house of Jacob forever, and of his kingdom there shall be no end." So also, the Psalmist as cited in the Hebrews : " Thou art a priest forever after the order of Melchisedek, which united the kingship over those for whom the priestship was exercised, — Melchisedek, which is by interpretation king of righteousness, and king of Salem, which signifies king of peace. Our Jesus rules in righteousness and peace over all for whom his atonement and intercession are accepted. The same thing is declared by the apostle : " Who gave himself for us, that he might redeem us from all iniquity, and purify unto himself a peculiar people (a people who are his own), zealous of good works." Redemption, purification, sanctification, are united in his care of his own people. " Thine they were and thou gavest them me," said he unto his Father in his mediatorial prayer.

The method of his governing his church is twofold : " He governs us," says the Catechism, " by his Word and Spirit."

His people are a willing people. The Saviour rules over them, not by force of mere authority, but with the consent of their hearts and minds. Hence he reveals his word, the Holy Scriptures, as the law and constitution of his kingdom, the rule by which his people shall serve him, and the source of the motives from which they shall serve him.

But our dispositions are naturally opposed to the divine will. " The carnal mind is enmity against God, and is not subject to the law of God, neither indeed can be ; " consequently, the more that the truth is pressed upon the unrenewed soul, the greater will be its enmity and its opposition. There is, therefore, a necessity of a divine energy to convert the soul to the love of God, and to a choice of the service he requires. " Thy people shall be willing in the day of thy power." This is the work of the Holy Ghost, who, because his influences are obtained through the merits and intercession of Christ, is called the Spirit of Christ. He, by his sovereign, mysterious agency on the soul and through the word, converts the heart to love, enlightens the mind to approve, and inclines the will to choose the word of God as the only rule of faith and practice. Nor shall this divine influence ever cease ; for not only will it bring the believer gradually to a perfect sanctification in heaven, but there perpetually maintain the glorified saint in a holy happiness. This kingdom of Christ is eternal. " He shall rule over the house of Jacob forever."

b. b. His kingdom over all things for the benefit of his people.

Inasmuch as the church is exposed to great enmity from wicked men and wicked spirits, besides finding many obstacles to its progress and final triumph from the state of things occasioned by sin, there is necessity for the divine defence and preservation of every

believer, and of the whole body, that the salvation purchased be secured. Therefore, all power is given to
him and exerted by him for his people. He is " Head
over all things to his Church." All power over earth
is his. The forces of nature, the discoveries of science,
the commercial intercourse of nations, the wars between
them, their revolutions and politics, all are controlled
and combined in his hand for the furtherance of his
cause. All power is his over heaven. As the Lord of
hosts, he brings all his angelic armies to serve him in
his mediatorship. Are they not all ministering spirits,
sent forth to minister for them who shall be heirs of
salvation? All power is his over hell. For he has
conquered death, and him that had the power of death,
that is, the devil. He does not, indeed, make the malignant spirits who contend against us his willing subjects, neither does he, for wise reasons, wholly prevent
their wicked activity; but, as he showed when on
earth, even the devils are subject to him. They can do
nothing without his permission, and, as will be seen in
the end, he will overrule all their machinations for his
glory and the prosperity of the Church, and of every
member of his church. It is in this that the apostle
exults: " If God be for us, who can be against us?
He that spared not his own Son, but delivered him up
for us all, how shall he not with him also freely give us
all things? . . . . Who shall separate us from the love
of Christ? Shall tribulation, or distress, or persecution,
or famine, or nakedness, or peril, or sword? . . . .
Nay, in all these things we are more than conquerors,
through him that loved us. For I am persuaded that
neither death, nor life, nor angels, nor principalities,
nor powers, nor things present, nor things to come,

nor height, nor depth, nor any other creature, shall be able to separate us from the love of God, which is in Christ Jesus our Lord." This kingdom over all things having been bestowed upon him for the specific purpose of bringing all his people triumphantly to glory, is not eternal; but, when that purpose is accomplished, and when at the final judgment he will have vindicated the justice of God in the condemnation of those who reject the offers of mercy, it will revert to God,—Father, Son, and Holy Ghost. As we learn from the apostle: " Then cometh the end, when he shall have delivered up the kingdom to God, even the Father (as the representative of the Godhead); when he shall have put down all rule and all authority and power. For he must reign till he hath put all enemies under his feet. The last enemy that shall be destroyed is death. For he hath put all things under his feet. But when he saith, all things are put under him, it is manifest that he is excepted which did put all things under him. And when all things shall be subdued unto him, then shall the Son also himself be subject unto him that put all things under him, that God may be all in all;" that is, providence, which for the church has been entrusted to the Son as the Mediator, will revert to the hands of God, and the Son as Mediator * with the Church, whose head he is eternally, will be subject to God, who, thenceforward, will reign immediately.

Thus is it our privilege, beloved Christians, to see in Christ all that is necessary for his office as our Saviour.

---

* Some think that by the Son here is intended the human nature of Christ (Thomas Aquinas in Epistolas) for which compare Heb. i. 1, Ps. viii. 5, 6, Heb. ii. 5 – 9. I prefer the interpretation given. The church, ever existing, will exist in its head; the humanity will ever be conjoined to the divinity. Hence the *person* of Christ is "subject unto him that put all things under him."

What he promises he obtains; what he obtains he secures for all those who put their trust in him. The covenant of our redemption is made, not between us and the Father; but between the Father and Son incarnate as our Mediator with the Father. The hope of the true believer, therefore, cannot fail; for it is established on the truth, the merits and the power of him whom the Father has, by the Holy Spirit, anointed to be our Prophet, our Priest, and our King.

SECONDLY : *Why are those who acknowledge Jesus as their Saviour called Christians ?*

We have no mention of the word Christian until we come to Acts xi. 26, where the historian says that about the time when Paul and Barnabas spent a whole year with the Church and taught much people at Antioch, the disciples were there first called Christians. Many contend that this name was given them by divine revelation or apostolic authority ; but if that had been the case it would in all probability have been so recorded ; and the more reasonable opinion seems to be that, owing to the remarkable success attending the labors of Paul and Silas, the disciples increased to such a considerable sect as to require a particular designation. Christian may have been the name pitched upon by the unbelieving out of derision, and, no doubt, it was used in contempt ; but it is certain that it was a very natural appellation, as all people are used to call the followers of an eminent teacher by his name, as Socratics, Calvinists, Wesleyans. The name, however, soon came to be applied and understood generally, as " Agrippa said unto Paul, almost thou persuadest me to be a Christian ; " and it received apostolical sanction, as it is used by Peter in his first epistle, iv. 16.

The Catechism takes occasion from its etymology, and very properly, to describe under it the privileges and distinguishing characteristics of all who are truly called after Christ.

The doctrine of the whole New Testament is, that believers are represented or covered by Christ; that the history of Christ's personal body is a parable of the Church, which is his spiritual body; and that all our blessings having been primarily conferred on our Head reach us through him, as all our services must be rendered unto God through his mediation.

I. Hence our Catechism makes the believer say: " I am a member of Christ by faith, and thus am partaker of his anointing." Belief in Christ is evidence of union to him and of participation with him; for, as the oil upon the head of Aaron ran down to the skirts of his garments, so does the anointing of Christ flow over his whole body, even to the most humble believer. We have seen that the anointing oil represented the Holy Spirit, which, for the assistance of our faith, came down visibly upon the head of Christ after he had passed through baptism to John and abode upon him; so not less truly, though invisibly, is every believer sanctified unto God by the Holy Ghost, which is Christ's Spirit, and reaches his people through his infinitely meritorious mediation. Not only are they regenerated, or born again of the Spirit, but the Holy Ghost dwells in them as an animating, enlightening, strengthening, elevating principle, maintaining their union to Christ, even as the Spirit of the Lord God consecrated, moved, instructed, upheld and maintained his humanity, until his work would be accomplished.

II. But as Christ Jesus was anointed to the several

offices necessary for his work of redemption, so the
effects of the Holy Spirit upon each anointed believer
must in some proper measure correspond to those
offices.

1. Christ is our anointed Prophet, the great Pub-
lisher of truth: so " all the Lord's people are prophets,"
for " the Lord hath put his spirit upon them." (See
Numbers xi. 29.) This imitation of Christ in his prophetical office is condensed here into *confession of his
name*. Every believer who openly professes to be a
Christian, gives his testimony from conviction and experience that the Gospel of Christ is, indeed, the truth
of God unto salvation ; then he adds to it the confirmation of a godly example, and according to the measure
he has of Christ's spirit, will he strive to send the
Gospel as Christ sends to all men in all the world.
This last prophetical duty of the believer is eminently
characteristic of a Christian life, and those who regard
the missions of Christianity with indifference, or assist
them reluctantly, may well doubt if they have Christ's
spirit, for they neither obey his commands, nor follow
his example. In a word, the life of a Christian is, by
the same Spirit which saves him, consecrated to the
spread of the Gospel throughout the world.

2. Christ is our Priest, through whose atonement
and mediation all the services of the Church are to be
acceptably offered ; for, many as were the religious services of both inferior priests and people under the Jewish dispensation, they all derived their value from the
expiatory sacrifice and intercessory prayers of the High
Priest. So, as Christ by the eternal Spirit offered himself unto God, the believer by the same Spirit offers his
whole life. The work of atonement and mediation is

peculiar to Christ, but, through his purifying and pre-
vailing merits, the believer presents himself a living
sacrifice of thankfulness to God. His whole life, all
his faculties, all his influence, all he has and all he is,
are a thank offering for the blessings of salvation.
Hence the true Israel are called by the prophet "a
nation of priests;" and the Apostle Peter unites with
the Apostle Paul in designating the Church as an holy
priesthood to offer up spiritual sacrifices (sacrifices dic-
tated by heart and mind), acceptable to God by Jesus
Christ. Thus, as priests as well as prophets, our whole
strength belongs to God by the consecration of the
same spirit which makes us members of Christ.

3. Christ is our King; therefore, as his subjects, his
willing people, are we to obey him wholly, making his
word our rule of Christian conduct, and following the
monitions of his Spirit in all things. But as we are
subject to sinful temptations from within, and from the
world, and from the devil, who makes use of both our
evil nature and the world to seduce and intimidate us, we
are animated by the consciousness of our acceptance with
God in Christ, resolutely, heartily and courageously to
contend against sin and Satan in this life, trusting in the
power of Christ to conquer our enemies, and in the grace
of his Spirit to conquer ourselves. Nay, we are to regard
ourselves, each one of us, as soldiers of that sacramén-
tal army, the Church militant, which, by the blessing
of God upon his word, is to subdue this revolted, angry
world, in spite of its oppositions and persecutions, its
wrath, its power, and its ostentations. We follow a
conquering King through battle and fatigue and suffering, but if we be faithful unto death, we shall share
his certain, inevitable, and glorious triumph. " Unto

him that overcometh will I give to sit down with me upon my throne, even as I have overcome and am sat down with my Father on his throne." Whatever honors preëminent he enjoys eternally, whatever kingdom he shall rule forever, his faithful ones shall share with him immortally ; for he who hath made them priests, has by the same word and spirit made them kings unto God and his Christ. His prophetical office shall cease, and theirs with his, for all prophecies shall fail when divine knowledge is perfect ; but his priestly office, and theirs in rendering worship and praise, his kingly office, and theirs in the power of the Father, are eternal. He the Melchisedek, king of Salem, king of righteousness, Priest of the most high God ; and they a royal priesthood. O Christ our prophet, O Christ our priest, O Christ our King, Lord Jesus Christ our only Saviour, behold us at thy feet, that we may catch the drops descending from thine anointment, and so walk worthy of the holy name of Christian, wherewith we are called ! Amen.

LECTURE XV.

THE SONSHIP AND GOVERNMENT OF CHRIST.

THIRTEENTH LORD'S DAY.

THE SONSHIP AND GOVERNMENT OF CHRIST.

QUEST. XXXIII. *Why is Christ called the only begotten Son of God, since we are also the children of God?*

ANS. Because Christ alone is the eternal and natural Son of God; but we are children adopted of God, by grace, for his sake.

QUEST. XXXIV. *Wherefore callest thou him our Lord?*

ANS. Because he hath redeemed us, both soul and body, from all our sins, not with gold or silver, but with his precious blood, and hath delivered us from all the power of the devil, and thus hath made us his own property.

IN our study of the section for the Eleventh Lord's Day, it was our delightful privilege to meditate on the fragrant name of Jesus, and in that for the Twelfth we learned the meaning of Christ, his title of consecration as our Mediator with God, the Prophet, Priest, and King of his people. There yet remain two other appellations by which the Catholic Church recognizes him as worthy of our divine homage and entire obedience; the first descriptive of his essential divinity, the other of his supreme authority: " The only begotten Son of God," " our Lord." " I believe in God the Father Almighty, and in Jesus Christ, *his only begotten Son, our Lord.*"

There is, therefore, no need of further preface to our use of the lesson before us, which, as we see at once, teaches us,

FIRST: *The reason why Christ is called, The only begotten Son of God.*

Thirty-third Question and Answer.

SECONDLY: *The reason why we call him our Lord.*
Thirty-fourth Question and Answer.

FIRST: *The reason why Christ is called the only begotten Son of God.*

" Why," asks the Catechism, " is Christ called the only begotten Son of God, since we are also the children of God ? "   " Because," we are instructed to answer, " Christ alone is the eternal and natural Son of God, but we are children adopted of God by grace for Christ's sake."

I. Sonship to God is, by the Scriptures, ascribed to other persons besides Jesus Christ, viz: *The holy angels*, of whom we read, " All the sons of God shouted for joy; " *men generally*, for the Evangelist Luke, in his genealogy of the Saviour, traces it back to " Adam, which was the Son of God ; " we are all of us commanded to pray, saying, " Our Father which art in heaven," and the Apostle Paul strongly approves the declaration of a Greek poet, that men are the offspring of God ; *worshippers of God*, when distinguished from those who do not worship him, as the sacred historian tells us that " the sons of God saw the daughters of men ; " *the children of Israel*, after they had been solemnly covenanted with God: " Ye are," said Moses to them by divine command, " the children of the Lord your God ; " *magistrates*, who are the ministers of God, in a certain sense, before the people, as the Psalmist to the judges: " I have said, Ye are gods (*i. e.* high persons), and all of you are children of the Most High ; " and, especially, *believers in Christ*, who, for Christ's sake, and being renewed by the grace of the Holy Ghost, are owned as the " sons and daughters of the Lord Almighty," having " received the spirit of adoption." Our Lord is distinguished infinitely above these by the character of his filiation, or sonship. Angels and men are called sons of God, simply because he has given them their being; worshippers of God, because they acknowledge his paternal rule and care; the covenanted Israelites, because he took them under his special guardianship; magistrates, because they represent his authority; and Christians, because he adopts them into his family through their union to Christ: the term in all these cases being used figuratively and implying no essential relationship to God. But our Lord is styled: *the* Son of God; his *own* Son; his *only begotten* Son; which expressions imply that he is the Son of God in an excellent, peculiar, natural, and therefore an eternal relation.

1. *The* Son of God. No one can read the New Testament, the epistles as well as the historical books, without seeing that this title as applied to our Saviour has a very eminent signification, and can by no means be confounded with the figurative sonship of angels or men. Belief in Christ as the Son of God, is comprehensive of all Christian faith. Thus the Evangelist John gives the testimony of John the Forerunner: "I saw and bare record that this is the Son of God." " He saith unto them: But whom say ye that I am? And Simon Peter answered and said, Thou art the Christ, the Son of the living God. And Jesus answered and said unto him: Blessed art thou, Simon Bar-Jona, for flesh and blood hath not revealed it unto thee, but my Father which is in heaven." " Whatsoever is born of God overcometh the world; and this is the victory that overcometh the world, even our faith. Who is he that overcometh the world, but he that

believeth that Jesus Christ is the Son of God?"
Now, surely, these expressions cannot mean that Christ
was the Son of God in any such sense as Adam was or
any Christian is. What need of the Baptist's solemn
assurance for this? Did such a conviction require a
special revelation? or could a faith that went no farther
overcome the world by its inspiring virtue? It is true
that the Son of God is a scriptural title of Messiah
recognized by the Jews themselves : yet that it was not
a mere synonym for Messiah, but meant more, is clear
from the fact that the two terms are used together. No
one could be the Messiah but the Son of God; and
because he was the Son of God he was the Messiah.
The Jews condemned him as a blasphemer, not because
he claimed to be the Messiah, which, if the claim were
false, would not have been blasphemy, but because as
the Messiah he avowed himself to be the Son of God.
" Jesus answered them and said : My Father worketh
hitherto, and I work. Therefore the Jews sought the
more to kill him, because he not only had broken the
Sabbath, but said, also, that God was his Father, making himself equal with God." So, at his trial before the
Sanhedrim, " the high priest said unto him : I adjure
thee by the living God that thou tell us whether thou
art the Christ the Son of the living God? Jesus saith
to him, Thou hast said (or, I am, see Mark xiv. 62.)
. . . . Then the high priest rent his clothes, saying,
He hath spoken blasphemy! What further need have
we of witnesses?" For this reason the Jews, after
Pilate had acquitted him, insisted on his crucifixion, for
said they : " We have a law, and by our law he ought
to die, because he made himself the Son of God."
They were right in their understanding of our Lord's

assertion of his sonship to God, for, if he were not actually the Son of God, he had blasphemed.

2. But that all cavil might be rebuked, the Scripture is if possible more explicit. Thus the Apostle twice in one chapter, (eighth of Romans,) calls our Lord, God's *own Son:* " God, sending his own Son in the likeness of sinful flesh, and for sin, condemned sin in the flesh ; " and again : " He that spared not his own Son but delivered him up for us all, how shall he not with him also freely give us all things ? " Here, the force of the reasoning depends wholly upon the peculiar sonship of Christ to God. For no such inference could be made if Christ who had been given were the Son of God only in a figurative or official manner. It is the love of the Father for his own Son which proves his great, his unspeakable love to us, in sending that Son under the likeness of our sinful humanity for our redemption ; nor can we, without great violence against the obvious meaning of words, understand by the phrase " his own," otherwise than that Christ is the Son of God in the fullest sense in which one can be the son of his father.

3. Does any objector yet hesitate, and suggest that " his own " may be nothing more than a term of endearment or approbation ? There is yet another expression repeatedly employed for the very purpose of declaring that the sonship is natural, by which we mean that he is essentially of the same nature of his Father : " God . . . sent his *only begotten* Son." As, in all cases, the son is of the same nature with his begetter, so is the begotten of God of the same essence as his divine Father. God calls his intelligent creatures, who, as to some qualities, resemble him finitely,

his children, but Christ he calls his only begotten, his only Son in his own nature. It is impossible that the force of language can go farther. This is the reasoning in the first chapter of Hebrews. The writer is establishing the infinite superiority of Christ to all those by whom God had made any previous revelation of his word ; and, beginning with the angels, he asserts that Christ hath by inheritance, or by his sonship, obtained a more excellent name or dignity than they. As a son derives his nobility from his descent, so Christ is divine in virtue of his sonship to God. "For," asks he "unto which of the angels said he at any time: 'Thou art my Son, this day, have I begotten thee?'" "this day," meaning after the Hebrew idiom, "in eternity." Again, "unto the Son he saith, Thy throne, O God, is forever and ever." God himself interprets the meaning of his own language, and styles his begotten Son, God, as truly God as himself. How could God himself be more explicit in asserting the divinity of Christ? Yet even against this direct testimony from the highest of all witnesses, the sceptic struggles, and would have us believe that the begetting refers to Christ's miraculous conception of the Holy Ghost. It is true that the human nature of Christ was, as it were, begotten by the Holy Ghost, and that he only has been so begotten ; but was it to a man, though divinely conceived, that the Father Almighty said: "Thy throne, O God, is forever and ever?" Nay, is it not clear that Christ was the only begotten Son of God before his incarnation? For the Father sent his only begotten Son into the world. Christ must, therefore, have existed before he was sent ; and existed as the only begotten Son of God. Again, in the first chapter of the Hebrews, it is asserted, that God made the worlds by the Son whom he, a little farther on, declares to be his begotten ; and the Evangelist John, in the preface to his Gospel, clearly identifies the Word which was " in the beginning with God," and which " was God," and by whom " all things were made," with him who " was made flesh and dwelt among us ; " whose glory his disciples beheld, " the glory as of the only begotten of the Father." So, also, the Saviour in his prayer before his passion, says : " Now, O Father, glorify thou me with thine own self, with the glory which I had with thee before the world was." Proofs of Christ's preëxistence might be multiplied ; but these are enough to show that the title, " only begotten," was his, independently of his incarnation, and antecedently to it. But in what state did he preëxist ? Certainly not as man, for he became man by his birth of the Virgin Mary (" blessed was she among women ! ") : not as an angel, for it is proved that " he had by inheritance a more excellent name than they." What else could the only begotten of God be but God ? Not merely divine, but truly, essentially God : as truly and essentially of the same nature as God the Father, as the son of a man is as truly and essentially a man. Not God in some lower sense than the Father, for it is only in his minority that a son is less than his father ; and as Deity is infinite, the Son of God must, like God the Father, be infinite ; and, therefore, they are equal. Is this reasoning too bold ? It is exactly what the Apostle asserts in so many words : " Let this mind be in you, which was also in Christ Jesus, who, being in the form (the mode of existence) of God, thought it not robbery to be equal with God, but made himself of no

reputation, and took on him the form of a servant."
How could he be God, and not equal with God; if
equal with God, infinite; if infinite, equal with the
Father? The begotten is of the same nature as the
begetter, the Son of God as God the Father; therefore
does the Church adore with equal praises the divine
Father, and the divine Son; the First, and Second
Persons of the holy Trinity; who, with the third Person, the Holy Ghost, constitute the one God in whom
we believe.

We must, however, be careful to remember that the
Scripture, in speaking of God and of the relations
between the Persons of the Godhead, uses language
framed for men, and to express their relations; nor is
it possible in such language to make known the infinite
truths of God's own being. Hence, the terms Father,
Son, begetting, or generation (which is the Latin
synonym), are to be understood in a sense as distinct
from that which they bear when applied to men, as the
divine nature is infinitely above the human, and it may
be true that theologians have speculated by inferences
from these terms to an unwarranted degree: but we
are certain from correlative Scripture that they imply
a real, natural, essential, though, from the nature of
the case, by us incomprehensible, relation between the
first and second Persons of the Godhead; which implies their equal divinity. Hence, also, we must believe
that, as the nature of God is unchangeable, the relation
between the Father and the Son, though clearly revealed (as to its fact) only in connection with the
Gospel, must have existed from all eternity. The
Father did not cause the Son to be; the Son did not
in his being follow the Father, but, whatever is the

ineffable relation which those words imply, it has been and will be coeternal with the existence of God.

The scope of the lesson for to-day is so great, that we have no opportunity to enter upon other corroboratory arguments for our Lord's divinity, nor even to draw out the many practical deductions from the matter to which we have confined ourselves ; but we trust in the Christian judgment of those who have followed us as we reasoned out of the Scriptures, so far as to believe that they will agree with the orthodox of all ages in the truth of Christ's natural and eternal sonship to God : to deny which is to deny his divinity, and to take all value from his atoning mediation.

SECONDLY : *The reason why we call Jesus Christ the only begotten Son of God, our Lord.*

" Because," says the Catechism, " he hath redeemed us, both soul and body, from all our sins, not with gold or silver, but with his precious blood, and hath delivered us from all the power of the devil, and thus hath made us his own property."

The true and essential divinity of Christ being established by his sonship to God the Father, his divine authority over us follows as a necessary consequence ; for he hath himself said : " that all men should honor the Son, even as they honor the Father. He that honoreth not the Son, honoreth not the Father which hath sent him." God is our Almighty, all-wise, infinitely holy Creator. Our being, with all its faculties, physical and spiritual, has come from him, from whom have come all things. We, therefore, belong to him, body, soul, and spirit, — all that we are, all that we have, all that we can do ; and he has the sole right, as he alone has the competent knowledge, to command and direct us in the way in which we may fulfil the end of our creation, which is his own glory. It is both wickedness and folly not to acknowledge and obey God as our rightful owner and master. Hence the uncommunicable name of the true God, which distinguished him throughout the Old Testament from all the false gods of the heathen, was JEHOVAH, used in the sense of SUPREME, which our translators render by LORD, printed in capital letters. Thus the Psalmist: " For the LORD (or Jehovah) is great and greatly to be praised; he is to be feared above all gods. For all the gods of the nations are idols; but the LORD (Jehovah) made the heavens." The term lord, signifying one having right and power to rule, is, however, applied to human sovereigns, dignitaries, and masters, who exercise dominion over their fellow-men. Hence, God the Creator receives homage and glory from the Scriptures, as infinitely supreme over all such forms of authority as may be claimed for, or by him delegated to any of his intelligent creatures; and Christ, as the Son of God, the second person of the adorable Godhead, is by virtue of his original, essential divinity, entitled to our homage and obedience as our Lord, and Lord of all.

But there is a peculiar and evangelical sense in which the only begotten Son of God, incarnate as Christ Jesus, the anointed Saviour, has become our Lord, — the Lord of all Christians, — to which the apostle refers when he says: " We know that an idol is nothing in the world, and that there is none other God but one. For though there be that are called gods, whether in heaven or in earth (as there be gods many and lords many), but to us there is but one God the Father, of whom are all things and we in him; and one Lord

Jesus Christ, by whom are all things, and we by him."
This is the Lordship of Jesus Christ, of which the Catechism here speaks, and concerning which it is now our
duty especially to inquire; although it is included in
Christ's office of king, already considered by us when
expounding his name, *Christ*.

I. The source of Christ's Lordship.

It is not original but derived. As the only begotten
Son of God, he had with the Father and the Holy
Ghost the supreme authority as creator, preserver,
and administrator of all things; but when, in executing the plan of redemption, he became the representative and took the place of his people, he " was made in
the likeness of men," and so " took upon him the form "
and condition " of a servant." In so doing, therefore,
he, so far as he was incarnate, laid aside his glory: he
appeared as man, as a servant; and as a man, and by
assumption of human nature, he was voluntarily but
truly a servant. Now the stress of all evangelical, as
well as antecedent, scripture shows that upon him as
the Son of God incarnate, as the representative of men,
the Father, representing the Godhead, conferred a delegated lordship, equal in all respects to that which God
exercises, within the limits and for the purpose designated by the plan of redemption. Thus says the
Psalmist, speaking for God: " I have set my King on
my holy hill of Zion; " that is, in the church. Again,
the angel in the annunciation: " Behold, thou shalt
conceive in thy womb and bring forth a son, and shalt
call his name JESUS. He shall be great, and shall be
called the Son of the Highest; and the Lord God shall
give unto him the throne of his father David. And he
shall reign over the house of Jacob forever; and of his

kingdom there shall be no end." Again, in commission-
ing his disciples, Jesus came and spake unto them, saying, " All power is given unto me in heaven and in
earth." Again, in Philippians : " God also hath highly
exalted him, and given him a name. which is above
every name; that at the name of Jesus every knee
should bow, of things in heaven, and things in earth, and
things under the earth ; and that every tongue should
confess that Jesus Christ is Lord to the glory of God
the Father." These are, as you know, but a few of
the passages in which Lordship supreme is conferred
upon JESUS the Emmanuel who was born of the Virgin
Mary, crucified under Pontius Pilate, raised from the
dead, and seated at the right hand of the majesty of God.

II. The object of this Lordship.

It is twofold : 1, His people, or church, comprising
all who believe on his name ; 2, All things for the sake
of his people.

1. His people. The right of God in them and over
them is delegated to Jesus Christ. " He shall reign
over the house of Jacob forever." Again, saith he in
his mediatorial prayer: " I have manifested thy name
unto the men which thou gavest me out of the world ;
thine they were, and thou gavest them me ; and they
have kept thy word : " and many other passages of the
same import.

2. We have already cited proofs that his power is
over all things ; and the apostle in Ephesians tells us
for what use this illimitable power is given : " That ye
may know . . . what is the exceeding greatness of
his power to usward who believe, according to the
working of his mighty power which he wrought in
Christ, when he raised him from the dead, and set him

at his own right hand in the heavenly places, far above all principality, and power, and might, and dominion, and every name that is named, not only in this world, but also in that which is to come; and hath put all things under his feet, and gave him to be the head over all things to the church, which is his body, the fulness of him that filleth all in all." In a word, his kingdom is over his people, and over all things, that he may secure their present and everlasting salvation, which includes a spiritual rule over their hearts and the administration of providence. Hence, his kingdom in this double sense is called his mediatorial kingdom; and the apostle speaks of it, when he says: "Giving thanks unto the Father, which hath made us meet to be partakers of the inheritance of the saints in light; who hath delivered us from the power of darkness, and hath translated us into the kingdom of his dear Son;" i. e. translated us into Christ's kingdom, that we by his gracious power be delivered from the power of darkness and be brought to a participation of the heavenly inheritance.

III. The right of this Lordship.

As it is not original but conferred, and conferred on Christ incarnate as the representative of servants, he can receive favor or privilege from God only as other creatures, who are servants of God; that is, as a reward of righteousness. The justice of God can allow it on no other principle. Indeed, it is on this moral necessity that the whole scheme of salvation by Christ proceeds — "to declare," as the apostle says, " his (God's) righteousness, that he might be just, and the justifier of him which believeth in Jesus." The righteousness required, therefore, is such a righteousness as is needed by those whom Christ represents, which is twofold: expiation of sin, and a meritorious obedience, both of which Christ offered unto God: the expiation in his death, the meritorious obedience in his honoring of the law by his whole life. Because of this perfect righteousness which, through the union of the divine nature with the human in which it was offered, is of infinite merit, the Father bestows the mediatorial kingdom or Lordship on Christ. "Being found in fashion as a man, he humbled himself and became obedient unto (until.) death; wherefore God also hath highly exalted him, and given him a name which is above every name," &c. Again: "Who (Jesus Christ) gave himself for us, that he might redeem us from all iniquity, and purify unto himself a peculiar people (*i. e.* a people belonging unto himself), zealous of good works." Again: "The righteousness of God which is by faith of Jesus Christ, unto all and upon all them that believe, . . . being justified freely by his grace, through the redemption that is in Christ Jesus." Christ has thus purchased for his own all that believe, and they bear his name stamped, as it were, upon them in token of their being secure in him of everlasting life. "In whom also," says the apostle, "after that ye believed, ye were sealed with that Holy Spirit of promise, which is the earnest of our inheritance until the redemption of the purchased possession, that we should be to the praise of his glory." Hence, throughout the New Testament, the title Lord is given only and emphatically to Jesus Christ; the Holy Ghost thus showing us, that now all the divine government in all things respecting the church is committed to him alone, as the only mediator between God and man.

Thus you have confirmed out of Scripture the doctrine of the Catechism, as to the reason why all true
Christians call Jesus Christ " our Lord ": " Because
he hath redeemed us, both soul and body, from all our
sins, not with gold or silver, but with his precious
blood, and hath delivered us from all the power of the
devil, and thus hath made us his own property."

INFERENCES.

First : The safety of all who believe in Christ.

The Son of God is their king.   Incarnate as our
elder brother, we know that he has a sympathy for
us ; appointed and accepted as our Redeemer, we know
that he has a right to save us ; bringing to his office all
the power and authority of his divine nature, we know
that he is able to save us.   Were he not man, we might
doubt his willingness ; were he not God, we might
doubt his ability ; but when we see in him God and
man, we may trust him while we adore.

Secondly ; The duty of all who believe in Christ.

To serve him as we would serve God, who has given
us to him ; to avow openly our allegiance to him before
the world, and to build up his kingdom as the divinely
ordained method of glorifying God in the redemption
of the world.

LECTURE XVI.

THE INCARNATION.

FOURTEENTH LORD'S DAY.

THE INCARNATION.

QUEST. XXXV. *What is the meaning of these words: " He was conceived of the Holy Ghost, born of the Virgin Mary?"*

ANS. That God's eternal Son, who is and continueth true and eternal God, took upon him the very nature of man, out of the flesh and blood of the Virgin Mary by the operation of the Holy Ghost: that he might also be the true seed of David, like unto his brethren in all things, sin excepted.

QUEST. XXXVI. *What profit dost thou receive by Christ's holy conception and nativity?*

ANS. That he is our Mediator; and with his innocence and perfect holiness covers in the sight of God my sins, wherein I was conceived and brought forth.

HAVING demonstrated the true and essential divinity of Jesus Christ, from the express declaration of Scripture that he is " the only begotten Son " of God ; and, also, his right to be honored by us as our Lord, in consequence of the delegated authority he has received from the Father to be Lord or head of the Church, and Lord or head over all things for the sake of the Church ; we now come to inquire how it is that we offer this divine homage and render this entire obedience to one who is presented before our faith in the form and substance of a man like ourselves: which leads us to consider the great mystery of

THE INCARNATION,

or the taking of human nature upon himself by the only begotten Son of God, or, as the Evangelist John

expresses it, his " being made flesh," or, as the apostle
Paul states it, his being " sent forth, made of a woman."
This incarnation was necessary for the fulfilment of
all prophecy, from the first promise that " the seed of
the woman should bruise the head of the serpent," to
the declaration of the last of the Old Testament writers, that " the *Lord*," the object of all godly faith and
desire, as " the messenger of the covenant," would personally " come into his temple."   It is necessary to the
truth of all the evangelical Scriptures, which set forth
Jesus of Nazareth as the Saviour in whom we are to
trust, and describe him with the perfections of eternal
God.   Hence the Church Catholic requires each of her
members to say : " I believe . . . . . in Jesus Christ,
his (God's) only begotten Son, our Lord, *who was conceived by the Holy Ghost, born of the Virgin Mary ;* " —
which is a declaration of our faith respecting the constitution of our Lord Jesus Christ's person after such a
manner that he was " God manifest in the flesh."   Our
lesson to-day expounds the meaning of these words, and
has two parts : The *first* asserting the fact of the incarnation (35th Question and Answer) ; the *second*
showing the reasons for the incarnation (36th Question and Answer) ; both of which we shall handle
as succinctly as the importance of the subject will
allow.

FIRST : *The fact of the Incarnation.*

" God's eternal Son, who is and continueth true and
eternal God, took upon him the very nature of man, out
of the flesh and blood of the Virgin Mary, by the operation of the Holy Ghost : that he might also be the
true seed of David like unto his brethren in all things,
sin excepted."

We derive our knowledge of the incarnation only from the word of God, who alone could reveal it; and we believe the great truth which it contains solely on divine testimony. The Scriptures which recite the glorious mystery, are so familiar to us, and so very many, that we need not quote them at full length; but may take out of them the principal particulars referred to by the Catechism in the place before us: and these we shall arrange under three propositions concerning our Lord Jesus Christ: I. He is truly man. II. He is truly God. III. He is both God and man in one. We say *is*, not *was;* for what our Lord became at his incarnation, he is now on the throne of his glory, and will continue to be forever.

I. He is truly man.

A man is compounded of a substantial body having certain physical qualities and faculties, and of a spiritual soul having will, understanding, and affections. So did our Lord become man.

1. As to his body. It was *substantial* — not a mere phantom or appearance of a body, but having all the qualities which distinguish substance from spirit. "Handle me and see," said he to his disciples after his resurrection; "for a spirit hath not flesh and bones as ye see me (or perceive me to) have."

It was a *human* body. Flesh is a term used generally for the substantial part of man. " The word became *flesh*," says the Evangelist; "Forasmuch as the children were partakers of flesh and blood, he also himself took part of the same." His glorified body has undergone that change which the apostle describes, when, in the xv. of 1 Corinthians, he speaks of the body which the believer will have after the resurrection; but his body, while he was on earth, was as truly human as ours are, and, if we be his people, ours will be glorified as his is now. " He," says the apostle in Philippians, " shall change our vile body, that it may be fashioned like unto his glorious body;" which could not be, if his body had not been first like ours. There was purity in our Saviour's body from the holy manner of its origin and his constitutional sinlessness, but, whether on earth or in heaven, it had and has all necessary human characteristics.

He was " born of a woman;" " the seed of the woman," according to the first promise; " made of a woman," as the apostle has it; " conceived in her," as the angel told Joseph; carried in her womb until " the days were accomplished that she should be delivered." The generative cause of the conception was miraculous from a divine energy : " conceived by the Holy Ghost," says the Creed, or, more properly rendered, *from* the Holy Ghost; " by the operation of the Holy Ghost " our Catechism explains it. " The Holy Ghost shall come upon thee, and the power of the Highest shall overshadow thee: therefore, also, that holy thing (creature) which shall be born of thee, shall be called the Son of God," is the declaration of the angel. The blessed Mary was a virgin; but all that a woman is to a child of which she is the mother, she was to our Lord's humanity; — not to his divine nature, for the Papists talk blasphemously when they call her the mother of God. The work of the Holy Ghost was threefold : in sanctifying the body of the Virgin for the purpose of our Lord's becoming flesh through her; in causing the conception, and in sanctifying the child : hence, the purity and sinlessness of our Lord's human-

ity, for he was not conceived in sin and brought forth
in iniquity, as we are ; hence, also, his freedom from
the moral connection which all others born of woman
have with the first Adam's apostasy. But in all other
respects, Christ derived his body as we have derived
ours.

The papists have many idle and preposterous fables
about the incarnation ; and a little while ago a council
of their bishops met to determine that the Virgin Mary
herself was conceived without sin, which would seem
also to require that her mother was as immaculately
born, and so backward to the first mother : but the
scriptural doctrine is, that the sanctification of Mary for
her maternal office was at the time of her conception
from the Holy Ghost. We reject with horror all the
profane inventions of a miserable idolatry, but we
should receive with adoring faith all that the divine
word teaches of the manner in which Jesus Christ is
truly human ; and how nobly does the sacred narrative
exalt the character of maternity above the disgraces of
the fall ! How absurd are the honors which the papists,
imitating Gnostic follies, would throw around a celibate
state ! If God chose a virgin to exalt her, the exaltation he conferred was making her a mother ! It could
be the privilege of but one woman to bear our Elder
Brother ; yet blessed are all those women whose maternal faith consecrates their offspring to be the sons and
daughters of the Lord Almighty, immortal heirs of his
heavenly kingdom !

2. Our Lord derived his human *soul* in the same
manner (mysterious beyond all guess at explanation)
that every man derives his soul with his body. All
further question is idle, for it would be prying into

what God has not revealed. But it were grave heresy to suppose that our Lord had not a human soul as truly as he had a human body; for without either he would not have been man. He needed to be made like unto his brethren in all things, "that he might be a merciful and faithful high priest, in things pertaining to God."

3. The history of our Lord after his birth confirms the truth of his full humanity. He was nourished as a babe at the breast. He increased in stature, from the weakness that needed the swaddling bands, and the support of his mother's arms. He went up as a Jewish lad when twelve years old to keep the Passover at Jerusalem, and afterwards passed through youth to the adult stature of man. He saw, he heard, he felt, he spake, he walked. He hungered, and eat; he was thirsty, and drank. He was weary, and he rested. When night came, he slept; and (oh, blessed proof of human sympathy!) he wept. He suffered extreme agony, sweating "great drops of blood," and, wrung with mortal anguish upon the cross to which his blessed hands were nailed and his feet bound, his meek brow bleeding under the thorns, his dear side pierced to his heart by the cursed spear, he died, breathing out his soul, was laid in a tomb, and the spices were prepared for his embalmment.

He thought as a man. He was taught and grew " in wisdom " and " in favor with God and man." He performed the moral duties of a man ; witness, his obedience to his mother and to Joseph her husband, to the Jewish authorities, to Cæsar, and to God. He loved as a son, and as a friend, and as a patriot. He was full of human sympathies ; pitying the poor, the diseased, and the sorrowful. He took little children up in

his arms; he was grateful for friendly kindness, and at
the grave of his friend he groaned in spirit, being
troubled. He prayed " with strong crying and tears."
He devoted himself with most intelligent and hearty
zeal to do the will of his Father. He " learned obedience by the things which he suffered." " For we have
not an high priest which cannot be touched with the
feeling of our infirmities ; but was in all points tempted
like as we are, yet without sin."

Yes! he was *pure*. The seed of the woman, conceived of the Holy Ghost, he fell not in Adam. Born
of a woman, yet begotten of God, he was our fellow-
man but not our fellow-sinner. Sanctified by the Holy
Ghost from the womb, " he did no sin, neither was
guile found in his mouth," but he was " holy, harmless,
undefiled, and separate from sinners." His holy soul
ruled the infirmities of his body, and he was " as a
lamb without blemish, and without spot."

Thus was he truly man : " the son of man," " the seed
of David ; " " the man Christ Jesus ; " " the man approved of God ; " " that man whom he hath ordained,"
" the second Adam." The perfect humanity of Jesus
Christ is an essential article of the Christian creed ; for
our Lord himself hath said : " Except ye eat my flesh
and drink my blood " (*i. e.* receive the doctrines of my
incarnation and atonement), " ye have no life in you."

II. He is truly God.

This we have already sufficiently proved in our exposition of several sections, but especially the last, when
we showed that the Son whom God the Father sent
into the world to be made of a woman, is the only begotten Son of God ; by which phrase we can understand
nothing else than that he is truly and essentially of the

same nature as his Father.   The same " Word " which
was God in the beginning, " became flesh and dwelt
among us," says the Evangelist; " and we beheld his
glory, the glory as of the only begotten of the Father,
full of grace and truth."   If, therefore, he was God
before his incarnation, he must continue to be God after
his incarnation; that is, God is essentially eternal, and
the only begotten Son of God must be God from everlasting to everlasting.   Thus the Evangelist applies to
the incarnation the very distinct prophecy of Isaiah :
" Behold, a virgin shall be with child, and shall bring
forth a son, and they shall call his name Emmanuel,
which, being interpreted, is, God with us."   So St.
Paul also : " Who, being in the form of God, . . . took
upon him the form of a servant and was made in the
likeness of men."   So the apostle again : " Great is
the mystery of godliness : God manifest in the flesh."
So also the Catechism : " God's eternal Son, who is
and continueth true and eternal God, took upon him
the very nature of man."   We may then pass on to
our remaining proposition : —

III.   He is God and man in one person.

God the Son *dwelt* in the man Christ Jesus.   The
Word became flesh and dwelt among us ; or, more literally, tabernacled among us.   He took the humanity,
so miraculously prepared, for a tent, a habitation, a
covering under which he humbled himself, radiating
his divine glory through it as the mediator between
God and man.   The writer to the Hebrews calls it the
vail of his divinity : " The rent vail, that is to say, his
flesh."   " For in him dwelleth all the fulness of the
Godhead bodily."   He entered the flesh within the
Virgin Mary, for the " holy thing which was born of

her is called the Son of God." Nor was this dwelling
only in his body, but in the man Christ Jesus, soul and
body; in the mind, the affections, and the will of the
holy man, using the spiritual as well as the physical
faculties of the humanity: for the human obedience,
active and passive, which he came in the flesh to render acceptable, because infinitely meritorious, was of
the soul as well as of the body.

But it was more than a mere indwelling, such as that
of the Holy Ghost in every believer. "The Word was
made flesh." The passive verb is there used to indicate the concurrent action of the Father, who sent his
only begotten, and of the Holy Ghost, who overshadowed the Virgin with the third person of the ever-
blessed Trinity (Glory be to the Father, and to the Son,
and to the Holy Ghost!), and of the Son, who, of his own
personal will and by his own personal act, came into the
world as the seed of the woman. "He took upon him
the form of a servant." "Forasmuch as the children
are partakers of flesh and blood, he also himself likewise took part of the same," *i. e.* participated in our
human nature. Here, in the word *took*, we have the
nearest approach we can have to an explanation of the
manner after which the divine and human natures of
our Lord were united. He took the human nature to
his own divine nature. The human nature — body and
soul — in all its parts, qualities, faculties, and functions,
physical and spiritual, became his, his own; not in essence but in relation, by assumption and adjunction.
Hence, the pains of the man, his sorrows, his very
death, became, as the language of many scriptures asserts, the pains, the sorrows and death of our Lord Jesus Christ. He is truly man as he is truly God. His

divinity was not transformed into humanity; he is still
God. The humanity was not transformed into divinity:
he is still man. The divinity was not commixt with
the humanity, nor the humanity with the divinity, else
he would be neither God nor man. He is both God
and man. The divinity was not made less, for infinite-
ness is essential to it; the humanity is not made more,
for finiteness is essential to it. He is entitled to all the
divine attributes while he disowns nothing that is human except sin. He is the only begotten Son of God,
yet our brother. The human nature is adjoined to the
divine. He is our Lord Jesus Christ, the incarnate
God, God manifest in the flesh; Emmanuel, God with
us. God, yet man; man, yet God: the God distinct
from the man; the man distinct from the God: else
God would have been a sufferer, or the works of the
man been finite in merit. Yet, we repeat, the humanity is so united to the divinity that he is one Lord Jesus
Christ. This perfect union is described by theologians,
for want of a better term, as in one *person;* that is,
one individual. The divinity so pervades, sanctifies,
and renders meritorious the nature, obedience, and sufferings of the man, that the Father accepts them and
we rely upon them as the one infinitely worthy atonement of our Lord Jesus Christ. Objections have been
made by those who deny our Lord's personal divinity,
to this use of the word person, and, did we use it in its
ordinary sense, the objection would be plausible; but the
singular, anomalous nature of the case warrants us in
using a term, when we have no other, according to our
definition of it: which is that oneness that constitutes
the two natures of Christ, as one agent or representative for us with the Father.

Other questions which may be here suggested have been treated, or will be elsewhere, in our expositions of the Catechism; and we wish to add only that it is important for our understanding of the true catholic doctrine to remember the precise conditions which have been specified. Thus Hooker, whom theologians worthily call the judicious, says that "in four words we may fully, by way of abridgment, comprise whatsoever antiquity hath at large handled" respecting the person of our Lord, "either in declaration of Christian belief, or in refutation of heresies, viz: truly, perfectly, indivisibly, distinctly. Truly, as to his being God; perfectly, as to his being man; indivisibly, as to his being of both one; distinctly, as to his continuing both in that one." Indeed, it should be noted that the first four and greatest councils of the church were called to define and establish the catholic doctrine on these several points: the Council of Nice, to condemn the Arians, who denied the proper divinity of Christ; the (first) Council of Constantinople, to condemn the Apolinarians, who attacked the proper humanity of Christ; the Council of Ephesus, to condemn the Nestorians, whose leader, Nestorius, was wrongfully charged with asserting that there were two persons in Christ; and the Council of Chalcedon, to condemn the Eutychians, who confounded the two natures of Christ. All these heresies are full of mischiefs, and, therefore, our pastors should imitate the ancient church in guarding the people against them.

SECONDLY : *The reasons for the Incarnation.*

QUEST. 36. *What profit dost thou receive by Christ's holy conception and nativity?*

ANS. That he is our Mediator, and with his innocence and perfect holiness covers in the sight of God my sins, in which I was conceived and brought forth.

These heads of doctrine have been already treated of in our lecture on the lesson for the Sixth Lord's Day, but a brief review of them may not be unprofitable.

The incarnation was necessary,

I. To establish an intercourse between God and man.

The sinner convinced of his guilt would not dare to approach God, whom he had offended, and whose wrath he knows himself to have incurred. Whence we find those of God's servants to whom he had manifested himself, trembling with fear, and becoming as dead men. It is the difficulty which Job felt when he exclaimed : " If I wash myself with snow-water, and make my hands never so clean, yet shalt thou plunge me in the ditch, and mine own clothes shall abhor me ; for he is not a man as I am, that I should answer him, and we should come together in judgment. Neither is there any daysman betwixt us, that might lay his hand upon us both. Let him take away his rod from me, and let not his fear terrify me : then would I speak and not fear him ; but it is not so with me." The proposition of a reconcilement must, therefore, come from God to man. On the other hand, God in his holiness cannot approach the sinner and not destroy him. " Thou art of purer eyes than to behold evil, and canst not look upon iniquity," says Habakkuk. There must, therefore, be an intervention of some pure medium between holy God and sinful man ; one equal with God, yet equal with man, who may put his hand upon both ; and that Mediator is found in the constitution of Christ as Emmanuel, God-man. In him we behold God united to humanity, but a humanity sinless ;

humanity united to God, but to God in loving-kindness
and tender mercy. God looks well pleased on man
represented by his incarnate only begotten; man looks
with penitent confidence on God represented to him by
his elder brother. As God, the blessed Christ enters
into the wisdom of God and is his Counsellor; as man,
he assures the believer of his kindred and is his Redeemer. Christ for us hath by his atoning merit taken
away the rod of his Father's wrath; and now, having
passed into the heavens for us, his flesh once torn on
the cross becomes a new and living way which he has
consecrated for us, by which we have access with boldness unto God, even on his throne. Christ is the reality of that ladder which Jacob saw, whose top rested
on heaven while it was set on earth, by which our
prayers ascend to God, and the blessings of God descend to us.

II. To make a sufficient ground of our reconciliation
with God.

Whatever be the merciful purpose of God towards
the sinner, he must be just; and God, not laying aside
his justice, yet bent upon mercy, provides a method by
which his violated law is magnified, yet his grace vindicated from reproach; and that method is the substitution of the Emmanuel to expiate our guilt and provide a righteousness on the credit of which we may be
rewarded. " He made him to be sin for us who knew
no sin, that we might be made the righteousness of God
in him." It was necessary that this substitute should be
divine, for every creature is himself subject to God,
and requires all his powers to discharge his own duty.
It was necessary that he should be in the form of a servant, for God himself cannot be under his own law.

It was necessary that he should be a man, because man was the sinner to be redeemed; that he should magnify the law given to man, because that was the law which had been dishonored; that the law should be magnified on earth, because it was given to rule man in this life. It was necessary that the penalty of the law should be endured in the nature of man, and in the sphere of his rebellion, because here the curse had passed upon human nature. But it was necessary that an infinite merit should be communicated to the obedience and sufferings of the substitute in human nature; and so the divinity in the humanity pervaded the actions of Christ, honoring the law infinitely more than the obedience or eternal punishment of a whole world.

III. To sustain man in his weakness.

With the wrath of God have come on man a thousand woes. The natural, as well as the penal, consequence of sin, is death, with all its precursive evils and all its following torment. Bitter is the cup which time presses on every human life. Without some strong sustaining power man would sink under his calamities. The child of God, even while he looks forward to heaven, is not relieved from his pains and sorrows. Still the body of sin and death is around his spirit. Still he lives in a fallen, faded, polluted, and hostile world. Still he must meet the malice of the Satanic tempter and the contradiction of sinners. Grace has, indeed, made a blessed change. Afflictions are to him no longer evidence of divine wrath, but proofs of a father's care to chasten him for heaven. Yet he must be assured of this blessing and be upheld, for his flesh is weak, though his spirit be willing. And this is given in the person and sorrows of Christ, who was tried

with all our temptations, whose heart bled in all our
griefs, who shuddered under the deep shadows of his
Father's wrath, and poured out his soul amidst the anguish of a cruel death.   He himself learned obedience
by the things that he suffered ; and now on the throne
of his glory, he knows how to succor them that are
tempted ; and, while he assures the believer of his human sympathy, he assures him also of the same divine
strength that sustained him under the griefs and difficulties that we are passing through.   With what strong
consolation is the Christian met as he flies for refuge to
the hope set before him, and sees the great sufferer on
the right hand of God ; the crown of universal glory
on the brow yet scarred with thorns, and the hand
pierced by the nail holding forth to him the sceptre, that
he may touch it and live forever.   Looking unto Jesus,
the author and finisher of our faith, who, for the joy
that was set before him, endured the cross, despising the
shame, he lays aside every weight and the sin that so
easily besets him, and runs with patience the race set
before him.   Nothing short of this can sustain and
cheer and make us victorious.   Oh, the life of my life
will go out unless I can see my nature in him sustained
by the divine strength I need ; unless I can see the same
hand that wipes away my tears wiping away his own ;
unless I can trace his footsteps down into the dark valley and know, however painful my path may be, that
he has trodden it before me, and now waits to welcome me to his joy when I have drunk the cup which
he drank for me.

IV. To elevate our fallen nature.

"We are all *by nature* the children of wrath." Cavil
at it, modify it as men will, there is no getting over the

fact that in Adam our nature was cast down from its pristine dignity to shame and dust. " By man sin entered into the world, and death by sin." By man must that nature be raised from the dust, and its dignity restored. The second Adam must repair the ruins of the first, and, in the Son of Man, the Lord from heaven, we see all that we have lost more than restored and secured to us by a covenant never to be broken because its surety cannot fail ; nay, which has already fulfilled all its conditions. By man we lost the image of God, his presence and communion. In Christ we behold God again dwelling in man, and offering to us fellowship with the Father and with himself. By man we lost the empire God gave him over all things here ; in Christ we behold man head over all things to his church. In man, we fell under the tyranny of death and him that hath the power of death ; in Christ, we behold the seed of the woman bruising the head of the serpent, and, having conquered death and hell in the enemy's own dominions, dragging them bound to his chariot-wheels, and making ostentation of his spoils, openly triumphing. O Death, where is thy sting, when thou comest as a radiant angel to call us home ; when every cord of flesh thou dost rend is but the parting of another stay that binds the aspiring soul to earth ; when thy severest agonies are but the wrenching of fetters from our wings ! O Grave, where is thy victory, when, through the tomb which Jesus has broken for us, we pass to the holy, glorious heavens ! There, the second Adam has entered the second paradise ; and there, when the resurrection shall change our vile body to be like his glorious body, shall our entire humanity be pure, sinless, innocent, and blessed forevermore ;

but oh, with what greater bliss when we walk amidst
the garden of delights, not alone, as Adam walked at
first, or as afterwards with but one to second his praise;
but in fellowship with an innumerable company of
saints and angels plucking freely of the tree of life,
and drinking of the river of God's pleasures that flows
from out the throne of God and the Lamb! And the
bliss shall be eternal: for sin can never enter there,
because the second Adam is the Son of God who cannot die; because he has died on the cross and now liveth forevermore.

Great is our confidence, because we believe in the
Lord Jesus Christ, the only begotten Son of God, who
was conceived of the Holy Ghost and born of the Virgin Mary.

LECTURE XVII.

CHRIST'S SUFFERING AND CROSS.

CHRIST'S SUFFERING AND CROSS.

QUEST. XXXVII. *What dost thou understand by the words:* HE SUF-
FERED?

ANS. That he all the time that he lived on earth, but especially at the
end of his life, sustained in body and soul the wrath of God against
the sins of all mankind; that so, by his passion, as the only propitiatory sacrifice, he might redeem our body and soul from everlasting
damnation, and obtain for us the favor of God, righteousness, and
eternal life.

QUEST. XXXVIII. *Why did he suffer under Pontius Pilate as his judge?*

ANS. That he, being innocent and yet condemned by a temporal judge,
might thereby free us from the severe judgment of God to which we
were exposed.

QUEST. XXXIX. *Is there anything more in his being crucified than if he
had died some other death?*

ANS. Yes, there is; for thereby I am assured that he took on him the
curse which lay upon me; for the death of the cross was accursed of
God.

THE doctrine held by the reformed churches, according to the word of God, respecting the propitiatory
and vicarious nature of our Lord's sufferings, has necessarily been handled at large in our comments on several previous lessons, especially on those for the Fourth,
Fifth, and Sixth Lord's days; and, therefore, it is not
requisite, that, in studying the article of the creed before us, we should do more than consider such particulars in it as have not been already treated of.

"I believe . . . in Jesus Christ our Lord, . . who . .
suffered under Pontius Pilate, was crucified, dead and
buried."

The *death* and *burial* of our Lord are reserved for

the next lesson; and we are now to learn: What is meant by his *suffering;* Why it is stated that he suffered *under Pontius Pilate;* and the reason for his suffering *on the cross.*

First: What do we understand by the words: *He suffered?*

The Catechism tells us in the Thirty-seventh Answer, which has just been read in our hearing.

Here are several things to be noted: the purpose of his sufferings; the cause of his sufferings; and the duration of his sufferings.

I. The *purpose* of our Lord's suffering.

"By one man sin entered into the world, and death by sin, and so death passed upon all men, for that all have sinned." That is the history of our ruin. The sentence which fell upon our first parent has fallen upon us all, for like him we all have sinned. That sentence is death: "In the day thou eatest thereof, thou shalt surely die." Death is the mode and execution of divine wrath against the sinner; but it means more than the separation of soul from body, which we ordinarily call death. It is such an infliction of divine punishment as turns the life of man, which God originally meant for happiness in the enjoyment of divine favor, to utter misery; and, as man sins in bodily acts consequent upon the will of his spiritual nature, and as the sentence is upon the whole man, both his soul and his body are under the curse. The misery of man is not at once extreme, because, instantly with his ruin, began the working of the remedial scheme by which the full execution of the sentence was delayed, that the sinner might have opportunity of repentance through faith in the redemption. Our first parents did not die, that is, their mortal life did not end, the moment that the sentence was incurred; but they at once began to die : their life was thenceforward a fatal disease until it terminated in the mortal agony, and then, had not the curse been averted by the redemption, they would have gone into everlasting, utter misery. So with us. We are born to die. Death meets us at the beginning of life, and we are dying all through our days on earth till we go to our graves; and then, if not saved by Christ, we must go to endure the never-ceasing agonies of eternal death.

But the purpose of God in Christ is to redeem us from death through the consecration of Christ to die in our stead, that so the penalty, being transferred to him, might no longer rest upon us who accept the grace. As the apostle says: " The righteousness of God [is manifested] which is by faith unto all and upon all them that believe, being justified freely by his grace through the redemption that is in Christ Jesus : whom God hath set forth to be a propitiation, through faith in his blood, to declare his righteousness for the remission of sins that are past, through the forbearance of God; to declare, I say, at this time his righteousness : that he might be just and the justifier of him which believeth in Jesus." On no other ground but the substitution of Christ to endure the penalty for us could the mercy of God to us be justified, and only through his suffering can we escape eternal death. So, also, on no other ground can be justified the suffering of the innocent Jesus when he was abandoned by God the Father, whose word is pledged for the reward of righteousness, to the malice of wicked men, the ignominy of crucifixion, and the curse of the violated law.

II. The *cause* of our Lord's sufferings.

The substitution of Christ for sinners exposed him to the wrath of God against sinners, and, as that divine wrath is manifested in the sufferings which are the punishment of sin, so, as the Catechism teaches us, the cause of Christ's sufferings could be nothing else than the wrath of God laying upon him the punishment which we deserve. There can be no suffering but that which proceeds from the wrath of God against sin. Yet the wrath of God was not against our Lord personally, because he was without sin; but against the sinners whom he represented. It was as if, when the bolts of divine vengeance were launched against sinners, our Lord put himself before them, sheltering them with his own person and receiving them on his own body and soul. He himself was, and continued to be, throughout the whole of his sufferings, the beloved of the Father; and it was because he was the beloved of the Father that his sufferings had their great merit of propitiation. Thus the prophet: " We did esteem him stricken, smitten of God, and afflicted; but he was wounded for our transgressions; he was bruised for our iniquities; . . . he had done no violence, neither was any deceit to be found in his mouth; yet it pleased the Lord to bruise him; he hath put him to grief." . . . " He shall see of the travail of his soul, and be satisfied; by his knowledge (*i. e.* knowledge of him or faith in him) shall my righteous servant justify many, for he shall bear their iniquities. Therefore will I divide him a portion with the great, and he shall divide the spoil with the strong; because he hath poured out his soul unto death, and he was numbered with the transgressors, and he bare the sin of many, and made intercession for the transgressors." Or as the apostle expresses it: " For he hath made him to be sin for us, who knew no sin, that we might be made the righteousness of God in him." And again: " Christ hath redeemed us from the curse of the law, being made a curse for us; for it is written, ' Cursed is every one that hangeth on a tree: ' " which is equivalent to saying that, by his crucifixion, he bore the curse which we deserved, in our stead.

It follows, also, that the sufferings of Christ were of his whole human nature, or " both of his body and soul," as the Catechism has it. The sentence upon man because of his sin, is upon both his body and soul. Nay, as the body, not being itself of a moral nature, cannot sin except as it is the instrument of the soul, the suffering of the body has no other end or reason but the affliction of the soul; and, as we see in human suffering on earth, but as will be fearfully more apparent in the place of torment, the soul is and must be the great sufferer, not only from its sympathy with the body, but in the anguish of its own spiritual remorse and bitter grief. It is possible, as many a martyrdom or natural death-bed has shown, for a Christian to forget the keenest anguish of body in the joyful elevation of his spirit; but there is no escape from the internal anguish of the soul itself. So, during the interval between death and the resurrection, while the bodies of the wicked are senseless dust, their spirits are in torment; — though their torments will be fearfully aggravated when, their bodies being raised, their spirits are tormented through corporeal sufferings. Hence, as is manifest from many passages, our Lord suffered not only in the pains of his flesh, but far more in the agonies of his spirit. " He was a man of sorrows and acquainted with grief." " Now," said he, " is my soul troubled; " and again : " My soul is exceeding sorrowful, even unto death." The Saviour was sinless; but all the distress that sin could bring upon the soul of one, who, not conscious of personal guilt, stood in the room of the guilty, he felt; the sense of horror from the contact of sins laid upon him, the anguish consequent upon the withdrawal of his Father's countenance, the humiliating weight of the curse, the shrinking which the living feel from an ignominious, cruel death, — all were his. These were the causes of that fearful, indescribable agony in the garden; these filled to the brim that cup which he shuddered over before he could drink it, when, as yet, not a hand had been laid upon him, and the physical torture of the cross was in anticipation; and these wrung out of his meek heart that exceedingly bitter cry, " My God! My God! why hast thou forsaken me ? "

But our Lord stood not in the room of a single sinner; he bare the sins of many; and heaven, opened to us by the vision of John, shows a mighty host redeemed unto God by his blood. Hence his sufferings were incalculably more than the sufferings of any one mere man could have been. For, though we, unhesitatingly, and not without horror, reject the idea that his sufferings were weighed out to him in exact proportion to the sufferings which every individual of all he redeemed would otherwise have actually suffered, we must see that they needed to be so great as to justify God in taking away his wrath from all the Saviour's people. It was, among other reasons, for the purpose of strengthening our Lord's humanity to endure this

accumulated aggregation of suffering, that it was constituted in union with the divine nature, which also
gave to his sufferings their infinite value.   So the
Catechism says, that "he sustained the wrath of God
against the sins of all mankind."

This last sentence requires some little explanation
lest its meaning should be misunderstood; and we shall
give it conformably to the comments of the learned and
pious Ursinus, the author of the Catechism, and, therefore, the best expositor of its sense.   The idea of the
sentence is that of several scriptures: as where our
Lord declares that "God so loved the world" as to
give his only begotten Son; and the writer to the
Hebrews, that Christ "tasted death for every man;"
and Paul, that "he gave himself a ransom for all;" and
John, "that he is a propitiation for our sins, and not for
ours only, but also for the sins of the whole world."
Yet Scripture must be read in harmony with itself;
and, as we know that all men are not actually saved,
but only those who, through grace, being ordained to
eternal life, do believe and repent; it cannot be that
our Lord bore the wrath of God against the sins of the
whole world in the same sense or degree that he bore
it in the room of his people.   They were actually redeemed by his blood, he having taken the penalty they
deserved on himself, so that their salvation was certainly secured by his vicarious satisfaction; but the rest
of mankind, though they have, so far as the gospel is
preached to them, opportunities of salvation, are condemned to death eternal, without violence being done
to the covenant of the Son with the Father, in the
plan of salvation.

Thus Christ died for all mankind, because in him

the blessings of salvation are not confined as were those
of the Abrahamic dispensation, to one particular people.   The Gospel is sent throughout all the world to
be preached to every creature; and whosoever will, be
he a Jew or Gentile, may take of the water of life
freely.   And again: The merit of our Lord's sufferings, through the union of his human to his divine
nature, is infinite; displaying the wrath of God against
the sins of the whole world, and so justifying the offer
of divine mercy to every sinner that believes on his
name.   As several of the later fathers, following Ter-
tullian, phrase it: " His merits are sufficient for all; but
efficient for the elect;" and Aquinas, whom the Papists
call "the Angelical Doctor," teaches: "The merit of
Christ as concerns its sufficiency equally belongeth to
all men; but as to its efficacy, . . . the effects and
fruits of it are mercifully bestowed on some, and, by the
just judgment of God, withheld from others."   Nor
can this be otherwise, since it were preposterous to
make Christ the substitute of those that refuse his representation.   But it is, on the other hand, positively true
that the benefits of Christ's merit do actually, though
not in a saving degree, extend to all men: because, for
the sake of Christ, all temporal mercies come to all,
and the world is kept by his intercession from becoming
a hell of extreme torture and despair; and very precious blessings, though not the most precious, are bestowed on mankind through the restraining influence
of Christianity and the light which it sheds on every
mind wherever the healing beams of the Sun of Righteousness shine.   It is enough for us to know that, if we
believe in Christ with our whole heart, his merit will
certainly save us; but, if we refuse the grace he offers,

not all the mercy of God in Christ warrants the slightest hope of escape from everlasting death.

III. The duration of our Lord's sufferings.

On this particular we need not greatly enlarge; for, as we have already shown that the penalty of death which was inflicted on men was not merely the mortal agony of the dissolution of soul and body, but all the evil consequent upon our mortality, which is, in the language of our Church, " a continual death," or, as we expressed it, a long mortal disease of which what we ordinarily call death is the critical symptom, it was necessary that the imputed death should come upon our Lord at the very moment of his life's beginning. All his life on earth, he was stricken, smitten of God, and afflicted. His spirit was under the shadows which preceded the utter darkness of the cross, and, learning obedience through the things which he suffered, he became our sympathizing Saviour, and knows how to succor us who are tempted, that we may overcome the world, and, notwithstanding our manifold tribulation, enter into the kingdom of God. All his precursive suffering would not have been enough (as we shall hereafter learn) without the consummation of his death on the cross; but, had he not suffered from his manger to his giving up his spirit on the cross, he would not have suffered the death we deserve to die, nor have secured for us the grace by which alone we may " live unto God " while " we die daily."

SECONDLY: *Why is it stated that he suffered under Pontius Pilate?*

The main reason, doubtless, for the insertion of this man's name here, was that the date of our Lord's suffering on the cross might be precisely fixed. The several gospels repeatedly speak of Pontius Pilate as the Roman officer, or procurator, charged by the emperor with the government of Judea at the time of which they write. Luke, the evangelist, had before said that Pontius Pilate was governor of Judea when the Baptist began to preach. Now we know from other histories that Pilate was removed from his procuratorship just before the death of Tiberius, and after he had exercised his government ten years. This fixes the period of his administration between A. D. 25 and 35, which corresponds with all reasonable accuracy to the sacred chronology,* and proves that our Lord was crucified in the fifteenth year of the reign of Tiberius. Justin Martyr, in his Apology (or defence) for Christianity, about the beginning of the second century, boldly appeals to the record of the acts of Pontius Pilate, then, like the reports of all governors, on file at Rome, for the truth of the facts respecting the passion of our Lord. There is also a remarkable passage found in some editions of the Jewish History by Josephus, which speaks of an extraordinary person, well known by the name of Christ, who taught new and extraordinary doctrines, and wrought miracles, and persuaded many people to follow his opinions, who were called after him Christians ; but, being brought before Pilate by impeachment of the principal Jews, he was crucified. Yet his followers did not desist, but claimed through their preachers to have seen him alive three days after his death. The passage has, however, been thought by many, though not all, learned men to have been a forged interpolation of the text of Josephus, and, therefore, we need not insist upon citing it as cor-

---

* See Lardner, Cred. Gos. His., vol. i. b. ii. c. 2.

roboratory proof. My own opinion is that the passage is genuine; but modesty may well prevent me from urging it when Lardner is against it. But there is a passage in the Annals of Tacitus which cannot be impeached, and states that "Nero persecuted with exquisite torments a sect of men commonly called Christians, — called so from Christus, who in the reign of Tiberius was executed under Pontius Pilate, the procurator of Judea." There are other highly convincing testimonies of writers not Christian; but these may suffice to show the reason for this sentence in the Creed.

It is proper, however, from deference to the teaching of the Catechism, and for our greater edification, that we note here several important truths connected with our Lord's suffering under Pontius Pilate.

1. It coincides with prophecy. For, —

a. Shiloh could not come until the sceptre had departed from Judah; which was not the case until after the death of Herod the Great, and the appointment of a Roman governor over Judea as a conquered province. Hence the Jews, by appealing to Pilate, acknowledged their lack of authority.

b. The Jews, and the Romans, now the masters of the world, may be said to have comprehended all mankind; and our Lord was " to be despised and rejected of men : " not of the Jews only, but of men generally. So the Psalmist : " Why do the heathen rage, and the people imagine a vain thing ? The kings of the earth set themselves, and the rulers take counsel together against the Lord and his anointed ; " and the company of believers after the Pentecost interpret " the people " as the people of Israel (Acts iv. 27), and, following the same view, we may suppose that by " the rulers" are meant the rulers of the Jews, who united with the Roman authorities in the execution of Christ, or the Lord's anointed ; as Jesus himself had told his disciples : " The Son of man shall be betrayed unto the chief priests and unto the scribes, and they shall condemn him to death ; and shall deliver him to the Gentiles to mock, and to scourge, and to crucify him."

c. It was necessary also that he should " be taken from prison and from judgment." So was he imprisoned and put to death under the double sentence of the Jewish Sanhedrim and the Roman governor.

d. It was distinctly foretold that the Messiah should bear the curse by hanging on a tree ; but, as we shall presently see, crucifixion was a mode of punishment never used by the Jews, who, if they had executed the Saviour, would have stoned him to death, — the punishment of blasphemy by their law.

2. There was a most fitting significance, as the Catechism says, in his being, " though innocent, condemned by a temporal judge that he might free us from the severe judgment of God to which we were exposed." We see him, the just, crucified as the unjust. His innocence is acknowledged. Pilate's wife from her miraculous dream, the penitent thief by his side, the centurion who glorified God after his death, and all the people that stood beholding and smote their breasts, but especially Pilate himself, in explicit and repeated declarations, testified his innocence : yet was he nevertheless condemned and crucified under the will of God, acting through the hands of ostensible authority. So may we, as we look upon the sufferer, see him taking our place, bearing our condemnation, and dying, not

himself guilty, the death which we deserved. Nor should we overlook the strong consolation that, though the world may unjustly reproach, condemn, and persecute his people for his sake, all its malice is of little account, so that we are able, through faith in his guiltless sufferings, to have the pardon and favor of God his Father. God may chasten the Christian even by the hands of his enemies, but will not forsake him or suffer him to be overwhelmed. Nay, though he slay us we may yet trust in him.

THIRDLY : *The reason for our Lord's suffering on the cross.*

" Thereby," says the Catechism, " I am assured that he took on him the curse which lay upon me, for the death of the cross was accursed of God."

This is in agreement with the apostle (Galatians iii. 13) : " Christ hath redeemed us from the curse of the law, being made a curse for us ; for it is written, Cursed is every one that hangeth on a tree." Let us, however, for greater explicitness, consider first the nature of crucifixion, and then the reasons why our Lord was put to death in that manner.

1. The nature of crucifixion.

It was probably a most ancient mode of punishment : for nothing was more natural than that men, determined to execute a criminal or an enemy, should, if they refused him the mercy of the sword, hang him on the nearest tree ; and this especially when they meant to make him a spectacle of ignominy, vengeance, or warning. Examples of this are frequent among all people. When, however, they desired to protract the agonies of the victim, they would fasten him upon the tree to perish with pain and hunger. The tree would afford an opportunity for this by its forked or transverse branches : hence, one of the Latin terms for such an instrument of torture was *furca*, or fork, like the letter Y ; and another, *patibulum*, (from *patere*, *quasi* to stretch apart,) which would seem to intend the crosspiece to the perpendicular, forming the letter T. In process of time the cross came to be artificially constructed of two beams in this last form, or, sometimes, though at a much later period, like the letter X. The Jews, as we learn from several passages, used to hang persons convicted of certain crimes on a tree, as criminals among us are hung by the neck on a gallows ; but their law did not allow them to protract their sufferings, nor to leave the bodies hanging after sunset. Among the Greeks, and, especially, the Romans, crucifixion was common, but was ever considered the most disgraceful and extreme mode of punishment, — being awarded only to slaves and the worst malefactors, though sometimes to their barbarian captives, whom they considered as slaves.

When a person was condemned to the cross, the command of the magistrate to the executioner was : "Go ; bind his hands, scourge him, cover his head, hang him on the unhappy tree." Scourging in every case preceded the crucifixion. It would seem, also, that the convict was made to bear his cross to the place of punishment. When there, in some cases the cross was first laid along on the ground, and the man so bound to it that it might be lifted with him and fixed uprightly ; or the cross was first erected, and he, being seated on a bar projecting at a proper height,* was then fastened upon it : which was done by driving strong spikes

---

* *Sedilis excessu*. Tertull. adv. nationes, LII.

through the palms of the hands, the arms being stretched out on the transverse beam, and by a spike driven through both feet, or one through each foot. Some have doubted whether or not our Lord's feet were nailed to the cross; but the prophecy is explicit: " They pierced my hands and my feet." (Ps. xxii. 16.) The limbs were, however, most probably, bound with cords, as else the weight of the body would have torn it off at the nails. No vital part being touched, the wretched sufferer would hang often for days,* until he expired from the mingled agonies of shame, hunger, thirst, and pain. The anguish of crucifixion (from which we derive our term, *excruciating*) must have been, physiologists tell us, very great. Cicero, in his impeachment of Verres, who had crucified a Roman citizen, calls it " the most cruel and terrible " of all punishments, which " no man should see, or hear, or even think of." The great nails were driven through the parts of the hands and feet abounding in nerves and tendons; the arms being stretched back and apart made the slightest motion aggravate the pain; the action of the air on the open wounds, increased it, by inflammation, yet more ; and, besides, the blood was necessarily forced in unnatural quantity on the brain and the stomach, which itself would cause intolerable torment. To this physical torture must be added, what to a pure, noble spirit would be far more poignant, a consciousness of disgrace, and an exposure to the jeers and taunts of an idle, brutal mob, always gathered around an execution. Plato, in a passage which has ever excited great astonishment from its striking resemblance to prophecy, makes crucifixion to be the

* Often till the third, sometimes even the seventh day.

utmost possible extreme of dishonor and suffering to
which a man can be brought by the malignant persecution of men.   He is describing a just person, such as
philosophical imagination portrayed, maintaining his
integrity against every possible disadvantage, and says :
" This man, though he has done nothing but good,
shall be accused of all manner of wrong, and, though
innocent, pass through life under censure as the
most wicked of men, yet maintain through all a most
unshaken virtue, until he shall be seized, scourged, tor-
tured, bound, have his eyes put out, and finally, after
having endured the extreme of all other cruelties, shall
be crucified."*

Our Lord's head was not covered, neither were his
eyes put out, and the mercy of the Jewish law,
(strangely remembered by that bigot people in their
savage fury,) which commanded that " strong drink
should be given to him that is ready to perish," doubtless, prompted (perhaps at the suggestion of some
pitying bystander, though the soldiers may have done
it insultingly,) the offering of a sponge, but with sour
wine and bitter infusions, to his painful lips ; for there
was no such custom among either Greeks or Romans.
But, in all other respects, he suffered crucifixion as it
has now been described : he was bound, was scourged,
was tormented by the soldiers ; they laid the heavy
wood on his blessed shoulders, and then nailed him on
the cross.

In the addition of the crown of thorns, as of the
purple robe, the reed placed between his bound hands,
and the superscription on the cross-piece (*patibulum*),
where the Romans usually put the crime of the sufferer,

* Plato, Report, II. § 5.

we see the mockery of his claim to be King of the Jews, — the only thing in our Lord's conduct which the callous-hearted Pilate appears to have cared about, it being rebellion against the Roman authority. We are now prepared to learn

II. The reason why our Lord was put to death on the cross.

1. It was death on a tree. The sin fatal to our race was committed by an offence against a tree which God had commanded should not be touched. It was also a tree, which, in the arrangements of Paradise resembling the apocalyptical description of heaven, bore the fruit of which if a man ate he should live forever. There is an exquisite fitness in our Lord's atoning for sin on a tree, thus turning the occasion of a deserved death into the ever-verdant, fruit-laden source of life eternal. As we look back to that disastrous scene where the tempter triumphed in the sin of the first Adam that brought the curse on us all, we see the second Adam, by his infinite righteousness, triumphing for us over all the force of our enemy, achieving our immortal blessing.

2. It being requisite that our Lord should die under Jewish as well as Gentile law, there was yet no mode of mortal punishment in the Mosaic law by which his suffering would have been consistent with prophecy; for, of the four methods known to them, slaying by the sword would not have answered, because it involved no disgrace; nor stoning, because then his bones would have been broken, which the Holy Ghost had foretold should not be; nor burning, because then the flesh of the great Paschal Lamb would not have remained to be the food of his people, for strangulation would have

rendered his flesh unclean. It was, however, necessary that his blood should be shed, because, without the shedding of blood, there is no remission ; that he should be lifted up to the eyes of faith as the serpent was lifted up in the wilderness ; that he should suffer extreme agony, because his pains were to be expressive of divine wrath against sin ; and, above all, that he should die on a tree, because that was the only mode of death which God had specially pronounced accursed. These requisites could be found only in crucifixion.

3. It, more than any other imaginable method, is calculated to impress us with the religious lessons which the death of the Lamb of God for us should teach every believer on his name.

a. With what horror should we regard those sins which brought such shame, and anguish, and curse on him, our devoted Friend and patient Surety !

b. With what confidence may we rely upon the acceptance of his atonement for his people when it pleased the Father so to bruise him, and put him to grief !

c. With what readiness should we give up the world when duty requires it, as we see it rejecting, persecuting, and maligning our divine Master, Example, and Saviour ! There, as we behold him crucified, should we see " the world crucified unto us," and so " crucify ourselves unto the world."

d. With what patience and long-suffering should we bear the certain, inevitable trials of a Christian life, so fully and painfully set forth in the crucifixion of our elder brother, while we arm ourselves with his patience, and assure ourselves of his sympathizing grace ! The cross is the badge of our profession ; we all must bear it; but it is the sign of our victory, because Christ in the midst of its agonies, overcame for us.

e. With what instant earnestness should we flee to take shelter in the Saviour's atonement, while, on the one hand, we see that God will by no means clear the guilty, and the fearfulness of the punishment which is sure to follow unrepented sin; on the other, see how greatly Christ desired the salvation of our souls when he opened for us the entrance to life by devoting himself to the cross, with all its shame, and curse, and anguish!

O Lord Jesus, fain would we bear the cross for thee, as thou didst bear it for us! But we are weak and sinful; how shall we bear what thou didst faint under? O Saviour, stamp its image on our hearts! Crucify us to thyself! Then shall the sorrow be easy, and the burden be light!

LECTURE XVIII.

CHRIST'S DEATH AND BURIAL.

SIXTEENTH LORD'S DAY.

CHRIST'S DEATH AND BURIAL.

QUEST. XL. *Why was it necessary for Christ to humble himself, even unto death?*

ANS. Because, with respect to the justice and truth of God, satisfaction for our sins could not be made otherwise than by the death of the Son of God.

QUEST. XLI. *Why was he also buried?*

ANS. Thereby to prove that he was really dead.

QUEST. XLII. *Since, then, Christ died for us, why must we also die?*

ANS. Our death is not a satisfaction for our sins; but only an abolishing of sin and a passage to eternal life.

QUEST. XLIII. *What further benefit do we receive from the sacrifice of Christ on the cross?*

ANS. That, by virtue thereof, our old man is crucified, dead, and buried with him, that so the corrupt inclinations of the flesh may no more reign in us; but that we may offer ourselves unto him a sacrifice of thanksgiving.

QUEST. XLIV. *Why is there added: He descended into hell?*

ANS. That, in my greatest temptations, I may be assured and wholly comfort myself in this, that my Lord Jesus Christ, by his inexpressible anguish, pains, and hellish agonies, in which he was plunged during all his sufferings, but especially on the cross, hath delivered me from the anguish and torments of hell.

OUR lesson for the last Lord's Day led us to consider carefully, and, as we trust, not without profit, the sufferings of our Lord, especially his condemnation under Pontius Pilate, and his bitter anguish on the cross. To-day we are called to behold the great Sufferer *dead*, and not only dead, but *buried*.

The doctrine of his death could not be separated from an understanding of his *crucifixion*, which was the

mode of it, and, indeed, has been fundamental to all
that we have hitherto been taught respecting the way
of salvation ; therefore, the Catechism simply reiterates
the main truth under the 40th Question. With like
brevity, the purpose of his *burial* is stated to be proof
that his death was really accomplished (41st) ; and an
inquiry as to the reason why we must die, notwithstanding his dying for us, is met by showing what the
death of the Christian has become, through the propitiation of Christ (42d). Then follows a recital of
some further benefits, or, rather, of some not as particularly dwelt upon before, derived from the cross (3d) ;
after which is set forth the fulness of comfort to be
found in the fact asserted of our Lord by the Creed,
that *he descended into hell.*

There are so many interesting questions connected
with the last point, that it requires a separate discourse ;
and we shall postpone its formal treatment, using it,
however, as far as needed in our present study. The
other matter of the lesson may be conveniently arranged
under three heads : —

FIRST: *The necessity for our Lord's humiliation even
unto death.*

SECONDLY: *His burial, and the reasons for it.*

THIRDLY: *The benefits which we receive from his
death and burial.*

FIRST: *The necessity for our Lord's humiliation even
unto death.*

The infinite merit of our Lord's vicarious sufferings
having been already shown, the question now is : Why
was it requisite that he should actually die? Were not
those sorrows of his that wrung his heart all his life
long, his terrible agony in the garden, his anguish of

both body and soul on the cross, enough to testify the
divine wrath against us without this extreme humiliation ?   If Enoch and Elijah were taken into heaven
without having passed through the mortal agony, why
might not the Father have assumed his well-beloved
Son to his glory from the cross, in the sight of his enemies, as he did afterward from Bethany, from the midst
of his adoring disciples ?   Would not the arrest of his
passion by such majesty have vindicated the excellence
of his atonement more than even his resurrection after
the disgraces of the tomb ?   My brethren, if such
thoughts arise in our minds, it is because we forget
the penalty which the Mediator undertook to pay
on behalf of his people.   The sentence was explicit :
" The soul that sinneth, it shall die ; " " Without the
shedding of blood, there is no remission."   The life of
the sinner was forfeited ; and, therefore, the life of the
substitute was required.   He had covenanted to die
that they might live.   We must believe that nothing
less, nothing short of this, could have answered the
broken, dishonored law.   All the sacrifices in which
the victims were slain outright, all the prophecies
which declared that he should pour out his soul unto
death, all his own testimonies respecting the decease
which he should accomplish at Jerusalem, all the subsequent teachings of his apostles, show that his obedience was not complete until death, nor his expiation
but in death.   All his antecedent sorrows and pains and
tortures were but precursors of his death : death was
in them all, but not complete until, as in our death, his
spirit was separated from his body, leaving the clay lifeless, and prone to mingle with the dust out of which it
was taken.   It was no seeming death, no deep trance

nor syncope simulating death, from which he recovered on the third day; but an entire dissolution, so that he ceased to live until at his resurrection he began to live again. " Father," said he, in the midst of the great darkness, as the vail of the temple was rent in twain, " into thy hands I commend my spirit ! and, having said thus, he gave up the ghost," or, as it is in the Greek, he expired: the breath went utterly out of his torn, exhausted frame; his body yet hung on the cruel nails, but his anguish was over; his blessed heart was still, his holy head drooped, his gentle eyes were closed; he had lived our life to its last pang; his soul had gone up to his Father; and Jesus of Nazareth was dead.

The death-sentence passed upon man included far more than the mere mortality of the body: death was a name for the wrath of God upon body and soul; wrath eternal, because never could man have suffered sufficiently to expiate his sin, and, without the renewing grace of God, he would be continually incurring fresh condemnation by fresh offence: so that death implies all the torments of hell, as well as the penal effects of sin in this world; but the death which is the end of our course here, was a component, essential part of the death-punishment, besides being a most striking emblem and foreshadowing of the wrath which follows it. Our blessed Lord did suffer the wrath of God in his spirit, as well as his body: the very wrath which makes the hell of the wicked. " The sorrows of death compassed " him ; " the pains of hell gat hold upon " him ; or, as the Catechism says (44th), he was in inexpressible anguish, pains, and hellish agonies, during all his sufferings, but especially on the cross : as far as a pure, sinless spirit can suffer hell, he suffered it ; but, so completely did he expiate our guilt, so fully satisfy divine justice, so utterly exhaust death by his sufferings, that he needed not to pass, after the article of dissolution, into the torments which await the wicked beyond this life.   As he bowed his head and gave up the ghost, he said : " It is finished ! " because, in that last submission, he bore the last pang of the curse, he drank the last drop in the cup of wrath, he felt the last stroke of the avenger, and the Father, in receiving his soul, accepted his atonement.   Then was it apparent to the universe of observing intelligence that he died for us, as at his resurrection it was apparent that his death was infinitely sufficient for our eternal life.   Hence we, after the example of Scripture, testify our belief in the redemption, by our confession of Christ's death, and, obeying his own command, celebrate his death by a sacrament which symbolizes the breaking of his body and the shedding of his blood.

O beloved Christians, what strength and sweetness there is in this article of our faith !   If Christ walked never so closely with us during all our previous temptations and sorrows, but turned away when the last enemy approached, shaking his fearful dart, how should we shrink back in terror, and cry, in his own " exceeding bitter cry," " My God, why hast thou forsaken me ? "   But now that we have seen him dead, we know that he will not leave nor forsake us, but will be our guide even unto death ; we mark the prints of his bleeding feet down every step into the valley dark as darkness itself, and know that he will go with us through the mystery.   Then we fear no evil, because his rod and his staff shall comfort us.

SECONDLY : *His burial, and the reasons for it.*

41st. *Why was he also buried?*

Ans.   Thereby to prove that he was really dead.

1. This is a very important reason ; for, on the reality of his death depends the perfection of his sacrifice, and the fact of his resurrection ; and, consequently, the truth of all Christianity.   It was at the third hour (nine o'clock in the morning) that our Lord was fixed on the cross, and about the ninth hour (three o'clock in the afternoon) that he expired.   Many lived on the cross for days before they died ; and it would seem that both the malefactors executed with him were alive toward the close of the day, for the soldiers brake their legs to kill them outright ; but in six hours his sufferings were over, his spiritual agonies hastening the catastrophe.   The next day was a Sabbath, a high solemnity, — one of the three Sabbaths of holy convocation, and immediately previous to the wave-offering (Lev. xxiii. 10, 11) ; so that the Jews, whose law forbade them to let any one remain on a tree over any sunset, were specially anxious that this notable Sabbath should not be defiled, and besought Pilate that an immediate end should be put to the sufferers.   Strange bigotry, that could tolerate such malignant injustice as the crucifixion of an innocent one like Jesus, yet stickle at a form ! Yet such is formality in religion : its scrupulosity in outward rules survives the spirit of piety.   Pilate, easy to comply when it cost him nothing, commands the soldiers, not without witnesses from among the Jews, to fulfil their wish : but Jesus is so manifestly dead, that neither soldiers nor Jews doubt it ; yet, to make all sure for us as well as for them, one of the Romans thrusts a spear into his side.   The spear reaches his heart, or, at the least, gives a mortal wound ; for out of

the fissure flows not only " blood," but what the evangelist calls " water," or the serous fluid found within
the sac encasing the heart (*pericardium*); though it is
possible that it was from the effusion which great agony
often sends into the *pleura :* but, in either case, the proof
is clear that death had actually occurred.   If there had
been the slightest chance for denial, the Jews, after the
resurrection of our Lord, would not have spared it ;
but, though they bribed the soldiers to say that his disciples had stolen his body in the night, they did not
pretend to say he had not been really dead.

Had not divine Providence prevented it, the sacred
body would have been roughly buried in the place appointed for executed malefactors, near the scene of the
crucifixion ; but, now that he had " poured out his soul
unto death," he is spared from farther indignities.   Joseph of Arimathea, of whom we know little more than
that he was " a rich man," a Pharisee, " an honorable
counsellor, which also waited for the kingdom of God,"
" a good man and a just," who " had not consented " to
the decree against Christ, but was " his disciple, though
secretly, for fear of the Jews," — remorseful at having
forsaken his Master, and impressed by the awful miracles attending his death, now goes " boldly " to Pilate
and asks " that he might take away the body of Jesus ; "
and Pilate, willing to please a man of his rank, and all
the while persuaded that our Lord had suffered unjustly, gives him leave.   Joseph had a new tomb prepared
for himself, hewn, as was the custom of the rich Jews,
out of a rock in the midst of a garden ; and there he
determined to lay the precious remains.   But Nicodemus, his brother counsellor, and like him in concealed
discipleship (for it was the same that came to Jesus by

night), now claims a part in the sad offices. The Jews, who abhorred burning, and the disembowelling necessary for the embalmment common among Eastern people, or any other mode of treating the bodies of their dead than burial, — yet craved the solace of fragrant obsequies, and were accustomed to wrap them with fine linen in spices, which were sometimes burned in great quantities. So, as Joseph had the honor of giving the tomb, Nicodemus brings the perfumes, not less than a hundred-pound weight of myrrh and aloes, — a costly, even magnificent provision, — such as would have been made for a person of highest rank; and together, the true-hearted Marys standing by if not assisting them, they wind the body in linen cloths with the spices, hoping to do it farther honor when the Sabbath had passed by. So they laid him in the rocky tomb, causing its door to be closed by a great stone rolled into its mouth; and there in a garden the second Adam rested in death, as in a garden death had come upon the first. But the wretched, persecuting Sanhedrim, though they could not oppose Pilate in his grant of Joseph's request, are not satisfied; and the next day demand of the Procurator that the sepulchre should be made sure until the third day, lest his disciples might come and steal the body, and so claim that Christ's own prophecy of rising on the third day was fulfilled. Pilate, out of patience with their wicked pertinacity, tells them to use their own watch-guard, which was a body of sixty soldiers assigned to guard the temple, and make as sure as they can. They, therefore, seal the stone, so that any movement of it might be detected, and set sentinels to prevent any entrance. It is not necessary to believe as some do (Theophylact and others) that the whole of the temple guard were put to the service; but the Jews had it in their power to employ all that was sufficient, and doubtless did. How did God, through their own act and intention to frustrate the truth of Jesus, thus provide for their discomfiture and our assurance!

The death of the Saviour is even yet more certain. How could he, even if his wounds were not mortal, have survived the enrolment of his head and person so closely? — or his confinement within the rock-bound cell whose entrance was so entirely sealed? Or how could his terror-stricken friends, against all these precautions, have abstracted the mangled body, and restored him to the full, vigorous life in which he appeared on the day of his resurrection?

2. Neither, without his burial, would all the prophecies respecting his work for us have been fulfilled. Until then, though he had had his place with the wicked, he had rest with the rich in his death;* neither was there opportunity for the Father to ransom his chosen from the power of the grave, and over the grave give him the victory. These prophecies are, however, so connected with what has been already said, and will be said hereafter, that we may refrain from farther reference to them now.

3. But what comfort and hope is offered to our hearts as we linger with the weeping women before the door of the Saviour's tomb! We need not be pilgrims to the Holy Land for this; our faith in the blessed Evangelists brings us to the scene. How calmly, how quietly, he rests within! They have done unto him

---

* A grave *was appointed* for him with the wicked, but with the rich **man** was his tomb (high place). — Is. liii. 9.

whatsoever they listed, but they cannot reach him now
with their savage cries, and brutal insults, and merci-
less tortures.   They have driven him out of the world
which he made for them, so fair and beautiful; out of
his own Jerusalem, which he had loved so well, and
wept over with so fond a pity; out of the mortal life
which he had made so lovely by his innocence, and so
beneficent by his miracles, and so eloquent of truth by
his teachings, and so full of promise to the sorrowful
by his tears, and to the penitent by his prayers.   Oh,
what a darkness was that when the sun hid his face
from the murder of the Holy One, and the convulsed
earth quaked in sympathy with her Maker!   What a
night was that when the stars looked down on the
world, whose Saviour and Lord lay dead and buried.
Think of the poor disciples, shrunk into hiding-places
like timorous sheep whose shepherd is slain, and of the
broken-hearted women, loving without hope, but faithful
in their despair!   Yet the sufferer is at rest.   He
sleeps.   His labors are done, his pains are past, his
enemies have accomplished their worst; his last cry
was the escape of his spirit, and his dear, holy, mangled
flesh awaits in peace a speedy awakening far beyond
sorrow and ignominy, within the glory of his better
world, where all the heavenly host will acclaim him an
infinite homage, because the signatures of the cross
attest him the Lamb that was slain.   Odors, fragrant
and rich, fill the air, as the spices breathe their honors
around him, and the flowers of the garden are redolent
through the dews.   All is as sweet as it is calm.   O
faithful Master, thanks be to thee, that thou didst not
refuse to lie down in the grave!   The grave is gloomy
and cold and sad, — the disgrace of our humanity, the

hiding-place of our shame.   Disguise it as we may, with marbles and epitaphs, and graceful trees, and summer-blooms, and evergreens, till it looks like a palace-garden, it is yet the place of silence, darkness, and corruption; nature revolts from the thought, nor can philosophy cure us of the shudder, for reason justifies it: —

> " To lie in cold obstruction and to rot,
> This sensible, warm motion to become
> A kneaded clod — . . . .
> . . . . . . 't is too horrible ! "

But oh, how sad it is when we are forced to carry there and put deep within its shades, away from our touch, and sight, and care, the dear forms in which the beloved of our hearts, — the good, the kind, the true, have lived but live no longer; the pleasant faces through which their souls shone on us, the bosoms that yearned for us, the hands that ministered to our comfort, the limbs active in serving our faintest wish, — to lie out amidst loathsome damps, under the beatings of the storm, and the winter's snows, because they are dust and to dust they must return !   Yet, how changed is the sepulchre since we have followed in his funeral, and seen the place where the Lord lay !   He is not there now, — he is risen; but he has been there; the fragrance yet fills the tomb; the garden still blossoms around it: as, in the beginning, he, by his own rest, made the Sabbath a rest for our souls, so has he, by his own burial, made the grave a rest for the bodies of his people.   There the wicked cease from troubling them; there they have a refuge from temptation, from tears and sin; there the High Priest of our profession has set a company of the guard from the heavenly temple to watch their sleeping dust — his own seal is on the door — and in his own time, when all the mortality, and dishonor, and corruption, and weakness, have crumbled away, will he roll back the stone from its mouth, and they shall come forth immortal, glorious, incorruptible, and full of power, to enter upon the kingdom where he is now gone to prepare places for them. Oh! now we know what our church means when it bids us say that, though Christ has died for our sins, we must also die. Death and the grave are no longer the penalty and the disgrace of our nature. Christ hath taken out the sting from death, the victory he has wrested from the grave; and now death to all who believe is the abolishing of sin, the grave a passage to eternal life. The pious dead are not lost: they only sleep in Jesus, — a blessed sleep from which he is coming to awake them. He has taken up their spirits now to the Father who took up his; and he will once more descend in the latter day to the earth, that he may restore their full humanity to paradise, — far more lovely than that the tempter entered, where no enemy nor ill can reach them forever. O spirit of the Holy One, who didst anoint Christ with grace for his death and burial, prepare us for ours, that we may follow him with the countless train of those who, through faith and patience, inherit the promises! Then shall death be to us a gain unspeakable, and the grave a welcome rest. We need rest, O Lord, for we are often weary; and, if it please thee, we would not bear our burden long.

" We would not live alway, thus fettered by sin,
 Temptation without, and corruption within ;
 Where the rapture of pardon is mingled with fears,
 And the cup of thanksgiving with penitent tears.

> We would not live alway — no, welcome the tomb;
> Since Jesus hath lain there we dread not its gloom;
> There sweet be our rest, till he bid us arise,
> To hail him in triumph descending the skies."

But we had wellnigh anticipated what we proposed to treat of —

THIRDLY: *The benefits we receive from Christ's death and burial.*

The Catechism says " further benefits," because it has already made us dwell largely on the benefits of Christ's sacrifice ; but we shall briefly recapitulate, and add to these stated in the present answer (43d), those given in the 44th, as taught in our Lord's descent to hell.

1. Christ as our infinite surety has borne the wrath of God for all who believe on his name. When the Father accepted the substitute, he did it under covenant to release those whom Jesus represented. He took the guilt of their sins from them in the very act by which he laid it on the sinless elder brother. So, when he paid the penalty, they paid it ; when he was stricken of God it was with their stripes ; when he was crucified they were crucified with him ; when he died they died in him ; when he was buried he sanctified the grave for them ; and so, also, when the Father received his spirit, and raised him from the dead, in sure token that justice was satisfied and heaven opened for the atoner, the Father accepted them, adopted them as his sons and daughters, assured them of deliverance from eternal death, set open wide the gate of heaven for their spirits when they leave the body, and for their bodies after the purification of the grave which Christ has made fragrant with holy peace. How certain, then, is the salva-

tion of the Christian, since justice and mercy with interlinking arms stand pleading for him before the throne on which the Lamb that was slain sits at the right hand of God !

2. The sympathy of our Lord with his people is entire. " In that he himself hath suffered, being tempted, he is able to succor them that are tempted." He has not only the power but the knowledge from experience to apply the power ; and as, in the language of the New Testament, temptation and trial are synonymous, one word in the original representing both, his sympathizing grace covers all the experience of the Christian ; for there is no form of trial through which the Christian can be made to pass that he did not pass through on his way to victory and rest.

All that we ordinarily call temptations, — the motives, arguments, and provocations to sin, to which we are exposed during our mortal life in this world, he knew ; we have a notable example of this in the conflict he had with the devil immediately after his unction by the Holy Ghost. All that we ordinarily call trials, — our sicknesses, our pains, our persecutions, our wrongs from the false judgments, and slanders, and oppositions of men, our sorrows for those we love in their sicknesses, and deaths and burials, — we know that he knew from the record of the evangelical witnesses.

So far as his innocent spirit could feel the anguish and self-abhorrence and shame of sin, he knew what the penitent suffers when, under the thunderings of the law, he trembles and avows his guilt ; for all his Israel's sins were gathered around his soul, compassing his spirit about, hiding his Father's face from him, causing him to shrink with horror from the vile contact, and pressing on his mediatorial conscience the fact that the punishment he bore was just. Nay, those very doubts which oftentimes assail the believer's mind, causing him to shrink from duty, to fear the future set before him, and even to think that God has forsaken him, assaulted the humanity of Jesus. " Now," saith he, at one time, " is my soul troubled, and what shall I say? Father, save me from this hour." What else was that agony in the garden, when he prayed: " Father, if it be possible let this cup pass from me!" and "there appeared an angel unto him from heaven strengthening him?" And how else can we understand that bitter cry out of the thick darkness, " My God! my God! why hast thou forsaken me?" There could not be a single form of pain, or anguish of body or soul, that follows sin, of which the Redeemer, who took the cup filled with our deserts, did not taste; and this is what the Catechism declares when it says (44th), that "our Lord Jesus Christ, during all his sufferings, but especially on the cross, was plunged in inexpressible anguish, pains, terrors and hellish agonies," that he might deliver us from the anguish and torments of hell.

Here then, believer, — tempted, afflicted, weak and trembling, is there full comfort for you. The Master knows your trials and your infirmity. Only imitate his steadfastness, — be faithful to him as he was to you; and he who received a gift of strength from on high to go through his passion, will send you strength according as your day.

3. For there is here a promise of sanctification. He crucified our old nature when the body he took on him, out of the flesh and blood of the Virgin Mary, was

crucified. There in his death, the tyrannous power of
sin, by which the devil holds captive the impenitent,
was broken from his people ; and in his grave he finally
buried the mortal flesh that he might raise it in newness of life, holy and eternal. Thus has he promised
to quicken from their death in trespasses and sins, all
who by faith are crucified with him, with him die, and
with him are buried. As he was raised up to heaven,
so shall they, even in this life, be raised up to sit with
him in heavenly places: privileges so like heaven, that
the apostle can give them no less an epithet than
"heavenly." Yet, this grace is only vouchsafed to
those who, relying on the working of God in them,
work out with fear and trembling their own salvation.
But, believer, what a motive as well as encouragement
is here? What so separates a man from the world as
death and burial? Yet so, by our profession of representation in Christ, do we profess to have died with the
world of sin, and to have put off our old man with its
affections and lusts. We are not dead with him, if we
be not buried with him. We have not been buried
with him, if we be not risen with him. Our true life,
our Christian life, now lies on the other side of the
grave as to its affections and aims and delights. "If
ye, then, be risen with Christ, seek those things which
are above." All our motives and rules must be brought
by us from heaven, "into which the Forerunner has
for us entered." "Truly," says an apostle, "our conversation is in heaven." Yes, beloved brethren, this is
the grace into which we profess to stand, who profess
by our Lord Jesus to have received the atonement.
We cannot go back to the world except we trample

over the grace of Jesus, and reject the arguments of his cross.

O Son of the Highest, remember us on thy throne! Thou hast vanquished sin for us in the atonement of thy death ; now vanquish sin in us by the intercession of thy life!

LECTURE XIX.

THE DESCENT INTO HELL.

SIXTEENTH LORD'S DAY.

THE DESCENT INTO HELL.

"He descended into hell."

THIS article of our creed, which, because of its peculiar interest, requires a closer study than we could
give it when considering, on a late occasion, the lesson
for the Sixteenth Lord's Day, should be approached
with cautious modesty, as it has been so disputed over
by theologians of the highest rank, that an attempt to
determine the truth among their widely different views
would be presumptuous, if we had not a " more sure
word of prophecy." Rejecting, as we do, the preposterous notion which the papists have adopted from the
good but fanciful Bishop of Milan (St. Ambrose), —
all the fathers before him saying nothing of the kind, —
that the creed was composed by the inspired apostles, we
cannot receive any dogma it contains on less authority
than divine Scripture ; yet, since we have adopted it as
the symbol of our catholic, evangelical belief, we must
understand its articles " according to the proportion (or
rather analogy) * of faith," as the apostle calls the
consistency of Christian doctrine.

But, FIRST : it should be noted that the descent into
hell is not found as a separate, distinct article of the earlier creeds. In the Nicene (A. D. 325) we read :
" He suffered, and was buried, and the third day he rose
again," — the descent into hell not being inserted ; in that

* ἀναλογίαν τῆς πίστεως. — Rom. xii. 6.

vulgarly attributed to Athanasius (A. D. 333) we read :
" Who suffered for our salvation, descended into hell,
rose again the third day from the dead," — the burial
being omitted ; from which comparison it would seem
that the two phrases were then thought to be synonymous.   But nearly all the learned, outside the papal
ranks, deny that Athanasius wrote the formula called
by his name.   Waterland, on strong grounds, ascribes
it to Hilary (Bishop) of Arles, which would bring it a
century later ; and certainly it was not known through
the church until the close of the sixth.   Rufinus,
Bishop of Aquileia * (a great city in the Venetian territory), says that his church had both articles in its
creed, but that the Roman and Eastern churches had
only the burial ; and he thought that the two meant
the same thing,† one, perhaps, being explanatory of the
other, if not a mere expletive.   It is not known at
what time they came to be interpreted distinctly,
though Erasmus thought that it began with Thomas
Aquinas (*circa* 1305) ; but, undoubtedly, some opinions
now held respecting our Lord's descent into hell were
promulged at an early period.   Witsius (the noble doctor of our mother-church) cites the historian Socrates,
to show that a company of about fifty Arians at Constantinople (A. D. 359) published a creed which says :
" He was crucified, and died, and was buried and pene-
trated ($\delta\iota\epsilon\lambda\eta\lambda\upsilon\theta\acute{o}\tau\alpha$) into parts beneath the earth ($\kappa\alpha\tau\alpha$-
$\chi\theta\acute{o}\nu\iota\alpha$), at whom hell ($\mathring{a}\delta\eta\varsigma$) itself was struck with terror."   But Witsius might have found in the same his-
torian a creed rejected by the council of Ariminum
(Rimini), who deposed the Arian bishops ‡ that had

* Nona inter claras, Aquileia, urbes. — *Ausonius.*
† Vis tamen verbi eadem videtur esse in eo quod sepultus dicitur.
‡ Ursatius and Valens.

presented it (A. D. 356), which has these expressions:
" Was crucified and died, and descended into parts
infernal, and set in order what was to be done there,
at (the sight of) whom the doorkeepers of hell trem-
bled." *   Such language intends considerably more
than mere burial.

We are careful to observe these historical facts,
because they prove that the insertion of the article,
" He descended into hell," as meaning more than his
burial, was made by heretics ; † and that, though now the
papists connect with it their doctrine of purgatory, and
kindred follies, the creed of the early church had nothing between the burial and the resurrection.   The descent into hell is in the creed of the church of Rome
now.   How it got there nobody knows, but it certainly
was not before the fifth century, probably not until long
after.

SECONDLY : It is, nevertheless, a scriptural fact that
our Lord descended into hell, as we learn from a collation of Psalm xvi. 9, 10, 11, with Acts ii. 23–32.   In
the psalm we read : " My flesh also shall rest in hope ;
for thou wilt not leave my soul in hell, neither wilt
thou suffer thine Holy One to see corruption.   Thou
wilt show me the path of life."   In the other scripture,
the apostle Peter at the Pentecost says : " Him (Jesus
of Nazareth) by wicked hands ye have crucified and
slain ; whom God hath raised up, having loosed the
pains of death, because it was not possible that he
should be holden of it.   For David speaketh concerning him : I foresaw the Lord always before my face ;

---

* Not having the Greek at hand, I quote the English translation, fol.
Cambridge, 1683, p. 272.

† At Seleucia, Acacius withdrew the passages, but no doubt from craft,
as he restored them at Constantinople.

for he is on my right hand, that I should not be moved. Therefore did my heart rejoice, and my tongue was glad; moreover, also, my flesh shall rest in hope: because thou wilt not leave my soul in hell, neither wilt thou suffer thine Holy One to see corruption. Thou hast made known to me the ways of life; thou shalt make me full of joy with thy countenance. Men and brethren, let me freely speak unto you of the patriarch David, that he is both dead and buried, and his sepulchre is with us unto this day. Therefore, being a prophet, and knowing that God had sworn with an oath to him, that of the fruit of his loins he would raise up Christ to sit on his throne; he, seeing this before, spake of the resurrection of Christ, that his soul was not left in hell, neither his flesh did see corruption. This Jesus hath God raised up, whereof we all are witnesses." Thus the apostle, as well as the psalmist, in saying that our Lord was not left in hell, implies that he had been there; and since we must believe the words of Scripture, we should rightly understand what those words mean.

1. The Hebrew and the Greek originals have each two words of different signification, to render which our translators had but the one word, *hell*. The Hebrew has *gehenna* (בֵּיהִכֶּם) and *sheol* (שְׁאוֹל): *gehenna* signifying the place where the wicked after death are in fiery torment, or hell in the present sense of that word among us; *sheol* signifying the region beneath the surface of the ground, but most frequently the place of the dead, or the grave — though in a few texts, by a natural figure, destruction. *Sheol*, not *gehenna*, is the word in the psalm: " Thou wilt not leave my soul in *sheol*," *i. e.* in the place or state of the dead, or

the grave.   The writers of the New Testament adopted *gehenna* from the Hebrew, and use it to signify the place of future punishment (γέεννα, rendered throughout our translation by *hell ;*) but whenever they speak of the state or place of the dead, they use the word *hades* (ἅδής) as equivalent to *sheol.*   Thus Luke in the parable has : " The rich man also died and was buried ; and in (*hades*) hell, he lifted up his eyes, being in torments, and seeth Abraham afar off, and Lazarus in his bosom."   Both were in *hades,* or the state, — place, if you will, — of the dead ; but one in torments, the other a great way off, in Abraham's bosom.   Throughout our English Vulgate, *hades* is rendered by hell,* except in 1 Corinthians xv. 55, where we have *grave :* " O death, where is thy sting ?   O grave (*hades*), where is thy victory ? "   *Hades* is the word in Peter's citation of the psalm.

Thus neither the psalmist nor the apostle says that our Lord went into the place of punishment, but the contrary ; as otherwise the reasoning of Peter would be that David had gone to torment, and is there still, — a conclusion from which every one would shrink.

2. Then, again, the Hebrew word rendered soul, *nephesh* (נֶפֶשׁ), does not necessarily, nor even radically, signify what we understand by soul, — the spiritual, moral part of man.   Its primary sense is *breath,* or the *life,* whether of man or beast.   Nay, there are passages where it signifies a corpse or exanimate body, as Haggai ii. 13 : " If one that is unclean by a dead body " (*nephesh*) ; and Lev. xix. 28 : " Thou shalt not make

---

* There is no doubt that *hell* has both the senses: the place of punishment, and the place of the dead, — the last the primary one.   Hölle (G.), hell;   höhle (G.), hole.   Hence the common people associate hell with gloomy caverns, — hell-gate, hell's-mouth, devil's chimney, etc., etc.

any cuttings in your flesh for the dead" (*nephesh*).
So, also, xxi. ; but especially Numbers vi. 6 : " All the
days that he separateth himself to the Lord, he shall
come at no dead body " (*nephesh*).   Thus we might
consistently translate it in the psalm : " My flesh also
shall rest in hope ; for thou wilt not leave my body in
the grave, neither wilt thou suffer thine Holy One to see
corruption."   For the most part, however, *nephesh* is
used as the word *person* by us : that which presents the
idea of the man to us ; as we say, " there were so many
persons present," or, so many souls were there ; and,
" not a soul," or, " not a person was present."   It is,
in fact, a frequent orientalism for the personal pro-
nouns ; so that it would be also consistent to read :
" Thou wilt not leave *me* in the state of the dead."
Either of these renderings would be justified by that
peculiarity of Hebrew poetry called *parallelism*, which
repeats in the second, with some difference of phrase,
the idea of the first line : " Thou wilt not leave me, or
my person, or my body, in the grave ; nor wilt thou
suffer thy Holy One to see corruption."   Certainly *Holy
One* can scarcely apply to an exanimate body merely,
but must refer to the person whose body is in the
grave ; for the term rendered *Holy One* in both the languages is not holy in the sense of dedicated, but in the
absolutely *moral* sense of *pious*, or godly ; and the
psalmist would not speak of a pious or godly corpse.

The apostle's term for soul (*nephesh*) is ψυχὴ : a term
corresponding to the Hebrew word in many particulars,
though not in all, but certainly, as many passages from
the classics show, * to the sense of person ; and we

---

* Euripĭdes, Helena, v. 52.   Her. Furens. v. 452.   Theocritus, Id. xvi.
24.   *C. Muleæ.*

should interpret it accordingly.   This is in accordance .
with the common habit of language.   Martha said of
her brother Lazarus: " Lord, by this time *he* stinketh,
for he hath been dead four days."   So our Lord said :
" Where have ye laid him ? " and the apostle Paul
(Acts xiii. 35, 37) " Wherefore he (David) saith also
in another Psalm : Thou shalt not suffer thine Holy
(pious) One to see corruption ; but *he*, whom God raised
up again, saw no corruption."   We see, therefore, that
soul, here, does not necessarily, nor even probably, mean
our Lord's spiritual soul in the first parallel, any more
than *Holy One* does in the second.

This is a fair critical interpretation of the passages
on which the descent into hell is mainly founded, and
the one admitted by the great part of the learned, especially by all the eminent doctors of the reformed
churches from Calvin down ; yet, since it has obtained
a place in the creed of the catholic church, a great
variety of opinions have been given concerning it by
theologians, both Papist and Protestant.

We shall, therefore, state some of these: first, those
of the Papists, and of such as agree with them partly,
among the Protestants ; then, those of the reformed
churches, to whose communion by the blessing of God
we belong.

1. The ancient Jews, to whom " life and immortality " were not revealed as they have since been by the
gospel, had an indistinct notion of a great region
beneath the surface of the ground, whither not only
the bodies of men went (in burial), but their spirits
lived after death, — the good in bliss, the wicked in misery.   This corresponded with the Egyptian and classical notions : we might say with the universal idea of

cultivated nations. Men at death were said to descend, — go down somewhere, ("*Facilis descensus*" "*ad inferos.*") The neo-platonic philosophers, who were in full force at Alexandria during the earlier Christian centuries, and mingled Greek with Egyptian doctrines, had, also, according to their wont, adopted many myths from the popular superstitions, as all the Orphic writings show. Some of the fathers, learned in both Christian and neo-platonic systems, but converted at a time of life when few men can wholly change their inveterate sentiments, still less their phraseology, transferred, without any scriptural authority, not a few figments of superstition to their new faith; especially mingling these about the state of the dead with the Christian doctrine. The Arians, sympathizing with the Alexandrian notion of the *Logos*, would be likely to carry their bias farther. Hence, we are not surprised to find them (as has been shown) interpolating the creed with their fancy respecting our Lord's descent into *hades*. The opinion obtained some favor even with the more orthodox, as it tallied to a certain extent with the rabbinical teachings that had obtained popular credence among the Jews, and given a tinge of language to some scriptural passages. We have no more respect for the Rabbins than for the Hermaic teachers; but we are disposed to consider what they quote who have adopted their general idea. The principal texts are these three: Eph. iv. 9, where it is said that our Lord " descended into the lower parts of the earth; " 1 Peter iii. 18, 19, 20, where it is said that our Lord by the spirit went and " preached to the spirits in prison; " Luke xxiii. 43, where our Lord said to the penitent thief, " This day shalt thou be with me in paradise." Misinterpret-

ing these texts, they divided the abode of the dead —
sheol, hades, hell, — into two main parts : one the place
of the pious ancients who believed in Messiah, but
died before his " manifestation to Israel ; " the other,
the prison (*gehenna*) of the wicked ; with some minor
partitions we need not stay to describe.   Christ, said
they, descended to this lower region first, to make
known to the pious spirits his full gospel, that, through
faith in his finished work, they might obtain full salvation, which they did by rising with him when he rose ;
but, also, to confound with his power and glory the
devils and wicked souls.   Afterwards, by degrees,
these notions were somewhat modified and enlarged,
until they composed out of them the doctrine of purgatory, with its kindred follies ; which is, that the spirits
of even Christians (except martyrs and some few others) after death need a *purgation,* or cleansing by fire ;
and are, for that purpose, shut up in suffering until
either sins are burned away, or they are freed from the
necessity by the prayers of the church, accompanying
the repeated sacrifices of Christ's body in the mass.
This is what the papists mean by saying masses for the
repose of souls.   The doctrine of purgatory has been,
as is well known, a most fruitful source of simoniacal
gain and profit to that artful mistress of abominations,
who leaves no means untried to subject mankind by
terror of her pretended authority, here and in the next
world ; but time would fail to give even the briefest
account of the many follies uttered by them in connection with the main dogma.   It is remarkable, however,
that it (the doctrine of purgatory) was never formally
affirmed by the church of Rome until the council
of Florence, 1439, and has been steadily rejected by

the Eastern churches of all ages. Strange that it should have taken thirteen centuries for an infallible church to find out a doctrine of religion ! The immaculate conception, however, lagged far behind. God deliver us from such developments of church-life !

There is, also, out of the church of Rome, and principally (if not altogether, nowadays) among high-church Episcopalians, a party more considerable for learning than numbers, who, adopting the ancient notion of *sheol*, or *hades*, contends that at death neither the righteous go to *heaven*, nor the wicked to hell (prepared for the devil and his angels) ; but that, until the resurrection, the good are in bliss, the wicked in torments, though far apart, and that neither the bliss of the one nor the misery of the other, will be complete until the soul is again united to the body. This region, or condition, intervening between the death of the body and the resurrection, they call, for want of a better term, the separate state ; because there disembodied souls exist apart from living men on earth, and from the angels in heaven.

It is not easy to see why this notion is so much insisted upon ; as while, at the best, its advocates are able to give but a vague, shadowy idea of what they mean by it, they gain no practical benefit over the vast majority of the orthodox who hold another opinion, but, as we think, lose much comfort ; for all well-taught Christians believe that, though the disembodied soul of the wicked man goes to the hell of fire, and the soul of the pious man goes to heaven, at once, the one will receive a great accession of misery, the other of bliss, when souls are united again to their proper bodies ; because then the *entire man* will suffer or enjoy with

greater intensity.   But as was said before, the number
even of Episcopalians holding this doctrine is comparatively small, many of the same creed opposing it stren-
uously, others speaking of it very doubtingly ; nor has
it any place in their articles or liturgy ;* and, as it is
based on the same texts as the Romish doctrine of
purgatory, a due examination of those texts will suffice
to refute both.

a. When the apostle in Ephesians (iv. 9) asserts
that our Lord " descended into the lower parts of the
earth," he simply, according to his Hebraistic habit of
language, means to describe the Saviour's extreme
humiliation for us, in submitting to poverty of life, the
shame of the cross, and even to the disgraces of the
grave in his burial under ground.   He could not as a
man descend lower.   It was from the uttermost depths
of human ignominy that he ascended to the sublimest
height of glory in heaven, bearing up with him his
cross-scarred, once dead and buried body, to the right
hand of his Father's throne.

b. The text in 1 Peter (iii. 18, 19), quoted to prove
that our Lord went after his death, and preached to the
spirits in prison, teaches no such thing.   For, if we
read from the 14th verse, we see that the apostle is
exhorting Christians to steadfastness and patience under

---

* The XLth article adopted in the reign of Edward VI. condemns the
doctrine of the soul sleeping between death and the resurrection, but says
nothing about a separate state.   The expressions in the prayer of the
Burial-Service: " Almighty God, with whom do live the spirits of them that
depart hence in the Lord, and with whom the souls of the faithful, after
they are delivered from the burden of the flesh are in joy and felicity;"
. . . . and that God would hasten his kingdom " that all the elect might
have their perfect consummation and bliss both in body and soul," are
quite as much in conformity with our opinions, if not more so, and were,
no doubt, like many other things in the book, adopted, at the farthest, as a
compromise of sentiments on things not essential.

calumny and persecution : " If ye suffer for righteousness' sake, happy are ye, and be not afraid of their terror, neither be troubled ; but sanctify the Lord God in
your hearts ; and be ready always to give an *answer* to
every man that asketh you a reason of the hope that
is in you, with meekness and fear ; having a *good conscience ;* . . . . for it is better, if the will of God be
so, that ye *suffer* for well-doing than for evil-doing."
Then, to encourage them in this patient steadfastness,
he gives two examples of fidelity and deliverance :
" For Christ also hath once suffered for sins, the just
for the unjust, that he might bring us to God ; being
put to death in the flesh," — persecuted to that last extremity, — " but," not abandoned by God, " quickened
by the Spirit, even by the Holy Ghost who raised him
gloriously ; " then again : " by which," the same Spirit
which moved him to his mission of suffering and mercy,
and delivered him triumphantly, " also he went and
preached unto the spirits in prison, which sometime
were disobedient, when once the long-suffering of God
waited in the days of Noah while the' ark was a preparing, wherein few, that is, eight souls, were saved by
water." He did preach to the spirits in prison, but
not when they were in prison, neither did he go personally after his death to preach to them : he preached
to them by the Holy Spirit in Noah, when they were
living on earth at the time the ark was a preparing ;
for the neglect of whose warnings they were drowned,
and cast into the prison of hell where they have been
ever since, as they were at the time Peter wrote.
Christ, in Noah, by his Spirit, preached to them before
the flood, just as in his ministers he preaches to us by
his Spirit now.

Noah, acting under the influence of this Spirit of Christ as a preacher of truth, *suffered* many trials, but was delivered out of them all in the ark which bore him safely over the waters that submerged the wicked to hell. Now, reasons the apostle, " the like figure (that is, the ark on the water) whereunto, even baptism, doth also now save us " who are suffering persecutions by making us one with Christ — " baptism (not [like circumcision which was] the putting away of the filth of the flesh but [see verses 15, 16] the *answer* of a *good conscience* toward God,) by the resurrection of Jesus Christ," which is the earnest of our eternal, complete redemption. This is the only view of the passage that will connect its several parts from the 14th verse to the end ; while, on the other hand, there is no fitness between Christian steadfastness, which is the apostle's theme, and Christ's preaching to souls in purgatory. There are other good reasons against the papistical interpretation, but what has been said is sufficient.

c. It has also been contended that the *Paradise* into which (Luke xxiii. 43) our Lord promised the penitent thief admission with himself, the very day they died, must be some other place than heaven, and, therefore, the separate place of faithful souls. We cannot allow either supposition ; but see the contrary. By sin man lost paradise, where he had enjoyed the favor of God, and was driven out of it ; and, now that our Lord had expiated sin for the restoration of his people to divine favor, what more natural or appropriate than to call the state of his people's recovered blessedness, paradise ? What more in harmony with the great truth than that he, as the second Adam, should, his work of salvation being finished, reënter paradise as the head of his new race, taking, as a trophy of his merits and as an earnest of his church, the converted malefactor into its holy, blissful beauty? We cannot imagine a better name for the heaven of the recovered humanity, than paradise. Why should there not be a second paradise when there is a second Adam?

Besides, the first paradise was not the abode of un-embodied spirits, but of man integrally, body and soul: with what propriety or intelligibleness can its name be given to a sphere where man never is, bodily? Is not heaven, which has always been the abode of pure, holy spirits, the more fitting place for the spirit of a just man when disembodied?

There is, moreover, no warrant in Scripture for such a definition of paradise. The word, which literally means a garden, is used by the Seventy for the Garden of Eden, and in the New Testament occurs in only two places besides our text: once in 2 Corinthians xii. 4, and in Revelation ii. 7:

In the first, the whole passage taken together inter-prets itself. "I knew," says he, speaking of himself, "a man in Christ above fourteen years ago, (whether in the body I cannot tell, or out of the body I cannot tell: God knoweth) — such a man caught up to the third heaven; and I knew such a man (whether in the body or out of the body, I cannot tell: God knoweth) — how that he was caught up into paradise, where he heard unspeakable words." Now, here, before we go farther, we must note two things that make it most unlikely for Paul to have had the views of paradise which they have, against whom we argue. They declare roundly that it is the separate place of faithful spirits only; but Paul, who must have known this if it were so, cannot tell whether he went there in his body or out of it. Had he gone to such a place, it must have been in spirit, as they say Christ did. Then they situate paradise in *sheol*, or *hades ;* and throughout in Scripture, men are said to *go down* into *sheol*, as here in the creed: " He *descended* into hell ; " but Paul was " *caught up* into paradise : " went there in the same direction — upward — that he went to the third heaven. The utter discrepancy is manifest.

But, on taking the whole passage, the two statements only describe, to any unbiased judgment, one rapture, — not two, as our opponents think ; for it is only after the second statement that he states what occurred in his vision, *i. e.* he " heard unspeakable words." After his manner, writing as he did for Gentiles and Jews, he repeats his first statement, using for the state of the blest the word to which his Hebrew readers were accustomed. Not improbably (as we think), he meant to teach them that, contrary to the popular opinion derived from the rabbins, paradise was not in *sheol*, or " the lower parts of the earth," but in the third heaven, which all admit is the immediate presence of God.* If there was only one rapture, therefore, our point is proved ; but if there were two, it by no means proves that paradise is a state separate from heaven.

For, in Rev. ii. 7, we read : " To him that overcometh will I give to eat of the tree of life, which is in the midst of the paradise of God." Now, where the tree of life is, there is paradise ; but in the 22d chapter (1, 2) we read again : " He showed me a pure river

---

* Paul certainly had two raptures or visions, at least, before this: one at his conversion, near Damascus; another shortly after, at Jerusalem. Acts xxii. 17. But both were more than fourteen years before the date of the epistle, that, at the earliest, was written A. D. 56 — probably later.

of the water of life, clear as crystal, proceeding out of the throne of God and of the Lamb ; in the midst of the street of it, and on either side of the river, was there the tree of life." Where the throne of God and the Lamb is, there is the highest heavens, the place of final blessedness (see Rev. vii. 9) ; but the tree of life is planted near the throne; therefore, there is paradise. Compare, also, with the text, Rev. iii. 21, where, to him that overcometh, Christ promises a seat on his throne. The promises are parallel. In a word, what more natural than that, when the Spirit describes the restoration of man to blessedness, he should describe it by the images of the first paradise, and the tree of life, of which man was not there permitted to eat.

Before we entirely dismiss these controverted texts, let us put alongside of them several which are not controverted. The apostle in Philippians i. 21–23, says, " For to me to live is Christ, and to die is gain. . . . . For I am in a strait betwixt two, having a desire to depart and to be with Christ, which is far better." Now Christ is, all admit, in heaven, — body and soul. When, therefore, Christ in life, that is, the living to Christ here, is exchanged for departing to be with Christ, it must be because the soul will then go to heaven, where Christ is ; which is, indeed, " far better." The reply offered to this is that Christ by his divinity is omnipresent, and, also, by his Spirit present with his saints in their separate state ; but this is rather a quibble than an argument, since it was not necessary for the apostle to depart to be with Christ in that sense ; as he is here in his omnipresence and by his Spirit until the end of the world. The apostle evidently means a *personal* nearness to his Lord. So he says, 2 Cor. v. 5–8,

even when anticipating the fulness of the resurrection :
" Now he that hath wrought us for the self-same thing
is God, who also hath given unto us the earnest of the
Spirit.   Therefore, we are always confident, knowing
that, whilst we are at home in the body, we are absent
(not at home) from the Lord : for we walk by faith, not
by sight (that is, in this life) : we are confident, I say,
and willing rather to be absent* from the body (not at
home in the body), and to be present (at home) with
the Lord."   Certainly, this means personal nearness
and actual vision ; for the contrast is of sight to faith.
And where is the Christian's home — his dwelling, not
in a foreign land, but with his people ?   In *sheol*, or
heaven ?   In corroboration of this, see what Stephen
the martyr saw and said at his death, Acts vii. 55 :
" He, being full of the Holy Ghost, looked up steadfastly into heaven, and saw the glory of God, and Jesus standing on the right hand of God. . . . And they
stoned Stephen, calling upon God, and saying, Lord Jesus, receive my spirit ! "   Where would the Lord Jesus
receive the soul of his saint, but where he himself is ?

Other corroboratory passages might be added, but
these will answer our purpose.

II. The doctors of the reformed churches, finding
the article in the creed, and not wishing to reject it,
though having no respect for the dogmas of the papists,
expounded it in a sense conformable to the word of
God.   Thus Calvin (Ins. ii. 16, 10) : " Nothing had
been done if Christ had endured only corporeal death.
To interpose between us and the anger of God, and
satisfy his righteous judgment, it was necessary that he

---

* 'Εκδημέως — ἐκ and δῆμος — exiled, expatriated, away from one's
people.

should feel the weight of divine vengeance. Whence, also, it was necessary that he should engage at close quarters, as it were, with the powers of hell, and the horrors of eternal death. He undertook and paid all the penalties which must have been exacted from them (for whom he was Surety), the only exception being that the pains of hell could not hold him. Hence, there is nothing strange in its being said that " he descended into hell," as he endured the death which is inflicted on the wicked by an angry God. It is but a frivolous and ridiculous objection to say that this perverts the order of the creed, putting after the burial what preceded it. For, after explaining what Christ endured in the sight of man, the creed appropriately adds the invisible and incomprehensible judgment which he endured before (in the sight of) God, to teach us that not only was the body of Christ given up for our redemption, but that there was a greater and more excellent price : " That he bore in his soul the tortures of condemned and ruined men."

The same view is given by the authors of the " Heidelberg Catechism," in the 44th Question and Answer : " Why is there added : ' He descended into hell ? ' That, in my greatest temptations, I may be assured, and wholly comfort myself in this, that my Lord Jesus Christ, by his inexpressible anguish, pains, terrors, and hellish agonies, in which he was plunged during all his sufferings, but especially on the cross, hath delivered me from the anguish and torments of hell." With this the reformed theologians universally agree.

That our Lord did so suffer the wrath of God, and the curse due to us in his spirit, there can be no doubt; but that such was the meaning of the article when added to the creed after the burial, is not so clear. Yet the edification and comfort so derived is not less ; nor are we forbidden to think, if we choose, that it was inserted to comply with the scripture of the 16th Psalm, as quoted by the apostle at the Pentecost.

It may, however, be properly asked, how, if we reject, as we do, the notion of an intermediate state, was the time between his death on the cross and his burial spent by our Lord ?

To this our answer is, that, as he commended his departing spirit into the hands of his Father, and promised to take the penitent thief the same day into paradise, we believe that the soul of our Lord did go immediately to God in heaven. The next day being the Sabbath, the second Adam rested with God, after accomplishing the new creation, as the first Adam rested with Him after the former creation, in paradise.

The rest of the Sabbath being over, the soul of our Lord descended on the morning of the first day of the week, from heaven into *sheol*, or the grave, or the state of the dead ; not to be under the power of death, but as a conqueror, to take up again his body from under the earth. In the metaphorical language of Scripture, we may suppose that there was a conflict between our Lord, now the Lord of life, and " him that had the power of death, that is, the devil ; " for he is said to have vanquished the last enemy, — his spoils being his own ransomed body, which he displayed openly. Thus we read : " Whom God hath raised up, having loosed the pains of death, because it was not possible that he should be holden of it " (Acts ii. 24). So, also, in the 68th Psalm (18th v.) : " Thou hast ascended up on

high ; thou hast led captivity captive ; " upon which
the apostle (Ephes. iv. 8–10) comments : " Wherefore he saith, When he ascended up on high, he led
captivity captive, and gave gifts unto men.   Now that
he ascended, what is it but that he also descended first
into the lower parts of the earth ?   He that descended
is the same, also, that ascended up far above all heavens,
that he might fill all things."   And again in Col. ii.
15 : " Having spoiled principalities and powers, he
made a show of them openly, triumphing over them in
it," or by it, — his resurrection and ascension.   As a
conqueror in an ancient triumph showed not only the
spoils of his conquest, but exhibited his vanquished foes
in chains about his car, so did Christ, bearing aloft his
own body, the earnest of all the bodies of his people,
manifest his power.   Thus Hosea (xiii. 14) : " I will
ransom them from the power of the grave ; I will
redeem them from death.   O death, I will be thy
plagues !   O grave, I will be thy destruction ! "   On
which the apostle (1 Cor. xv. 54–56) : " Then shall
be brought to pass the saying that is written, Death is
swallowed up in victory.   O death ! where is thy
sting ?   O grave ! where is thy victory ?   The sting
of death is sin, and the strength of sin is the law ; but,
thanks be to God, who giveth us the victory through
our Lord Jesus Christ ! "   Or, as Heber sings in his
magnificent hymn for Easter : —

> " Now empty are the courts of death,
>   And crushed thy sting, Despair ;
> And roses bloom in the desert tomb,
>   For Jesus hath been there.

> " And he hath tamed the strength of hell
>   And dragged him through the sky ;

> And captive behind his chariot wheel
> He hath bound captivity.

> " God hath gone up with a merry shout
> Of his saints that sing on high;
> With his own right hand and his holy arm
> He hath won the victory ! "

Is it presumptuous to say that this view of the subject meets the questions, and corresponds with the testimony of Scripture?

PRACTICAL INFERENCES.

FIRST: *The completeness of Christ's work for us.*

He exhausted the curse in his sufferings, and there remains no hell for the believer.

He follows us even into the regions of the dead, and bursting the bars of death, opens the way for our resurrection.

He hath made death our servant and friend.

SECONDLY: *The blessedness of the believer's death.*

It is following Christ out of this life to heaven.

It is the departure of the soul, not into prison, or sleep, but into the presence of God.

It is leaving the body of sin and death in the grave, to be kept and purified by Christ until a glorious resurrection.

LECTURE XX.

THE RESURRECTION OF CHRIST.

SEVENTEENTH LORD'S DAY.

THE RESURRECTION OF CHRIST.

QUEST. XLV. *What doth the resurrection of Christ profit us ?*

ANS. First, by his resurrection he hath overcome death that he might make us of that righteousness which he had purchased for us by his death; secondly, we are also by his power raised up to a new life; and, lastly, the resurrection of Christ is a sure pledge of our blessed resurrection.

"THE THIRD DAY HE ROSE AGAIN FROM THE DEAD."

IF you take this article away from our creed, the whole system of evangelical doctrine is dissolved and crumbles to the ground like a building from under which the corner-stone has been dragged out. The prophets before him, our Lord himself, and the apostles after him, stake the credibility of the gospel in all its parts and as a whole, on the one fact of his resurrection from the dead (*a*). Without it the divinity of his person (*b*), the genuineness of his mission (*c*), the efficacy of his atonement (*d*), and the eternal life of his people (*e*) would be, not only without proof, but proved to be falsehoods. "If Christ be not risen," says the apostle, "then is our (*a*) preaching vain, and your faith is also vain." Again, he speaks of himself as "separated unto the gospel of God . . . concerning his Son Jesus Christ our Lord, which was made of the seed of David according to the flesh, and (*b*) declared to be the Son of God with power, according to the spirit of holiness, by the resurrection from the dead." Again, preaching to the Athenians on Mars-hill, he opens the doctrine of the mediatorship: "Now commandeth" God "all men everywhere to repent: because he hath appointed a day, in the which he will judge the world in righteousness (c) by that *man whom he hath ordained:* whereof he hath given assurance unto all men, in that *he hath raised him from the dead.*" Again: "If Christ be not raised, your faith is vain ; ye are yet in your sins : " which corresponds with the testimony in Romans — " To us also it " (that is the righteousness of faith which Abraham had) " shall be imputed, if we believe on him that raised up Jesus our Lord from the dead ; who was delivered for our offences, and was raised again (d) for our justification." So, also, the apostle Peter : " Blessed be the God and Father of our Lord Jesus Christ, which, according to his abundant mercy, hath (e) begotten us again unto a lively hope (a hope of life) by the resurrection of Jesus Christ from the dead, to an inheritance incorruptible, and undefiled, and that fadeth not away, reserved in heaven for you, who are kept by the power of God through faith unto salvation, ready to be revealed in the last time." Indeed, the testimony of the Old Testament throughout foretold the humiliation and consequent exaltation of the Messiah, as our Lord showed when, walking with the two disciples to Emmaus, he said : " O fools, and slow of heart to believe all that the prophets have spoken. Ought not Christ to have suffered these things, and to enter into his glory ? And, beginning at Moses and all the prophets, he expounded unto them in all the Scriptures the things concerning himself." Hence the resurrection of our Lord has been justly denominated the cardinal fact of Christianity ;

and we cannot over-estimate the importance of rightly understanding its vital relation to all the principles of our most holy faith. This is taught us in the 45th Question and Answer of the Catechism, under three comprehensive heads, which suggest the proper order for our thought, after some preliminary observations on matter brought before us by the phraseology of the creed.

By the resurrection of Christ we mean what the words of the article literally signify: " He rose again from the dead." As he actually died and not merely swooned away (of which his murderers certified themselves before he was taken down from the cross), so he actually rose up from death, leaving the tomb in which he had lain a living man. The same body which he took on him out of the flesh and blood of the Virgin Mary, (blessed was she above women, and blessed the fruit of her womb!) was crucified; the same body in which he was crucified, was buried, and so the same body rose up from the grave. It was not a phantasm, or mere semblance of a body, but a real, substantial body, identical with that which he had before his death; and in it the wounds he received on the cross were clearly visible. Thus, when he appeared to his disciples in the evening, they were "terrified and affrighted, and supposed that they had seen a spirit, and he said unto them: Why are ye troubled ? and why do thoughts (disputes) arise in your hearts ? Behold my hands and my feet " (those dear hands and feet which had been pierced by the nails), " that it is I myself: handle me and see ; for a spirit hath not flesh and bones as ye see me have. And, when he had thus spoken, he showed them his hands and his feet. And while they yet be-

lieved not for joy, and wondered, he said unto them,
Have ye here any meat? And they gave him a piece of
a broiled fish and of a honeycomb; and he took it and
did eat before them . . . Then opened he their understanding, that they might understand the Scriptures;
and said unto them, Thus it is written, and thus it behooved Christ to suffer, and to rise from the dead the
third day." The evangelist John farther informs us
that Thomas, the apostle, was not present on this occasion, and when told of it by the rest, he doubted the
story and said : " Except I shall see in his hands the
print of the nails, and put my finger into the print of
the nails, and thrust my hand into his side, I will not
believe. And after eight days again his disciples were
within, and Thomas with them. Then came Jesus,
the doors being shut, and stood in the midst and said,
Peace be unto you! Then saith he to Thomas, Reach
hither thy finger, and behold (perceive) my hands; and
reach hither thy hand, and thrust it into my side ; and
be not faithless, but believing. And Thomas answered
and said unto him, My Lord and my God." So also
the apostle Peter, when preaching to Cornelius and his
friends in Cesarea, says : " Him God raised up the third
day, and showed him openly ; not to all the people, but
unto witnesses chosen before of God, even to us, who did
eat and drink with him after he rose from the dead."
These were palpable, unmistakable proofs that the visible form of Jesus was a real, substantial, living body,
— the same that was crucified.

At the same time, the manner and character of the
corporeal life which our Lord had when visible to his
disciples on earth after his resurrection must have differed in some important particulars from those of the

life he had had before his death ; and, for the same reasons, his body must have been changed, not as to identity or essential quality, but as to its mode of being.
It becomes us to speak here with a reverent modesty,
yet we cannot and ought not to blink the questions
which necessarily arise.

The life which he received and exercised then was
not derived, as his former life or our ordinary life, from
physical generation and growth, but from the immediate will of God. His former life was necessarily, because of his body's natural tendency to decay, mortal.
The death of Christ in his human nature was as much
the inevitable consequence of his being born of a
woman as ours is. Nay, one of the main reasons why
he became a partaker of our flesh and blood was, that
he might die and, as the writer to the Hebrews says,
" through death . . . destroy him that had the power
of death ; " which he could not have done in any other
nature than human. But the life of Christ after his
resurrection was in its nature immortal, and his blessed
body incapable of decay or any of those weaknesses
which arise from a tendency to corruption. It was
the same life that he has now at the right hand of
the Father ; and, therefore, his body had all those properties that his body has, and the bodies of his saints will
have after their resurrection, in heaven. This body
and the change through which it passes, is described by
the apostle in the 15th of 1 Corinthians : " It is sown
in corruption, it is raised in incorruption ; it is sown in
dishonor, it is raised in glory ; it is sown in weakness,
it is raised in power ; it is sown a natural (animal)
body, it is raised a spiritual body ; and so it is written,
The first man Adam was made a living soul (that is,

made for an animal life); the last Adam was made
a quickening spirit." Now no one may pretend to understand the full meaning of these remarkable antitheti-
cal phrases (we must wait till the light of heaven for
that) ; but this much we can, with the aid of other
scriptures, discover : The heavenly life of the man
Christ Jesus, and of his people after their resurrection,
having a spiritual, not an animal source, will be so far
spiritual as to be set free from all animal necessities and
infirmities ; such as dependence on food and breath, and
liability to passion, appetite, weariness, sickness, and
decay. So, by consequence, their bodies will be ethere-
alized, purged from all grossness, no longer a hindrance
to their souls, but sympathizing with, and partaking of,
spiritual activity and indefatigable self-supporting energy. In a word, though we have not now time to
enter upon the edifying comparison, the glorified body
of Christ, as it was seen by the three disciples, transfigured on the top of Tabor, was the pre-manifestation of
his heavenly body, and the pattern after which the
bodies of the redeemed will be transfigured at the resurrection. " Our conversation is in heaven," says the
apostle, " from whence also we look for the Saviour,
our Lord Jesus Christ ; who shall change our vile body,
that it may be fashioned like unto his glorious body,
according to the working " (energy, which is the operation of the Holy Spirit,) " whereby he is able to subdue
all things unto himself ; " or again in the aforecited
chapter of 1 Corinthians : " As we have borne the
image of the earthy " (that is, of the first Adam who was
formed from the earth), " we shall also bear the image of
the heavenly " (that is, of the second Adam, the Lord
from heaven). Let it not be objected to this view of

our Lord's body after his resurrection, that he did actually partake of food. So did the angels who appeared
in bodily shape to Abraham and Lot. It was but a
gracious condescension of Christ to the weak minds of
his disciples, the more readily to convince them that he
was the same Lord who had so often broken bread with
them before; not because he needed the sustenance
requisite for a mortal life. Our own Witsius on this
quotes with high approbation a passage of St. Augustine: "To be incapable of taking food, or to stand in
need of food, would be equally an evidence of imper-
fection in the revived body. The parched earth swal-
lows up water in a very different manner from that in
which it is taken up by the burning sun. The one
does it from need, the other by power." For a like
reason, our Lord did not, during the forty days, appear
to the disciples in his glory. They could not have
identified him in such radiance with the man of sorrows, neither could they with their sensual eyes have
looked upon him and lived, as we know from the experience of the three witnesses who, on the holy mount,
became as " dead men."

While, however, we believe that the body of our
Lord was gloriously changed, we must reject the vain
notions of papists and others, that it became infinitely
divisible and omnipresent, as they contend that it is in
the mass. It continued to be a human body, and,
therefore, limited to such space as a human body naturally occupies; nor is it possible, in the nature of
things, even for a miracle to transubstantiate the sacra-
mental bread in the priest's hands, so as to make it
part of Christ's body, which is in heaven.

We should note, also, the language of the article:

" He rose."   He rose from the dead by his own mediatorial power.   He had purchased the right of uprising,
by his blood shed in expiation of sin.   Yet, in many
passages we read that God, even God the Father,
raised him up; and, in several, the quickening is ascribed to the energy of the Holy Ghost.   The same is
said of his incarnation: " God sent his Son, made of a
woman ; " " the Holy Ghost came upon the virgin, and
the power of the Highest overshadowed her; yet he
" took upon him the form of a servant ; " he took part
of flesh and blood.   So with his death : " It pleased the
Father to bruise him," and to " make his soul (life)
an offering for sin ; and though he of his own will laid
down his life for his friends, it was through the eternal
Spirit that " he offered himself without spot to God."
There is no contradiction in these several statements,
but a declaration of the consent and coefficiency of the
three persons of the ever-blessed Trinity in the several
processes of the redemption.   Glory be to the Father,
and to the Son, and to the Holy Ghost, Amen !

The article farther particularizes that it was the
third day on which our Lord rose again from the dead.
This is according to several scriptures, particularly
Christ's own words shortly after his transfiguration
(Mark ix. 31), and was literally true ; for he expired
on the afternoon of the day before the Jewish Sabbath
(our Friday), and rose on the morning of the first day
of the week.   But other scriptures seem to have foretold that the interval would be three days, or three
days and three nights.   He himself said to the Jews,
speaking of his body, " Destroy this temple, and in
three days I will raise it up ; " and again : " As Jonas
was three days and three nights in the whale's belly, so

shall the Son of Man be three days and three nights in the heart of the earth." But there is properly neither discrepance nor difficulty in this, the two expressions in the Hebrew manner of speech meaning the same thing. They began the day of twenty-four hours in the evening, and called it the evening and the morning, like the Greek night-day; and also reckoned a part of a day as the whole. So, as our Lord remained dead part of three days, they would express it by three days and three nights. Any objection to the truth of our Lord is frivolous, and any attempt to explain it otherwise than we have done would be incorrect. Our Lord and his disciples would not make so manifest a contradiction of themselves as the use of three days and three nights in any other sense would have been. He continued dead long enough to disprove the suspicion that he had only swooned, but not long enough, especially as his dear body was wrapt around with spices, to "see corruption."

He rose on the first day of the week, thus ushering in a new world; whence the early Christians under apostolical authority, which was equivalent to revelation, for they acted under the inspiration of the Holy Ghost, transferred the weekly rest, or Sabbath, from the seventh day to that of the resurrection. After this we have no trace of their keeping the seventh day, but many instances of their meeting together for Christian worship, instruction, and communion, on the first day of the week, to which they gave the name of the Lord's day (Rev. i. 10). The doctrine of the Sabbath will be handled at large in its proper place; but, while we devoutly acknowledge the obligation of the Sabbath to be perpetual, we cannot err in following apostolical example in connecting the Sabbath rest with the resurrection of him who is Lord of the Sabbath. The change is but another honor done to the mediatorial kingship of Christ, who appointed his Sabbath as the Creator in the beginning had appointed his. The transference of divine authority to the Mediator was aptly signalized by a change of the day symbolical of worship. It meets the instincts of the Christian heart. Man yet guiltless, the representative of God over the works of his hands, might enjoy, as he needed, communion with the Creator to prepare him for his holy duty; but man the sinner, whose only hope is in the merits of him whom the Father honors, and whose evangelical duty is in the kingdom of the Son, needs and can enjoy divine communion with his Saviour, and only through him can he reach communion with the Father, our God in Christ.

The last day of the week has for us no associations or warrant of hope. It leads us only to the tomb, where he, who had promised to redeem Israel, lies dead and cold, and, to all human sight, vanquished by our great enemy; but, on the morning of the first day, we meet a risen Saviour, triumphant over death, and victorious for us. Then, throughout the day, more than on any other, does he delight to mingle with us by his spirit, whether in our solitary searchings for him as man, or in our social converse, like the two disciples talking together as they walked, or in the full assembly, as the ten with the devout women. Oh, who that has enjoyed such communion with the Lord, can doubt that God the Father, Son, and Holy Ghost, has blessed our Sabbath day, and hallowed it?

Now, on what authority does the article before us

require our faith in the fact that our Lord rose again
from the dead on the third day ?   We answer solely on
the authority of the apostles.   There are, it is true,
corroboratory proofs from external history, but as Christians we can base our belief only on inspired records.
The story, as told by the evangelists with such wonderful agreement, is, indeed, a testimony to its own truth-
fulness ; but two of the four were themselves apostles,
and the other two companions of apostles, — Mark of
Peter, and Luke of Paul.   So it is on the apostolical
testimony alone that we depend.   This was the divine
arrangement.   In all the dispensation of the gospel, it
is the order of God that they who are saved should be
saved by faith and not by sight.   The pride of human
scepticism must be broken down by the truth, mighty
through the accompanying power of God.   It had been
easy for the risen Saviour to have showed himself alive
to the Sanhedrim and all the people of Jerusalem ; but
such is not the divine method.   Our Lord during his
life did exhibit before them every sufficient and prophetical proof of his Messiahship ; yet they wickedly
rejected and crucified him.   After his death and resurrection, he demonstrates the truth of his gospel, not by
mere human suffrages, but by its own divinity and his
confirming spirit.   It was graciously due to those who
had believed on him during his life of humiliation, that
they should behold him risen ; and it is most probable,
we might say certain, that he did show himself alive
after his passion, to all such believers ; but for others,
the testimony of the appointed witnesses was to be
enough.   So the apostle Peter, in the first sermon to
the Gentiles, says : " Him God raised up the third day,
and showed him openly, not to all the people, but unto

witnesses chosen before of God, even to us, who did eat and drink with him after he rose from the dead; and he commanded us to preach unto the people, and to testify that it is he which was ordained of God to be the judge of quick and dead. To him give all the prophets witness, that, through his name, whosoever believeth in him shall receive remission of sins." In conformity to this we are told, that all true believers, who constitute by aggregation the church of God, are built on the foundation of the apostles and prophets, Jesus Christ himself being the chief corner-stone, — the testimony of the prophets before Christ, and the testimony of the apostles after him, being united in his person, history, and works, as the Saviour. Nay, one of the chief purposes for which the apostleship was ordained was to testify of our Lord's resurrection; and a main, indispensable qualification for the office was that the one chosen should have seen the Lord after his resurrection. Thus, in the aforecited passage (Luke xxiv. 46–8), our Lord, in the evening of the day on which he arose, after having showed them his wounds and illuminated them with a knowledge of the Scriptures, added: "Thus it is written, and thus it behooved Christ to suffer, and to rise from the dead the third day: and that repentance and remission of sins should be preached in his name among all nations, beginning at Jerusalem. And ye are witnesses of these things. And behold, I send the promise of my Father upon you: but tarry ye in the city of Jerusalem until ye be endued with power from on high." So, when the eleven before the Pentecost thought it necessary to put one in the place of Iscariot, Peter said that one must be ordained to be a witness of his (the Lord's) resurrection.

Paul, called afterwards to be the apostle to the Gentiles, received this qualification by special vision of Christ, and vindicates his claim to the apostleship, which it would seem some had challenged by demanding : " Am I not an apostle ? Am I not free ? Have I not seen Jesus the Lord ? " And in another place, he says, after speaking of the other witnesses to the resurrection : " Last of all, he was seen of me also, as of one born out of due time. For I am the least of the apostles, that am not meet to be called an apostle, because I persecuted the church of God."

For this reason among others, we of the reformed churches consider that the apostolical office ceased with the first college, and that it is wholly unscriptural to hold of any minister in the church since, that he is a successor of the apostles as such. The apostles were also preachers, and we should be sorry to deny the right of any ordained minister of any evangelical church, to follow the apostles as a preacher of the word ; but at the same time we confidently and flatly deny that any preacher or minister of any rank, of any church, can be a successor of the apostles in any other sense, and consider such pretensions preposterous, arrogant, contrary to the truth of God. For, besides its being necessary to an apostle that he should be appointed immediately by Christ, should have the gift of inspiration, should be able to work miracles and to confer the grace of the Holy Ghost, — none of which marks are discernible in those who claim the office nowadays — it were enough to vitiate their assumption that they have not seen the Lord Jesus.

While, however, we receive the fact on the authority of the Holy Ghost in the apostles, the same Spirit bearing witness in our hearts that their word is true, we should be irrational not to inquire on what grounds their testimony is put beyond impeachment.

If Christ be not risen, as they state, Christianity is the most consummate imposture, and the result of the basest conspiracy that the world has ever seen. But this is impossible ; for let us consider, first : The character of the witnesses. They were, — with the doubtful exceptions of Matthew, the publican, among the eleven who were with Christ from the beginning, and of Paul, who was added four years after the crucifixion, — simple, unlearned, inexperienced, born in a rude country and bred to humble callings, — men most unlikely to originate such a scheme or to dare the risk of carrying it on. They were, also, ordinarily shrewd and not easily deceived as to facts that came under their immediate observation. But, if they had been deceived by the pretensions of him they followed, his death of weakness and shame, had it not been succeeded as he had foretold by his resurrection on the third day, would have undeceived them. The resurrection was the hinge on which their opinion of Jesus turned; and, had it not occurred, there was no motive for them to continue their adherence to his cause, but every reason for their abandonment of it. Yet, though their faith was weak and often vacillating before his death, shortly after it they appear among the people cognizant of the crucifixion, courageous, unhesitating and explicit in declaring their full reliance on the truth and power of the doctrine he had preached. And what was that doctrine but a system of the purest morals, the most religious obligations, the utmost self-denial and steadfastness under persecution in the hope of obtaining from a just God a recompense of mercy, not in this world but in eternity? There have been many false religions, and each has had many devoted followers, but no instance has been seen where men lied for the sake of virtue; conspired to cheat that they might make others upright; and braved the vengeance of God, to teach the world his worship in the purest and most spiritual form: certainly none in which the devotees based their delusion on a palpable fact of which their senses were judges, yet which had never occurred.

Consider also the number of the witnesses. The prophets, from the fall downward until the baptism of Christ, had all of them foretold the humiliation and glory of Christ, some of them with great particularity as to time, place, and circumstances; John the Baptist, at the height of an unparalleled influence over the people, jeoparded it all by declaring that he was only the forerunner of Christ, in whose rising light his should wane like a star before the morning sun; our Lord himself, while presaging his own ignominy and death, promised his followers nothing for this life but tribulation, shame, and persecutions. All occurred as it had been foretold: then, after his death he was seen alive (for, if we admit the testimony at all, the particularity with which it is given precludes deception or mistake respecting his identity and life) by the eleven apostles, with Matthias, all of whose statements fully and minutely harmonize; by the pious women; and, at one time, by more than five hundred brethren assembled, the greater part of whom were alive, as Paul says, twenty-eight years after, and not one of whom ever denied the assertions of the apostles; but, on the contrary, all of them continued steadfast in their faith, despite of persecution and obloquy. Now how can we believe that a conspiracy could be formed of so many persons of all ranks, stretching over twenty centuries, at least, for the purpose of deluding the world, contrary to its prejudices and habits, into the adoption of the purest, most beneficent system with which mankind has ever been blessed!

Consider, again, the circumstances in which the apostolical testimony was given : not in some remote, obscure place, but at Jerusalem, before the very multitude and within hearing of the very Sanhedrim, who had been promoters of the trial and crucifixion of Jesus, as well as personal observers of the natural prodigies said to have accompanied his death and uprising ; nor this long afterward, but at the close of fifty days. The apostle Peter at the Pentecost boldly appealed to the citizens of Jerusalem, and to the mixed multitudes of Jews and proselytes from Judea and other countries, who had been present all the time, for the truth of his assertions respecting the life and works of Jesus, his crucifixion, and the supernatural events accompanying it ; and then plainly declared his resurrection and ascension. Surely, then, the more intelligent and influential Jews had the opportunity (and they did not lack the will), if it were possible, to disprove the story ; yet so far from this, the very people who had clamored against Jesus and followed him with execrations, listen astounded, and thousands upon thousands of them embrace the gospel. The new church is founded close to the cross and tomb of its Master. There it lingered for several years, challenging investigation ; and thence its adherents scattered themselves over the greater part of the then known world, disputing with erudite philosophers, attacking hoary prejudices, denouncing popular idolatries adorned with magnificence and attractive through their sensualism, daring the anger of infuriated priests and absolute tyrannies : while they required, as the only method of reconciliation to God, that men learned and unlearned, freemen and slaves, kings and people of all nations and lands, should bow at the cross of an excommunicated Jew ; yet with such success, that though, in the course of three centuries, three millions of them had been martyred and many more treated as infamous and deserving of all outrage, the little church, at first not six hundred strong, had become, even in what the world estimates as strength, mightier than the Roman empire itself, — absorbing within its bosom sects of philosophy, religious armies, aristocracies and populace, though never a sword had been unsheathed for its defence or progress, and its only weapon was the truth of the gospel, confirmed by the resurrection of Jesus.

And what motives could there have been for such a conspiracy ? Why should the apostles with their attesting brethren, after having had proof of the imposture, if imposture it was, have united, contrary to all their avowed love of divine truth, to propagate the name of the deceiver ? That priestcraft in all ages has been cunning, and bold with schemes to attain power and wealth and luxurious gratifications, history abundantly shows ; that even Christianity, when in favor, has been prostituted and defiled for such purposes by its priests and hierarchs, that astute but unscrupulous rulers have used its forced alliance to strengthen thrones or erect dynasties, is most lamentably true ; but where had the apostles such inducements ? Forewarned by their master that they should suffer trial in every form, openly foretelling their own persecutions and martyrdom, promising their disciples a no better lot than their own, they lived as they professed to live, for reward after death, in an eternity where, if they were conspirators, and blasphemers, and liars, as they must have been if Christ had not risen, they could have expected nothing short of utter damnation.

Now, to say nothing of other proofs, many of which might and should be adduced in a longer treatise, we may safely conclude, as sturdy Barron expresses it, " that this testimony is beyond exception ; that no matter of fact ever had, or could well have, a more valid and certain proof : . . . . so that to refuse it, is in effect to decline all proof by testimony, to renounce all certainty in human affairs, to remove all grounds of proceeding securely in any business or administration of justice, to impeach all history of fabulousness, to charge all mankind with insufficiency or extreme infidelity, and to thrust God away from bearing credible attestation in any case." Nay, my brethren, may it not be truly said that, to be sceptical of the great fact which we this day celebrate, requires a greater credulity than the most absurd superstition ? At this very hour, all Christendom is exulting in honor of our risen Lord ; earth ascends toward heaven, and heaven is stooping toward earth, that the church below and the church above may blend their anthems in one grand harmony of praise, to the Lamb that was slain for our offences and raised again for our justification.

Let us now follow the Catechism in ascertaining how we are profited by the resurrection of Christ.

The answer supplied us is : —

" First, by his resurrection, he hath overcome death, that he might make us partakers of that righteousness which he had purchased for us by his death ; secondly, we are also by his power raised up to a new life; and, lastly, the resurrection of Christ is a sure pledge of our blessed resurrection."

We have here, to reduce the doctrine under brief heads, the assurance by the resurrection of Christ,

FIRST : *Of our justification.*

" He hath overcome death, that he might make us partakers of that righteousness which he had purchased for us by his death."

SECONDLY : *Of our sanctification.*

" We are also by his power raised up to a new life."

THIRDLY : *Of our final and full glorification.*

" The resurrection of Christ is a sure pledge of our blessed resurrection."

FIRST : *The resurrection of Christ assures us of our justification.*

The divine method of justifying the sinner who believes in Jesus, through the imputation of the infinitely meritorious righteousness wrought for us by our divine Surety, incarnate as our elder brother, has been handled at large under several previous sections of the Catechism, and need not now be formally discussed. Let us, however, remember that, in his atoning work, Christ acted under a covenant which he had made as our representative head with the Father, as representing the godhead ; and the conditions of the gracious covenant were, that, on his rendering a sufficient honor to the law which they had broken, the salvation of his people should be intrusted, with all power in heaven and earth, to his mediatorial hands.   It was necessary,

therefore, not only that he should be divinely acknowledged as the appointed Mediator, which was done by
the descent of the Holy Ghost upon him at the beginning of his ministry, but that, when his atoning work
was finished, its sufficiency and acceptance. should be as
divinely certified; and this was done by his being
raised from the dead to the right hand of the Father.
Thus the apostle, in that wonderful verse which is an
epitome of the whole gospel : " Let this mind be in
you, which was also in Christ Jesus ; who, being in the
form of God, thought it not robbery to be equal with
God, but made himself of no reputation, and took upon
him the form of a servant, and was made in the likeness of men ; and, being found in fashion as a man, he
humbled himself, and became obedient unto (until)
death, even the death of the cross ; wherefore, God
also hath highly exalted him, and given him a name
which is above every name."   This exaltation was the
exaltation, not of the Son of God merely, for he needed
none, but of the Son of God *incarnate*, as a servant, in
our room ; and was the reward of his obedience
wrought out all his life, even to his death on the cross.
In other words, he had fulfilled his part of the covenant by rendering an infinitely sufficient righteousness ;
and the Father fulfilled his part by exalting the crucified Redeemer to infinite power, with " a name which
is above every name, that, at the name of JESUS, every
knee should bow, of things in heaven, and things in
earth, and things under the earth ; and that every
tongue should confess that Jesus Christ is Lord, to the
glory of God the Father."

The fitness of such a recognition is apparent.   The
death passed upon the sinner by sentence of the law is

eternal death, because no amount of punishment that the sinner can endure can satisfy the law's offended honor : he can never pay the penal debt, and, therefore, must suffer on forever, because never relieved from condemnation.   So, had Christ not risen after he died, there was no proof that the honor he had vicariously done the law was sufficient.   To all seeming, his death, like ours, would have been eternal, and our representative, like ourselves, remained under the curse.   But when he, from the infinite dignity which his divine nature gave to his human sacrifice, had honored the law by the obedience of his active life, and the expiation of his submissive death had rendered the law an infinite honor, he had utterly paid the penalty, disarmed the curse, and exhausted death.   The avenger had no power over him ; it was not possible that he should be longer holden of the pains of death ; and, therefore, of his own right, purchased under the terms of the covenant, the Mediator arose, in manifestation that his saving work was accomplished and accepted.   Thus the writer to the Hebrews declares that " the God of peace brought again from the dead our Lord Jesus, the great Shepherd of the sheep, through the blood of the everlasting covenant ; " that is, through the virtue of his own blood shed as the head of the church, under the agreement of the gracious covenant ; and, in another place, the same writer declares that the Son of God was sanctified by the blood of the covenant (Heb. x. 29). The whole argument of the evangelical scriptures proceeds upon this.   The victims, — goats, or sheep, or calves, slain upon the Levitical altar, were proved to be mere types, pointing to the true sacrifice, but in themselves insufficient to take away sin, not merely because of their unworthy nature, but because, when slain, they never revived. Hence the necessity of fresh blood ; the craving law was never satisfied, the penalty was not paid, the death substituted was not enough.   Nothing short of his resurrection could show that the sacrifice of the substitute was accepted as sufficient.   Thus the writer to the Hebrews : " For the law, having a shadow of good things to come, . . can never, with those sacrifices which they offered year by year continually, make the comers thereunto perfect.   For then would they not have ceased to be offered ? because that the worshippers once purged should have had no more conscience of sins. . . . And every priest standeth daily ministering and offering oftentimes the same sacrifices, which can never take away sins ; but this man, after he had offered one sacrifice for sins forever, sat down at the right hand of God ; from henceforth expecting till his enemies be made his footstool. For, by one offering, he hath perfected forever them that are sanctified." From the moment that he said on the cross : " It is finished ! " the justification of his people was secured ; even the lifeless body of the Surety passed from the hands of his enemies into those of his friends, having suffered no farther insult except the rude opening of that blessed fountain of blood and water which has filled for us the pool of healing ; and he lay in the tomb only long enough to sweeten it for our rest : but the assurance, the divine acknowledgment, of the justifying merit, was not given till his resurrection.   Then we see, by his victory of the grave, that the sting of death was plucked out, and that the law has no more strength to hold us, and bless with triumphant voices our Lord Jesus Christ.   So the apostle in Romans : " Who shall lay anything to the charge of God's elect? It is God that justifieth. Who is he that condemneth? It is Christ that, died; yea, rather, that is risen again." And in full sympathy with the divine word, we may exclaim, in the words of the seraphic Hall: "Oh, my dear Saviour, I bless thee for thy death, but I bless thee more for thy resurrection. That was a work of wonderful humility, of infinite mercy; this, a work of infinite power. In that, was human weakness; in this, divine omnipotence. In that, thou ' wast delivered for our offences;' in this, thou ' wast raised again for our justification.' "

But there was something more needed than the display of his acceptance with the Father; the salvation of his people, now purchased by his blood, was to be accomplished by his power. He was to ask and receive for them the grace of the Holy Ghost, and by that Spirit make them actually partakers of his righteousness. The smitten, feeble flock needed the care and guidance and championship of its great and good Shepherd; the powers of hell were to be crippled, and the powers of heaven and earth employed for the triumph of his church; the gates of hell were to be borne away, and the everlasting doors of heaven flung open for their exodus from the grave to immortality; the angelic armies were waiting for the Lord of their hosts, the Captain of our salvation, to lead and direct them in the service of his redeemed, and the Father expecting him on his throne, that, to his coequal divinity, the infinite rule of providence might be given. He could not be Lord of the living while he remained among the dead. None but the risen Lord could say to the sorrowful believer, Why weepest thou? and chase away his tears

by a word of love.   None but the risen Lord could say
to the doubting one, " Be not faithless, but believing,"
while he opens the scriptures concerning himself to the
illuminated understanding.   None but the risen Lord
could say to his messengers, " Go ye into all the world
and preach the gospel to every creature ; and lo ! I am
with you always, even unto the end of the world." "No !
if Christ be not risen, then is our preaching vain ; "
" if Christ be not raised, then is our faith vain ; we are
yet in our sins ; " " if for this life only we have hope
in Christ, we are of all men most miserable."

SECONDLY : *The resurrection of Christ assures us of
our sanctification.*

The union of the believer with Christ, his representative head, is vital and perpetual.   " I am crucified
with Christ," says the apostle, " nevertheless, I live ;
yet not I, but Christ liveth in me ; and the life that I
now live in the flesh, I live by the faith of the Son of
God, who loved me, and gave himself for me."   As
by faith he dies in Christ's death on the cross, so by
faith he lives a new life in Christ's life after death.   As
Christ's life after his resurrection was a heavenly life,
so the life of the believer, who knows the power of
Christ's resurrection, as well as the fellowship of his
sufferings, is made conformable to Christ's death by
dying unto sin, and aspiring to Christ's life in heaven.
This is the generous and elevating argument, as the
apostle gives it : " Where sin abounded, grace did
much more abound ; that, as sin hath reigned unto
death, even so might grace reign through righteousness
unto eternal life, by Jesus Christ our Lord.   What
shall we say then ?   Shall we continue in sin, that
grace may abound ?   God forbid.   How shall we, who

are dead to sin, live any longer therein?   Know ye not
that so many of us as were baptized into Jesus Christ
were baptized into his death.   Therefore we are buried
with him by baptism into death; that, like as Christ
was raised up from the dead by the glory of the Father,
even so we also should walk in newness of life.   For,
if we have been planted together in the likeness of his
death, we shall be also in the likeness of his resurrection; knowing this, that our old man is crucified with
him, that the body of sin might be destroyed, that
henceforth we should not serve sin.   For he that is
dead is freed from sin.   Now, if we be dead with
Christ, we believe that we shall also live with him;
knowing that Christ, being raised from the dead, dieth
no more; death hath no more dominion over him.   For
in that he died, he died unto sin once; but in that he
liveth, he liveth unto God.   Likewise reckon ye also
yourselves to be dead indeed unto sin, but alive unto
God through Jesus Christ our Lord."   Nothing can
be clearer than this expository logic.   Sanctification follows necessarily upon justification through the atonement of Christ, as his resurrection followed his death.
We have no part in the one, if we do not feel the
power of the other.*

Besides, as we learn from several scriptures, the
same Holy Spirit by whose power Christ was raised,
quickens his people by grace.   The gift of that Spirit
without measure to Christ was promised him in the
covenant: "For it pleased the Father that in him
should all fulness dwell."   All grace comes from the

---

* See Ephesians i. 19-23; ii. 6, 7.   The parallel is drawn between the raising up of Christ and the conversion of the sinner.   Throughout the epistle,
the power of God signifies the Holy Ghost.

Father, but only through Christ, and through Christ only by the operating energy of the Holy Ghost. Christ needs not the grace for himself, but receives the fulness of the Spirit, that of his fulness we all might receive, and grace for grace. Hence the apostle Peter, at the Pentecost, proves the ascension of Christ, and accounts for the miraculous effusion of spiritual influences by the same word. " This Jesus hath God raised up, whereof we all are witnesses. Therefore, being by the right hand of God exalted, and having received of the Father the promise of the Holy Ghost, he hath shed forth this, which ye now see and hear." That Holy Spirit purchased for us by his merits, and obtained for us by his prayers, he continues to send down upon Christians as individuals, and as a church, and will until the consummation in glory. The grace of the Spirit is the sanctifying life of the church, sent from the head of the body through all his members ; and " he ever liveth to make intercession for us." It is of this inner grace, as well as Christ's power over providence, that the apostle was thinking when he says : " God commendeth his love towards us, in that, while we were yet sinners, Christ died for us. Much more, then, being now justified by his blood, we shall be saved from wrath through him. For if, when we were enemies, we were reconciled unto God by the death of his Son, much more, being reconciled, we shall be saved by his life ; " that is, his life after his resurrection. Salvation is completed only through sanctification ; sanctification only by the grace of the Holy Ghost ; and that grace is obtained for us only by him who ever liveth to make intercession for us. So the apostle Peter, speaking of our lively hope from the resurrection of Jesus, says that the heavenly inheritance is "reserved" for those "who are kept by the power of God, through faith unto salvation." Notwithstanding all Christ's sufferings, we should despair of reaching heaven, were it not that he who died for us now lives for us, to make us more than conquerors over temptation without and corruption within. Thus it is that we are by his power raised up to a new life ; and now, because Christ that died is risen again, and is now at the right hand of God, and also maketh intercession for us, we know that the author will be the finisher of our faith, and may well be persuaded that nothing will be able, to separate us from the love of God, which is in Christ Jesus our Lord. " Because *he* lives, *we* shall live also."

THIRDLY : *The resurrection of Christ assures us of our final and full glorification.*

The answer in the Catechism is confined to our resurrection, and the ascension of Christ is the subject of the next article, the discussion of which will involve our assurance of an entrance with him into glory. But, though theologians distinguish, and very properly, the several degrees of our Lord's exaltation, the Scriptures often speak of his resurrection and ascension together, as though his ascension began in his rising from the grave, and finished in his sitting at the right hand of the Father. So in Philippians : " He was obedient unto death, even the death of the cross : wherefore God hath highly exalted him." " This Jesus hath God raised up," says the apostle at the Pentecost, " whereof we all are witnesses. Therefore, being by the right hand of God exalted, ... he hath shed forth this," manifestly from his throne ; and in his first epistle he says that, by the resurrection of Jesus Christ, we are begotten to a lively hope of our heavenly inheritance. If a view we took of the matter in our study of the last Lord's Day be correct, our Lord ascended to his Father immediately after he arose, though for obvious reasons he returned at intervals to show himself to his disciples, and to make a formal, visible ascension at the end of forty days. Certainly, the apostle Paul teaches that there will be no such interval (as, indeed, there is no reason for it) between the rising of the saints, and their reception into glory : " We shall not all sleep, but we shall all be changed, in a moment, in the twinkling of an eye, at the last trump." The change spoken of is into glory. So again : " The Lord himself shall descend from heaven with a shout, with the voice of the archangel, and with the trump of God ; and the dead in Christ shall rise first : then we which are alive and remain (that is, those Christians who shall be living at the time) shall be caught up together with them in the clouds, to meet the Lord in the air : so shall we be ever with the Lord." It is impossible, therefore, for us not to connect closely our glorification with our resurrection. The resurrection promised us is not a renewal of our animal life, nor a life to be spent upon earth, even in part, but an instant and full entrance to heaven, of which our Lord's ascension was both type and assurance.

He died and was buried, not as an individual man, but as the recognized head of his church ; and, therefore, he arose not as an individual, but as the head of his church, in which capacity he also ascended to heaven and now reigns at the right hand of the Father. But if the head ascends, the body ascends with it. Thus I find that the Latin translators of the Catechism insert the word "Head" here: "The resurrection of Christ *our Head* is a sure pledge of our blessed resurrection." All who by faith die with him, shall, through the indissolubleness of their vital union to him, rise with him, that, as they have partaken of his shame, they may partake of his glory. The consummation of this privilege is for wise reasons delayed, but the resurrection of Christ is the assurance of its certainty. For as without the resurrection of Christ we should have no proof that he is the Saviour, so except we shall be raised we can have no salvation.

The soul of the believer could not at death enter heaven unless it was made certain that in due time his body should be raised also. For the soul of the man is not the man; neither is the body of a man, the man: the man is not perfect, the whole man is not saved, except he be saved soul and body. The curse of death fell upon man, both soul and body; the grace of eternal life through the second Adam is given to the believer, both soul and body. The Son of God, when he came to be incarnate as our Surety, took to himself a human body and soul, else would he not have been a man: so he suffered for us the pains of the curse in both his body and his soul; and so he rose as our Surety, having accomplished the atonement, both body and soul. So, also, because of his acknowledged satisfaction, shall we who believe in him be redeemed, body and soul, and raised to the blessedness where he is. Thus the apostle: "Now is Christ risen from the dead, and become the first-fruits of them that slept. For since by man came death, by man came also the resurrection of the dead. For as in Adam all die, even so in Christ shall all be made alive. But every man (each) in his

own order : Christ the first-fruits ; afterward they that
are Christ's at his coming." The argument is brief, but
conclusive. Other questions on this doctrine will be
discussed, when we come to the article on the resurrection of the body.

For the present let us rejoice that " this mortal shall
put on immortality, and this corruption, incorruption."
Our life is brief, so was our Lord's ; it is full of sorrows,
but his incomparably fuller ; it is racked with pain, but
never so exquisite and manifold as his ; it is worse than
grief and torture, it is polluted with sin, and there we
are unlike him, the holy, harmless, and undefiled ; it
ends with agony and death and the grave, and to the
close we may track his blood-stained footsteps. But this
is not all of life : Christ has risen to a life eternal, heavenly, holy, and blest. So shall all his people live, where
sin or sorrow or pain or death can reach them no more
forever.

O beloved friends, shall all of us have part in that
blessed resurrection ? Have we all been crucified with
Christ ? Have we all been converted, are we all sanctified to newness of life ? Have we all set our affections beyond and far above this world, where Christ
sitteth at the right hand of God ? O let us see to it
that we are sealed with that Holy Spirit of promise ;
for a new heart, and a Christian life here, is the only
earnest of a glorious life hereafter.

O remember (God, for his Son's sake, make us all
remember!) that there is also a resurrection unto damnation, and that all who are not Christ's in faith, certified by practice, pass through death and the grave into
the second death, and hell, from which there is no return forever ! It is a terrible alternative ! Save us,

O heavenly Father! Save us, O Holy Spirit! Save us, O Jesus Christ! Standing beside the broken tomb of the crucified, and looking up through the rent vail to the throne of God and the Lamb, we pray, Save us from eternal death!

LECTURE XXI.

THE ASCENSION OF CHRIST.

EIGHTEENTH LORD'S DAY.

THE ASCENSION OF CHRIST.

"He ascended into heaven."

QUEST. XLVI. *How dost thou understand these words: "He ascended into heaven?"*

ANS. That Christ, in sight of his disciples, was taken up from earth into heaven ; and that he continues there for our interest, until he come again to judge the quick and dead.

QUEST. XLVII. *Is not Christ then with us, even to the end of the world, as he hath promised?*

ANS. Christ is very man and very God; with respect to his human nature he is no more on earth, but with respect to his Godhead, majesty, grace, and Spirit, he is at no time absent from us.

QUEST. XLVIII. *But if his human nature is not present wherever his God-head is, are not then these two natures in Christ separated from one another?*

ANS. Not at all; for since the Godhead is incomprehensible and omni-present, it must necessarily follow that the same is not limited with the human nature he assumed, and yet remains personally united to it.

QUEST. XLIX. *Of what advantage to us is Christ's ascension into heaven?*

ANS. First, that he is our advocate in the presence of his Father in heaven ; secondly, that we have our flesh in heaven, as a sure pledge that he, as the Head, will also take up to himself us, his members; thirdly, that he sends us his Spirit as an earnest by whose power we seek the things which are above, where Christ sitteth on the right hand of God, and not things on earth.

ALTHOUGH Christ's satisfaction for his people was complete when on the cross he said, "It is finished !" and bowed his head and gave up the ghost, and although its completeness was certified by his resurrection, which showed that death had no power over him, there remained. yet much to be. accomplished by him for the full redemption of his church in glory ; and since he came from the bosom of his Father, it was necessary to the manifestation of his consummate acceptance as our mediatorial Head that he should, according to his own word, "ascend up where he was before." Hence the ascension of Christ into heaven is a most important and edifying article of our Christian belief. Indeed, except we rightly understand and personally apprehend the doctrine of this great fact, it is impossible to enjoy the best comforts of our holy religion, or to acquire the divine strength essential for our perseverance in a Christian life. May God help us in our pious study!

Our church, in the lesson of the Catechism to-day, supplies us with an excellent method of thought, which, by the aid of the Holy Spirit, we shall endeavor to follow.

FIRST: *The fact of our Lord's ascension* (46th Ques. and Ans.), *with some explanations* (47th, 48th).

SECONDLY: *The advantage it is to us* (49th).

FIRST: *The fact of our Lord's ascension into heaven.*

The *testimony* recorded by the evangelical writers is abundantly sufficient for our faith.

The evangelist Mark declares (xvi. 19), that after Jesus "had spoken" unto his disciples, "he was received up into heaven, and sat on the right hand of God." The evangelist Luke, in the last chapter of his Gospel, and the first of the Acts of the Apostles, gives a particular account of the event. He ascended in full view of the eleven, and, probably, of the pious women, his mother, and some of his believing kinsmen (Acts i. 13, 14). After a cloud had received him out of their sight, two angels appeared, declaring that he had been taken up into heaven (11th). Stephen, the protomartyr, at his death, (vii. 56,) and Paul at his conversion, (ix. 1–17,) saw the Lord Jesus in heaven, as also did John in the apocalyptic vision (Rev. i. 13–18). The descent of the Holy Ghost at the Pentecost confirms it, when we compare the prophecy (Ps. lxviii. 18) : " Thou hast ascended on high ; thou hast led captivity captive ; thou hast received gifts for men ; yea, for the rebellious also, that the Lord God might dwell among them ; " with the apostle Peter's declaration (Acts ii. 33) : " Therefore (Jesus) being by the right hand of God exalted, and having received of the Father the promise of the Holy Ghost, hath shed forth this which ye now see and hear ; " and also that of the apostle Paul (Ephes. iv. 7, 8) : " Unto every one of us is given grace according to the measure of the gift of Christ (that is, the Spirit). Wherefore he saith, When he ascended up on high, he led captivity captive, and gave gifts unto men."

The *time* of our Lord's ascension was forty days after he had risen from the dead, he having been with his disciples repeatedly during that interval, for the purpose of proving to them his resurrection, teaching them more fully his doctrine, and giving them directions how they should serve him after his departure. Why this interval was forty days we are not told. Moses was the same time in the mount after he had brought down the moral law, which had the sentence of death, while receiving the typical law, which foreshadowed the kingdom of Christ (Ex. xxiv. 18). Elijah travelled forty days in the strength of the food brought him by the angel, until he reached Horeb, where he heard Jehovah in the still small voice, the type of the Holy Ghost (1 Kings xix. 5–12). Jesus himself fasted forty days between his unction and his triumph over the tempter ;

and several other instances show that to have been a
period often fixed by God, doubtless for wise reasons.
But the most interesting parallel is the forty days from
his birth to his presentation in the temple (compare
Luke ii. 22, with Leviticus xii. 2, 4, 6). " So," as our
Witsius observes, " on the fortieth day after his resurrection, which was a second nativity, he went to appear
before his heavenly Father in the temple not made with
hands." The time was long enough for the purposes
to which he put it, but brought to a close the moment
when the disciples showed a supposition that he was
about establishing a temporal kingdom on earth :
" Lord," said they, " wilt thou at this time restore the
kingdom to Israel ? " — and immediately after he had
answered them, referring to the gift of the Spirit, while
they beheld " he was taken up " (Acts i. 6–9). In
the course of these forty days he appeared, as recorded
by the evangelists, at least eight times, and the disciples
had the most convincing proof of his having risen
bodily from the grave.

The *place* from which he ascended was Bethany : not
the village, as that was fifteen furlongs from Jerusalem,
and he would hardly have chosen a spot where there
must have been many unbelieving spectators ; but the
district of Bethany, which lay on the near side of
Mount Olivet, adjoining the district of Bethphage, and
about a mile, or a Sabbath-day's journey, from Jerusalem (Acts i. 12 ; Luke xxiv. 50, 51 ; John xi. 18).
" He led them out *as far as Bethany* ; " that is, to the
spot where the district began. The Mount of Olives,
and the district of Bethany in particular, were dear to
Jesus from many delightful associations ; and, if we
adopt the etymology which makes Bethany signify the

place of sorrow, there is an eloquent fitness in his ascension thence from our sorrowful earth to his heaven of joy.

He *actually* ascended. It was no vision; in the clear daylight, the disciples saw him parted from them, and going up through the atmosphere.

God the Father, by the efficient Spirit, took him up. It is probable that he was borne aloft by invisible angels, as by those ministering spirits God executes his works; yet we are right, also, in saying that he went up, or ascended, by his own power, — the power of his personal divinity, the power of the Holy Ghost within him, and the power which he had, by prerogative of his mediatorship, purchased by his accepted atonement.

He went up *body* as well as *spirit*. He carried his entire humanity up with him; the very humanity which had been born of the Virgin Mary, which had gone through the sorrows, duties, and temptations of our mortal life; which had been " crucified, dead, and buried." This we know from many scriptures, as (Heb. iv. 14) where it is said that *Jesus* (our Lord's name as the Son of Man), " our great High Priest," " has passed into the heavens." Again (x. 12) : " This man (that is, this very same person), after he had offered one sacrifice for sins, forever sat down at the right hand of God." Again (19, 20) : " Having, therefore, brethren, boldness to enter into the holiest by the blood of Jesus by a new (freshly slain) and living way, which he hath consecrated for us, through the vail, that is to say, his flesh," etc. His recently slain yet living flesh is the way into the holiest (the presence of God), which he has consecrated for us, by which to pass through the vail. The same is taught by those pas-

sages which assert that the glorified body of the second
Adam, our Redeemer, is the pattern and earnest of the
glory that will invest the heavenly bodies of his saints
(1 Cor. xv. 42–49 ; Phil. iii. 21).

He went up into *heaven*. Heaven is the place or
state where God dwells in his highest, most resplendent
glory. The Jews supposed that heaven was supernal,
or beyond the earth's atmosphere, and the language of
Scripture is in accordance with their opinion. Thus,
from every part of the earth's surface, the way to
heaven is upward. It is remarkable, also, that heaven,
as on the Mount of Transfiguration, seems to have
descended, meeting the Lord as he rose. " A cloud
received him out of their sight " (Acts i. 9) ; not a
dark cloud, that would have been inconsistent with the
purport of the scene ; but, probably, as the early
church believed, a bright cloud, like the Shekinah, or
that on Tabor, (Matt. xvii. 5,) or the light to which no
man can approach, within whose brightness the king
immortal dwells (1 Tim. vi. 16). We may compare
this with Psalm xviii. 9 : " He bowed the heavens
also, and came down ; " and many other scriptures
which show that when God makes a special manifestation of his presence, he depresses heaven towards the
earth, as now he met Jesus in the air.

Thus our incarnate Lord ascended into heaven, to
his Father's immediate presence, for us ; " higher than
the heavens," " above all heavens," " through the
heavens ; " that is, to the very highest seat of the majesty on high ; not only entering the glory, but himself
glorified in it. As we read in a former part of the
gospel (John vii. 39) : " The Holy Ghost was not yet
given, because that Jesus was not yet glorified ; " and

he prayed before his passion : " I have glorified thee on earth ; I have finished the work which thou gavest me to do. And now, O Father, glorify thou me with thine own self, with the glory which I had with thee before the world was." To such a height of divine glory did Jesus carry our human nature with him.

The 47th and 48th questions and answers are intended to meet certain objections supposed to be made against the true doctrine of our Lord's person, and have reference to an opinion held by the Papists and some others, especially among the followers of Luther, that the Saviour's humanity may be omnipresent, as in the bread and wine of the sacrament, which they contend is transubstantiated to, or consubstantiated with, his body. These ubiquitarians (as they are called, from *ubique*, everywhere) cite in support of their notion the promise of our Lord to the church : " Lo, I am with you alway, even unto the end of the world." How, say they, can Christ be with his people, if he be not personally everywhere ? And since it is admitted on all hands that his divinity is omnipresent, how can his humanity be united to his divinity, if it be not omnipresent also ? Or how, if this be not so, can Christ " fill all things," according to the testimony of the apostle Paul ? To all this our church most conclusively answers by saying that our Lord, being both God and man, is, indeed, present with us in his divine nature, especially by his power, grace, and Holy Spirit ; but that his human nature, being essentially limited, cannot be with us on earth while it is in heaven. Nor does this bring into doubt the unity of his person, since he assumed the human nature to his divinity ; his humanity continuing finite, else it ceases to have a main quality of humanity, the divinity continuing infinite, else it ceases to be divine. For when it is said that God dwells in the flesh, it must not be thought that the divine nature is circumscribed by the human, but that it manifests itself through the finite nature thus adjoined. The divinity is ever present with the humanity; but the humanity is not everywhere present with the divinity. Thus our Lord expressly said to his disciples: "It is expedient for you that I *go away*: for if I go not away, the Comforter will not come unto you; but, if I depart, I will send him unto you." Christ did go away; his disciples saw his human nature ascend into heaven; and afterward at the Pentecost he did send, as since he has continued to send, his Holy Spirit from the right hand of the Father. Nay, on any other ground, what can be the meaning of those many texts which promise that Christ will come again to judge the world, and to receive his people to himself, that where he is they may be also?

Secondly: *The advantage to us of our Lord's ascension* (49th).

As we had occasion to say when treating of our Lord's resurrection from the dead, we must, as the Scripture teaches us, consider the resurrection complete in the ascension to glory. He came from heaven to accomplish the atonement in his death; therefore, his assumption from death to heaven proved that his vicarious righteousness was complete and accepted. Noting this point we pass to those of the Catechism, which are three.

1. Christ is our advocate in the presence of his Father in heaven.

This advocacy, or pleading on behalf of his people,

we are told by many scriptures, especially the Epistle to the Hebrews, is a large part of Christ's office in heaven. The Jewish high priest, the accurate type of Christ, once a year, after he had offered on the altar the great sacrifice of atonement, also a direct type of the suffering Saviour, passed within the vail that excluded all but himself from the Holy of Holies; bearing with him some of the victim's blood, which he sprinkled on the propitiatory, or mercy-seat, that covered in the ark the law broken by sin; and, having thus presented the sign of atonement in the presence of Jehovah, he then and there made intercession for the people whom he represented. Let us also connect with this the memorable fact that, at the dedication of the first temple, the type of the true church, "fire came down from heaven and consumed the burnt-offering and the sacrifices, and the glory of the LORD (that visible glory which symbolized the spiritual presence of Jehovah) filled the house," and so consecrated it as his own. Thus, when our great High Priest Jesus had completed his atonement for us, he carried with him into the highest, holiest heavens the immediate presence of God, — not merely his blood, for that was the sign of a dead sacrifice; but — his reanimated, immortal body which had been sacrificed on the cross, God rending the vail before him and leaving it rent, in token that all may draw nigh through him; and there, not like his sinful type pleading as a suppliant, but as the Son sitting at the right hand of his Father, claiming the covenanted prerogatives of his mediatorship, he asked, and, blessed be his name! ever liveth to ask the grace of the Holy Spirit to seal forgiveness and adoption on the hearts of his people as the divine assurance that his ransomed church is accepted and consecrated of God for his sake. The typical sacrifice was offered repeatedly, because it was only a type ; the typical high priest entered the Holy of Holies every year, because he was only a type ; but our true Sacrifice, having offered himself once for all, rose from the dead because his atonement was infinitely sufficient; and our true High Priest having entered heaven to receive the blessings of his purchase, " forever sat down at the right hand of God, from henceforth expecting till his enemies be made his footstool ; for by one offering he hath perfected forever them that are sanctified." Hence the effusion of the Holy Spirit — which had not before been given, or given only in preliminary drops, because Jesus was not yet glorified — upon the church at the Pentecost when Jesus was by the right hand of God exalted ; and hence, because he continues in his glory, the grace from on high continues to descend, and will continue until his whole ransomed church is complete in glory like himself. Yes, dear Christians, the ascension of our faithful Lord, of which we have proof in the grace of the Holy Ghost, is to us a demonstration that we have an advocate on high, who will not forget those whom he is not ashamed to call his brethren, who will ask for us all that we need ; and who can never ask, as our necessities can never require, more than his merits deserve or his almighty Father will delight to give. The vail is rent ; and though our mortal eyes cannot pierce the invisible world, our faith sees Jesus, our head, on his peerless throne. Let us then exult with the apostle and say to each other, as he said to the Hebrew Christians : " Having, therefore, brethren, boldness to enter into the Holiest by the blood of Jesus, by a new and living way, which he hath consecrated for us, through the vail, that is to say, his flesh ; and, having an High Priest over the house of God, let us draw near with a true heart in full assurance of faith." The weak prayers which, rising from our sinful hearts, a just God would not listen to, can reach the ear of our sympathizing brother ; and he, combining with them his mediatorial right and divine eloquence, will make them infallibly prevalent. None can fail who plead through Christ.

2. " We have our flesh in heaven, as a sure pledge that he as the head will also take up to himself us, his members."

Our Lord, as we have seen, actually ascended body and soul into heaven, and there he now lives, a perfect man, at the right hand of God. As truly as his blessed body was born, lived, suffered, died, and rose again, so truly is it at this moment in heaven. Hence we learn that there is no physical reason against our humanity being received into heaven and living there. It is true, as was shown in our last lesson, the life which Christ has had since his resurrection, differs from that which he had before his death, being derived not from birth of a woman, but from the immediate power of God ; yet his human nature continued unchanged in any essential quality, and will continue the same forever. It was our nature he had on earth, it is our nature he has in heaven ; where the man Christ Jesus lives we may live. He triumphantly entered heaven not for himself alone : as the eternal Son of God it was his by original right ; but, as the head of his church, the kinsman, redeemer of his people, he took possession of their heavenly inheritance, " which hope," says the apostle to the Hebrews, meaning the hope of heaven, " we have as an anchor of the soul, both sure and steadfast, and which entereth into that within the vail; whither the forerunner is for us entered, even Jesus, made an High Priest forever after the order of Melchizedec." The sublime elevation of Christ has not separated him from his people. He is still their head, and they his body. He still represents them as their champion, advocate, and king. " Where my flesh reigns, I reign," says Augustine. As in his death our shame was upon him, so in his majesty his glory will be upon us. " I go," said he to his disciples as the time approached when he should be received up, " to prepare a place for you ; and if I go and prepare a place for you, I will come again, and receive you to myself, that where I am, there ye may be also." The express purpose for which he ascended was to prepare places for us near his own, and his purpose would fail did he not take up to himself us, his members.

And here I cannot deny you, or myself, the pleasure of enjoying the eloquence of Witsius, whose soul burns with more than seraphic fire, while expatiating on this animating theme. " It was important to Christ, that he should possess the right which he had procured for himself, and that, having valiantly and successfully overthrown his enemies, he should be carried in a triumphal chariot, and amidst the shrieks of devils, and the acclamations of angels, amidst the amazement of the wicked, and the choruses of the faithful, make a glorious and joyful entry, not into a capitol like that of Rome, but into the heavenly Jerusalem, and the temple not made with hands, there to enjoy a delightful rest after the long travail of his soul. . . . . There (also)

had he to set up his chair as a prophet, that he might
instruct his people by his Spirit, who irradiates their
minds from above. There he had to appear in the
presence of God as a priest, . . . and as the high priest
to enter within the vail and make intercession for the
people. There he was to take possession of the throne
of his kingdom, that he might hear the angels around
the throne, shouting with a loud voice: 'Worthy is
the Lamb that was slain, to receive power, and riches,
and wisdom, and strength, and honor, and glory, and
blessing;' that, looking down from his lofty seat, he
might laugh at the impotent rage of his enemies, and
from that impregnable fortress afford the most effectual
succor, and liberally bestow the richest gifts on his
saints. . . . . Nor can any one of them fail to regard
with most lively interest an inauguration of their king
so splendid, and a triumph of their champion so magnificent. What can be more delightful for them than
to see their Lord, who, so lately overwhelmed with so
many waves of unparalleled trouble and sorrow, even
to the very abysses of hell, now shining in the fresh
splendor of a spiritual body, exalted far above the
stormy clouds and dreadful thunders ; nay, above the
sun himself, and the loftiest of the stars, made higher
than all heavens, and taking possession of the throne
as his father's equal, amidst the congratulations of angels, and of the spirits of just men made perfect! . . .
' God is gone up with a shout; Jehovah with a sound
of a trumpet. Sing praises to God, sing praises. Sing
praises to our king, sing praises. For God is the king
of all the earth ; sing ye praises with understanding.' "

3. " He sends us his Spirit as an earnest, by whose
power we seek those things which are above, where

Christ sitteth on the right hand of (the Father) God, and not things on earth."

We have already anticipated much of this head, and seen how the sending of the Spirit was, and continues to be, the proof and assurance of Christ's having entered heaven as the head and forerunner of his people; for he had said : " If I go not away, the Comforter will not come unto you ; but if I depart, I will send him unto you." Yes, dear brethren, none of us may know that we have the benefits of Christ's ascension, unless we have received his Spirit into our hearts, and are conscious of its sanctifying and elevating influences. As the apostle says : " After that ye believed, ye were sealed with that Holy Spirit of promise, which is the earnest of your inheritance until the redemption of the purchased possession, unto the praise of his glory." By faith we die with Christ in his crucifixion, we are quickened to a new life with Christ in his resurrection, and so we rise heavenward with Christ in his ascension. So again: " He hath raised us up together, and made us sit together in Christ Jesus." Again : " If ye then be risen with Christ, seek those things that are above, where Christ sitteth on the right hand of God. Set your affections on things above, not on things on the earth. For ye are dead, and your life is hid with Christ in God." It is therefore essential to a spiritual following of Christ, a necessary sign of our fellowship with him, that we cherish not only an expectation, but an earnest, longing, increasing desire for heaven. The things of earth are a snare and a hurt, except as we use them to help us on our way heavenward ; the duties of this life are not faithfully performed, except as we aim in them to fit ourselves through grace for heaven ; nay, the religious blessings we are permitted to enjoy here, fail of their end if they do not urge us onward to a full fruition in heaven.   Our Christian life is a course through this world, which we are to run looking unto Jesus at the right hand of the throne of God.   The mark of the prize of the high calling is in heaven.   Nay, it is the hope of heaven which keeps our souls surely and steadfastly.   No matter what other proofs of his being a Christian a man may think that he has, — what moral virtues, what present zeal, what reverence for God and sacred things, what kindness and faithfulness to his fellow-men, — if he have not this longing thirst for heaven, he should doubt his Christianity.   The regenerate soul can be satisfied with nothing short of awaking with the divine likeness.   We cannot pray aright without hoping for heaven, for there only will the askings of a pious heart be fully granted.   We cannot give thanks aright without hoping for heaven, for there are the consummate blessings of the Redeemer's purchase.   We cannot serve God aright without hoping for heaven, for there only is our faithfulness to be acknowledged, and our wages paid.   Our hope should be submissive, and our longing patient ; we should be willing to remain so long as God has work for us here, but ever with a yearning sense that to depart and be with Christ is far better.   Grace in the heart is an ascensive power, ever lifting its desires upward and upward, and so above the temptations of time and earth.   We can never drive this world out of our hearts, but by bringing heaven into them.   And heaven meets our affections when they ascend, as it met Jesus ; and he who so walks, climbing the arduous way from the valley of Baca to the temple on the mount (for we must walk until we get our wings of angelic strength), will so approach the heavenly threshold, as, like holy Enoch, he can cross it at a step.

Oh, dear friends, what an advantage have they whose Jesus is in heaven, over those first disciples when they had him with them personally on earth. They were for building tabernacles on Tabor, looking for a temporal kingdom, walking by sight and not by faith ; but our Lord now above draws up to a better, higher, holier home our aims, our desires, and our love. Have they who thus believe and hope, says an excellent father of our own church, " a double ensurance of heaven, since they have their nature there as a pledge, and the Holy Spirit in their souls as an earnest ? "

LECTURE XXII.

CHRIST ON THE THRONE AS RULER AND JUDGE.

CHRIST ON THE THRONE AS RULER AND JUDGE.

QUEST. L. *Why is it added " and sitteth at the right hand of God? "*

ANS. Because Christ is ascended into heaven for this, and that he might there appear as head of his church by whom the Father governs all things.

QUEST. LI. *What profit is this glory of Christ, our head, unto us?*

ANS. First, that by his Holy Spirit he poureth out heavenly graces upon us as his members; and then that by his power he defends and preserves us against all enemies.

QUEST. LII. *What comfort is it to thee that Christ " shall come again to judge the quick and the dead? "*

ANS. That in all my sorrows and persecutions, with uplifted head, I look for the very same person who before offered himself for my sake to the tribunal of God, and hath removed all curse from me, to come as judge from heaven; who shall cast all his and my enemies into everlasting condemnation, but shall translate me with all his chosen ones to himself, into heavenly joys and glory.

THE assumption of Christ Jesus into heaven testified the divine approval of his work on earth, as his uprising from the dead demonstrated the sufficiency of his expiation. The only begotten Son of God had been sent from heaven into the world to provide a righteousness for our justification through faith ; and when that end was fulfilled, he returned whence he came. But not as he came forth did he return to heaven. In order to accomplish his vicarious righteousness, he had assumed a human nature like our own, and made it one person with his adorable divinity. In that human nature he had humbled himself as a servant obedient until death, " despised and rejected of men," " stricken,

smitten of God and afflicted," oppressed to the lowest
ignominy of torture by the malice of the world, to the
deepest reproach and pains of hell both in body and
soul on the tree of the cross by the justice of his Father;
and all this that he might bear away our shame, magnify and honor the law which we had broken, expiate
the guilt we had incurred, and lift up from the ruin sin
had brought upon them, those whom he accepted as
brethren when he became " the seed of the woman."
Therefore, when his vicarious merit was complete, and
the crucified had by a divine life " conquered death and
him that had the power of death," " having obtained
eternal redemption for us," he did not forsake the nature
he had loved so well, but bore aloft through the rent
skies the body and soul he had made his own by a
union personal and indissoluble. He entered heaven
as the only begotten Son of God, but also as the Son
of man ; coequal with the Father, yet our elder
brother, the Emmanuel claiming his divine right, the
mediator claiming his covenanted reward, the forerunner claiming the inheritance which as a Son was his
own, and in which he had associated his people through
the adoption they receive by his representation.

But the Scriptures declare that his being received
into heaven was not enough ; and when our faith looks
up through the parted vail, we see that he

" Sitteth at the right hand of God." The Catechism,
also, in the lesson for to-day very properly unites to this
article of our creed that which asserts

" From thence he will come to judge the quick and
the dead."

Both will, with divine permission, make the subject
of our present study.

The Answer to the 50th Question gives the reason why it is added that Christ " sitteth at the right hand of God."

The 51st states the " profit which this glory of Christ, our head, is unto us."

The 52d declares the comfort we derive from the fact that Christ " shall come again to judge the quick and the dead."

We shall be able to cover all this ground, and with greater convenience, by considering the several topics under three heads :

FIRST : *The meaning of the phrase, " He . . sitteth at the right hand of God."*

SECONDLY : *The reason for this preëminent glory of Christ.*

THIRDLY : *The comfort which the believer derives from this doctrine of our Lord's exaltation.*

FIRST : *The meaning of the phrase, " He . . sitteth at the right hand of God."*

1. The assignment of a place on the right hand of a king denotes his confidence and satisfaction in the person so honored.   Christ " sitteth on the right hand of God."   The Scripture represents that it is God in his supreme dignity who thus honors Christ.   The Son, " when he had purged our sins, sat down on the right hand of the Majesty on high," says the writer to the Hebrews ; and again : " Looking unto Jesus . . who . . . is set down at the right hand of the throne of God ; " which fulfils the prophecy : " The LORD said unto my Lord, sit thou at my right hand, until I make thine enemies thy footstool."   This implies a conferring of authority with the honor, as when a king elevates one as chief minister in the administration of his

empire. But other scriptures show that more is intended than a place *beside* the throne on its right hand. The Son sitteth *on the throne itself* with the Father: "Unto him that overcometh will I grant to sit with me on my throne, even as I also overcame and am set down with my Father in his throne." So, also, we behold "the Lamb in the midst" "of the great white" "throne;" and the river of life issuing from "the throne of the Lord God almighty and the Lamb." This clearly signifies the association of Christ with the Father in the full exercise of all power over all things, as the Master says: "All power is given unto me in heaven and in earth."

2. The vastness of the power thus exercised by the Son proves him to be truly and infinitely God, and therefore coequal to the Father; for what less than omnipresence, omniscience, and omnipotence were equal to the administration of universal empire? So we read: "Unto the Son, he saith, Thy throne, O God, is for ever and ever."

3. Yet, while such dominion belongs unto the Son by right of his original divinity, the phrase "on the right hand" indicates that this eminent authority has been *delegated*. It is the Emmanuel, the Son of God incarnate, that sits on the throne, and we know that the human nature neither has by right, nor can of itself exercise such dominion. Hence we are told that, because Christ Jesus "being in the form of God took upon him the form of a servant, and was made in the likeness of men; and, being found in fashion as a man, humbled himself, and became obedient until death, even the death of the cross, . . God also hath highly exalted him (the God-man) and given him a name that

is above every name, that at the name of JESUS every knee should bow, of things in heaven, and things in earth, and things under the earth; and that every tongue should confess that Jesus Christ is Lord, to the glory of God the Father."

The phrase " sitteth at the right hand of God the Father almighty," signifies the elevation by God the Father, representing the Godhead, of Jesus Christ the Mediator, representing the church, to the glory and power of a universal kingdom, as we read: " That ye may know . . . what is the exceeding greatness of his power to usward who believe, according to the working of his mighty power, which he wrought in Christ when he raised him from the dead and set him at his own right hand in the heavenly places, far above all principality, and power, and might, and dominion, and every name that is named, not only in this world, but also in that which is to come: and hath put all things under his feet, and gave him to be head over all things to the church, which is his body, the fulness of him that filleth all in all."

SECONDLY : *The reason for this preëminent glory of Jesus Christ.*

1. That the Father might manifest to all intelligent creatures his infinite appreciation of our Lord's mediatorial work.

The redemption of sinners was, as the Scriptures assure us, purposed and planned in a council of the ever-blessed Trinity, Father, Son, and Holy Ghost, each adorable person taking his peculiar part : The Father representing and vindicating the honor of the Godhead which had been treasonably provoked by our sins ; the Son undertaking to magnify the broken law and satisfy the justice of the law, whose sanctions were eternal life as the reward of righteousness alone, and eternal death as the sure penalty of disobedience ; the Holy Ghost promising his efficient energies to make successful all the means employed in the economy of grace.

This redemption is the highest work of God, infinitely transcending all his other works of creation and providence, which for the same reason are made subservient and contributive to it. There God has his highest delight, and from its issues he looks for his chiefest praise. Hence it is styled emphatically " the good pleasure of his will ; " and it is " to the praise of the glory of his grace." But while we adore with equal thanks the Father, the Son, and the Holy Ghost for their most merciful offices in our redemption, it is obvious that the office of the Father and the office of the Holy Ghost necessarily demand a perfect discharge of the office committed to the Son. His vicarious righteousness is the basis of the Father's choice and the Spirit's efficiency ; for the Father sends the Son to work out the atonement, and the Holy Ghost applies the atonement to the salvation of the church. The Father " predestinates us to the adoption of children by Jesus Christ," and the Holy Ghost makes us " accepted in the beloved." Now, as we have seen, the Son having become incarnate had fulfilled all righteousness, made an infinitely sufficient basis for our atonement (or reconciliation) with God, and so justified the mercy of God in the salvation of the sinner who believes on Jesus, when he finished his sacrifice on the cross. Therefore was Jesus Christ his only begotten Son, in whom he was well pleased, — not simply as his only begotten Son, —

there needed no work of righteousness to recommend his coequal Son, — but his only begotten Son, the incarnate mediator who had perfected the work of propitiation. The only begotten had taken on him the form of a servant, in our nature representing us; and in him, as a servant representing us, is he well pleased. The Father rejoices over him as the magnifier of the divine law, the satisfier of the divine justice, the justifier of the divine mercy; and receives him back to heaven as the head of a once prodigal race that was dead but is alive again, that was lost and is found. With what glory shall he invest this well-beloved Son less than the robe of his best majesty! What place shall he assign him in whom he is so well pleased, less than a seat on his own throne! What reward shall he bestow on the Propitiator for such perfect righteousness, less than the administration of all power in heaven and in earth!

The incarnate Son, in the execution of this work, had stooped to extreme shame. He had been degraded by poverty, persecution, and contempt, even to the once infamous cross; his enemies had exulted over him as he lay in the guarded tomb to all semblance under the grasp of "him that had the power of death;" men and angels had seen that it even pleased the Father to bruise him and put him to grief; nay, had heard his cry of anguish and desolation come from the thick darkness, "My God, why hast thou forsaken me!" And now must the Father show by a glory infinitely greater than the ignominy, how much he delights in his faithful servant; so he raises him from the lowest parts of the earth, where he was stript of all things, to the highest seat in heaven, that he may fill all things.

Therefore the glory of Christ is to be measured only by the infinite riches of the glory of his grace; and such the manifestation of the Father to the man whom he delighteth to honor, that not only the church shall ascribe unto him glory and dominion forever and ever, " but every creature which is in heaven, and on earth and under the earth, and such as are in the sea, and all that are in them," shall say, " Blessing and honor and glory and power be unto him that sitteth upon the throne, and unto the Lamb forever and ever."

2. " That he might," says the Catechism, " there appear as the head of his church, by whom the Father governs all things."

Let us, for greater convenience, divide this sentence.

a. " That he might there appear as the head of his church."

The first Adam was driven, because of his sin, by avenging angels, from the presence of God in the first paradise, and all his descendants fallen with him are by nature and personal guilt in the same state of condemnation and consequent exclusion from the divine favor. Christ, as the second Adam, had undertaken to restore, by his representative righteousness, all sinners who believe on his name to the privilege and blessedness they had lost. As Adam was the head of his race, so does Christ act as the head of his church, which Isaiah calls " his seed," " the travail of his soul." But as the vicarious merit of the mediator is infinitely greater than the most perfect obedience of man could have been, the privilege and blessedness purchased by him must incomparably transcend what had been lost. Hence, the state of the church in the divine favor cannot now

be adequately shown on earth; and the second paradise
is opened amidst the glories of the divine presence in
heaven. Christ, therefore, having risen from the dead
after the consummation of his atonement, remains on
earth no longer than was required to confirm the fact
of his resurrection, but ascends with his human body
and soul to take possession of heaven as his by mediatorial right. He enters heaven not for himself alone,
but for us as the forerunner of his church. When his
pierced feet crossed the threshold of that holy place, he
demonstrated that all who believe on his name shall
follow in his majestic steps, and that the whole nature,
body and soul of every Christian, shall partake of the
same glory with which his humanity is now invested.
There in the second paradise, where the tree of life
offers its perpetual fruits, beside the river of the
waters of life, which flows from out the throne of
the Lord God almighty and the Lamb, shall Jesus,
our surety, forever enjoy the reward for which he
endured the cross, despising the shame, as he beholds
all his ransomed people safe, sinless, and happy like
himself.

Nor was it enough for this that he should merely
enter heaven. The angels enjoy heaven as the con-
comitant reward of their unswerving fidelity; — the
divinely incarnate Son who had not only accomplished
an infinite merit for his people, but also, in so doing,
fulfilled the highest good pleasure of the Father, must
have a recompense far above the angel's honor. The
only begotten Son must have his divine place on his
Father's throne, and he takes his seat with his inseparable humanity about him, the Immanuel in whom the
Father is well pleased. The ransomed sinners, in all

their multitudinous numbers, will enjoy heaven as the reward of his imputed righteousness, but he is the head of the body of which they all are members, and it is his right by which they are there; therefore must it appear that his dignity is infinitely preëminent; nay, that he is Lord of heaven, to open its gates and its treasures as his own for all his· people. He reigns for us, because he reigns in our flesh. There to Christ on his throne do our affections follow him, for there " all the articles of our faith lead us."

b. " That he might there appear as the head of his church, *by whom the Father governs all things.*"

Though the merit on which the salvation of the church was finished by Jesus Christ when he died upon the cross, his work as our Redeemer will not be accomplished until his whole church — every one of his ransomed people — is brought home to the glorious house of his Father. For wise reasons, (elsewhere treated of,) this process is gradual; gradual in each believer, and gradual in the church. There is a severe discipline through which the grace of God is manifested by the experience of Christians and the church on earth, and by which they are to be prepared for the holy consummation of heaven. They are to labor in services like his, for which their strength is utterly insufficient; they are to meet difficulties and oppositions and delusions far greater than their own power and skill to overcome. All the malice of the world and hell is against them. Yet must they overcome. Humanity must achieve its own triumphs. All things were put under man at the beginning, and all things must be again put under him in the end. The restoration else were not complete. Now we see not all things put under the church. Her battle is fierce and obstinate.   " But we see JESUS, our second Adam, at the right hand of God the Father," crowned with glory and honor.   God has put all things into his hands, the hands of the man Christ Jesus.   All power is given unto him in heaven and earth, not as the Son of God, — that power has been eternally his by right of his original divinity, — but to the Son of God incarnate, Jesus Christ as the head of his church, and for the benefit of his church.   Nothing less than his infinite divinity were sufficient to exert this universal power, but he exerts it through his humanity as the grand type of regenerated, glorified man.   He reigns as the second Adam by the power of his godhead. All providence, therefore, is his ; all things, all beings created, all events, all the laws of nature, all the affairs of nations, all the arts and sciences, inventions and enterprises of men are so ruled, directed, and overruled by him as to assist his people individually, and as a church in their struggles onward and open the way for their final triumph.   " The angels " who constitute the hosts of which he is Lord, are " all ministering spirits sent forth to minister for them who shall be heirs of salvation ; " even the devils, also, are subject unto him, their malice being restrained and their ultimate defeat made certain, for " he must reign till he hath put all enemies under his feet."   So that the apostle made no vain boast when he said, " We know that all things work together for good to them that love God," and that all things are theirs, because they are " Christ's, and Christ is God's."   The fulness of the church which is his body, is the fulness of Christ's glory, so hath the Father put all things under his feet and given him to be head over all things to his church that he

may see of the travail of his soul and be fully satisfied.

3. That he " may by his Holy Spirit pour out heavenly graces on us his members."

In the plan of redemption the Holy Ghost assumes
the office of rendering effectual the work of Christ, and
hence is said to proceed from the Father and the Son,
as the Son from the Father. When, therefore, the
mediator had finished his meritorious work, he took his
seat at the right hand of the Father, and asked and
received the promised agency of the Holy Ghost for
the carrying out of his redemption to its entire completion.   Hence the Holy Ghost is said to be the Spirit
of Christ, and he is said to send the Spirit from the
Father (John xv. 26). So at the Pentecost the descent
of the Holy Ghost proved the session of Christ on his
throne : " Therefore," said the apostle Peter, " being
by the right hand of God exalted, and having received of the Father the promise of the Holy Ghost
(*i. e.* the promised Holy Ghost), he hath shed forth
this which ye now see and hear."   All the gifts of
God through Christ to men, all the graces which
characterize believers, — knowledge, strength, holiness,
faith, hope, love, — with all their attendant train of
blessed dispositions, are the effects of the Holy Spirit
dwelling and working in them.   To obtain this
spirit in his various energies is the object of Christ's
priestly intercessions.   Whatever we need for our
Christian comfort, guidance, and courage, can come
to us only by the Holy Spirit ; as all that was necessary to consecrate and sustain the humanity of Christ
himself, came from the Holy Ghost sent down by
the Father upon him.   The Spirit was the holy oil

of his unction when he was crowned as the royal high priest and prophet of the church, and its precious perfumes flow down to the humblest member of his mystical body. Christ, therefore, sitteth at the right hand of the Father on his throne, that as he administers all providence for the external benefit of his church, he may also send each member of it all grace for the internal Christian life ; or, as the 51st Question and Answer has it, the profit which this glory of Christ, our head, is unto us, may be stated in two parts. " First : That by his Holy Spirit he poureth out heavenly graces upon us his members ; and then that by his power he defends and preserves us against all enemies."

4. There is yet another form of Christ's glory connected with his elevation as Lord of all, which, though stated in a separate article of the creed, the Catechism most properly unites with the consideration of his sitting at the right hand of the Father : his coming " to judge the quick and the dead."

Throughout the Scriptures, the final and general judgment of the world is ascribed to Christ, " because," says the apostle on the Areopagus, God " hath appointed a day in the which he will judge the world in righteousness by that man whom he hath ordained, whereof he hath given assurance unto all men in that he raised him from the dead." Here not only is the judge declared to be the Son of God incarnate, by the emphatic term man, but his judgeship is intimately connected with his office as mediator by the assurance of his appointment being given in his resurrection from the dead. We see, also, according to the creed, that he proceeds from his throne to execute the office :

" From thence he shall come to judge the quick and
the dead ; " not that he leaves his sovereign authority behind him, but that he derives his authority
to judge from his royal dignity. In a word, it is a
prerogative of his mediatorial headship over all. The
reason of this is twofold : first, from the relation of
the mediator to God ; secondly, from his relation to
the church.

a. In committing to Jesus Christ the administration
of mercy, the Father necessarily committed to him the
administration of justice. It became him to reconcile
mercy to the believer with justice to the impenitent ;
and, while he effected through his righteousness the
redemption of his people, though sinners, to carry
out the condemnation of all who rejected his suretyship. He could not, therefore, fulfil the trust of
all authority from the Father until he had not only
opened heaven for the penitent, but also sent away
the obstinately impenitent to their merited doom. The
gospel did not annul the law, but placed the law with
the gospel in the hands of the mediator. Hence, as the
final judgment is intended for the manifestation of the
divine holiness in the consummation of the present system, so it should be presided over by the mediatorial
Lord.

It is also for the benefit of the church, that its mediatorial head should be the judge to dissipate their
fear, fulfil his gracious promises to them, and forever
deliver them from all danger and dread of their enemies, by a complete and everlasting overthrow of all
wickedness.

Thus the disciple, in the answer to the 52d Question,
declares his unspeakable comfort from the judgeship of

Christ: "That in all my sorrows and persecutions, with uplifted head, I look for the very same person, who before offered himself for my sake to the tribunal of God, and hath removed all curse from me to come as judge from heaven; who shall cast all his and my ene- mies into everlasting condemnation, but shall translate me with all his chosen ones to himself into heavenly joys and glory." Even in this majestic splendor of the mediator, the believer is associated with the glory of his elder brother. It is in his kindred flesh that the Son of God shall sit on the judgment-seat; it is his head that shall display consummate power over the destinies of all men.

There are many very interesting questions and edify- ing truths beyond what we have touched upon con- nected with this subject; but as the Catechism does not bring them under the present lesson, and much larger space were necessary for their discussion than we have now at our disposal, we must leave them for other occasions, and proceed to consider

THIRDLY: *The comfort which the believer derives from this doctrine of our Lord's exaltation.*

This has been made to appear as we went through the previous discussion, but the several points may be profitably recapitulated.

1. Our right through grace to heaven is secured.

"Lord, it is good for us to be here," said Peter on the mount of transfiguration, when he beheld the glory of Jesus, and in his bewildered ignorance he would have continued on the top of Tabor; but just before his passion, when the master had gathered the twelve around him for the last time, he declared, " It is expe- dient for you that I go away." From the scene of his transfiguration he descended to pass through sorrow, shame, and death to his Father's presence; and after he had ascended out of sight of his exulting disciples at Bethany, they had to pass through trials like his to reach their crown. But it was "the joy set before him," which animated him to "endure the cross, despising the shame;" it was the reward he had promised them which nerved their spirits to be faithful until death. He was no longer with them on earth; but they knew that he was in glory at the right hand of the Father. They no longer heard his gentle voice or saw his affectionate smile, but they knew that he had not forgotten them, for he had carried up with him his human body, and was still their elder brother and high priest, who could be touched with the feeling of their infirmities, having been tempted like as they were, though without sin; they had seen him condemned, crucified, dead, and buried; and now they' were exposed, a scattered feeble flock, to the malice of the same enemies and a cruel death; but they knew that he whom they trusted was Lord of heaven, triumphant over all, and had taken his royal seat as their forerunner. There the man Christ Jesus, body and soul, was in glory, — a glory of which he had promised them that they should be partakers. Therefore, sinners though they were, partakers of flesh and blood, unworthy in themselves, and weak as they were unworthy, they knew that heaven was theirs; that they should enter heaven body and soul; that none could debar them entrance, because he, who had washed them from their sins in his own blood, and imputed to them his right eousness, and acknowledged them as members of his body, was now the king who had control over all the mansions of his Father's house, and had promised to come again and receive them unto himself, that where he is they should be also. They could have no doubt of his faithfulness, they could have no doubt of his power; for he had been faithful unto death, and was now head over all things to his church. Thus we find that an assured hope of heaven was the great stay and comfort of the apostles and of the primitive Christians. They set their hearts on heaven, and nothing short of heaven could at all satisfy their longing expectations. Doubt of their ultimate blessedness there, the possibility of their being disappointed, would have been to them the power of keenest torture: "If for this life only we have hope in Christ," said the apostle Paul, "we are of all men most miserable." Their hope was in Christ for the life to come. The same comfort is ours, beloved brethren. Our Saviour is in heaven; he is Lord of heaven — Lord of heaven in our nature; and in receiving him and crowning him, the Father has given an earnest of receiving us and crowning us, if we be indeed Christians. It was to gain heaven for us that our Lord Jesus suffered and endured; to reach heaven and be with him there, should be, as it is, the great aim of all his true followers, and our only comfort; but our unspeakable comfort is, that, whatever meets us here, heaven will be ours at last, because Christ has made it ours now. Let, then, our conversation be in heaven, our fellowship with the Father and his Son Jesus Christ, and the spirits of just men made perfect, and the holy angels. We are pilgrims now, but we are going home, and that home is heaven.

2. Our strength for the Christian life is secured.

Though the end of his pilgrimage be secured in

heaven, the Christian knows that great trials may, if his time on earth be prolonged, lie between his present state and heaven; nor can he help but fear, lest a promise being left him of entering into rest, he might seem to come short of it. He would not deliberately wander from his master's footsteps, nor yield to temptation; but he is feeble, his heart most wicked and deceitful, his knowledge little, and his judgment weak. How shall he restrain that wicked heart of his? How undeceive himself from its sophisms? How resist its long-indulged tendencies to draw back from the living God? Were he left to himself he would despair; but he is not. His master is not beyond his reach; there is a door open by which his faith can reach him still; and in faith he goes through the rent vail even to the throne of grace, and on that throne he sees Jesus, his intercessor, beside God the Father almighty, having received the gift of the Holy Ghost for all the members of his blessed body. As the Father honors the Son by receiving him as head of the church, so the Holy Ghost honors him by putting all his energies at his disposal for the church. The Holy Ghost enters the soul of each believer as the earnest of eternal life, shedding the light of truth through his understanding, the love of God through his heart, power from on high through his will. In a word, all that the believer needs within for his Christian life is assured to him, because he knows that Christ sits on his throne to "pour out by his Holy Spirit heavenly graces upon us his members." We may not, therefore, whatever be our conviction of our own sin and insufficiency, doubt of strength from Christ, so long as we have continual access to the throne of God and the Lamb. We have but to ask, and we receive, and receive in no small measure, grace to help in time of need, grace to cover all our infirmities, to supply all our wants, to transform us from all that we are by nature to the likeness of the second Adam, the perfection of humanity and the heavenly type of his ransomed seed.

3. As our strength within is secured, so is our defence from without.

Our Head, by his victory over death and him that had power of death, triumphed over all his and our enemies; nay, by right of the covenant, has power over all created instrumentalities as head of the church for the church. It is, therefore, no more a question whether or not we are able individually, or as a church, to contend against the forces adverse to our cause, or to advance towards an ultimate success the kingdom of which we have been made partakers; that has long since been settled. We are nothing, the whole church apart from its head is nothing, in comparison with the world and the devil. Now we ask with uplifted heads, is not Christ able? Has he not, whose is all power in heaven and in earth, who sitteth at the right hand of God the Father almighty, the force as he has the prerogative to overcome for us, and by us, that we may overcome with him? O believer, when by reason of difficulties around you and threatenings before you, your heart fails, look up! Look up to Jesus, where he sitteth at the right hand of God, whither all the articles of your faith lead you. Only set your affections on him; only cast your care on his almighty arm, and you shall be certain of deliverance and of success.

4. Our vindication is secure.

Our Lord left his disciples on earth to take his seat on his throne. Personally absent he is now, though present by his Spirit. But the separation will not be perpetual. We show forth in the holy sacrament of the supper his death ; but we show it till he come. When the disciples stood gazing up at the heavens through which their Lord disappeared in glory, angels were sent to stand by them, and say, " This same Jesus, which is taken up from you into heaven, shall so come in like manner as ye have seen him go into heaven ; " and he himself had said before, " If I go away, I will come again and receive you unto myself, that where I am ye may be also." So says the article of our creed : " From thence he shall come to judge the quick and the dead." For wise reasons he will permit his church to be tried, assisting them by his Spirit and his power, but withholding from them a full success. They will be accused, mocked, baffled, and persecuted. Yet only for a time. He sits on his throne expecting till his " enemies be made his footstool ; " and we, though on earth, have a gracious privilege of sharing in the expectation ; for when he comes again, it shall be to judge the quick and the dead. The Lamb that was slain shall sit on the judgment-seat, to justify the believer from the curse by his own righteousness ; to condemn the unbeliever because his mercy has been rejected ; to open with his nail-pierced hands the kingdom of glory for his friends ; to banish, by the fierceness of his own wrath, his enemies to an everlasting doom. Before assembled angels and an observant universe will he acknowledge and glorify the most despised of his little ones, while he pours eternal contempt upon the proud who resisted his love.

O Christian, O unbeliever, consider who can stand before him in the judgment! If we trust in ourselves, our condemnation is sure; if we trust in him, our vindication shall be complete.

END OF VOL. I.

INDEX TO VOLUME I